Peru's APRA

Peru's APRA

Parties, Politics, and the Elusive Quest for Democracy

Carol Graham

Lynne Rienner Publishers ■ Boulder & London

Published in the United States of America in 1992 by
Lynne Rienner Publishers, Inc.
1800 30th Street, Boulder, Colorado 80301

and in the United Kingdom by
Lynne Rienner Publishers, Inc.
3 Henrietta Street, Covent Garden, London WC2E 8LU

Library of Congress Cataloging-in-Publication Data
Graham, Carol, 1962-
   Peru's APRA : parties, politics, and the elusive quest for
democracy / Carol Graham.
      p.   cm.
   Includes bibliographical references and index.
   ISBN 1-55587-306-5 (alk. paper)

   1. Partido Aprista Peruano—History.   2. Peru—Politics and
government—1980-   I. Title.
JL3498.A6G7   1992
324.285 '07—dc20   92-240
                                                              CIP

British Cataloguing in Publication Data
A Cataloguing in Publication record for this book
is available from the British Library.

Printed and bound in the United States of America

The paper used in this publication meets the requirements
of the American National Standard for Permanence of
Paper for Printed Library Materials Z39.48-1984.

To John, for waiting;
To my parents, for their inspiration;
To Marianne and Richard, and Anita and Andres,
for their ever-welcoming hospitality;
And to Alan, for reading about the APRA
on sunny Santiago Sundays—and many other times

I also thank the women of Huascar, whose kindness
and generosity in the face of their plight is one of the
few sources of hope in the morass of today's Peru.

Contents

Illustrations

Abbreviations

AD	Acción Democrática (Venezuela)
AP	Acción Popular
APRA	Alianza Popular Revolucionaria Americana
ARE	Alianza Revolucionaria Estudiantil
ASI	Acuerdo Socialista Izquierda
CAEM	Centro de Altos Estudios Militares
CEN	Comité Ejecutivo Nacional (APRA)
CGTP	Confederación General de Trabajadores Peruanos
CIA	Central Intelligence Agency (USA)
CONAPLAN	Comision de Plan de Gobierno
COOPOP	Cooperación Popular
COPEI	Comité de Organización Política Electoral Independiente (Venezuela)
CTP	Confederación de Trabajadores Peruanos
CTRP	Confederación de Trabajadores Revolucionários del Perú
CUA	Comando Universitario Aprista
DIRCOTE	Dirección Contra Terrorismo
ENCI	Empresa Nacional de Comercialisacion de Insumos
FREDEMO	Frente Democrático
FRENATRACA	Frente Nacional de Trabajadores y Campesinos
IDE	Izquierda Democrática Estudiantil
IDESI	Instituto para Desarrollo del Sector Informal
IMF	International Monetary Fund
INP	Instituto Nacional de Planificación
IPC	International Petroleum Company
IU	Izquierda Unida
JAP	Juventud Aprista Peruana
JUA	Juventud Universitaria Aprista
MIR	Movimiento de la Izquierda Revolucionaria
MOTC	Movimiento de Trabajadores Clasistas
MRTA	Movimiento Revolucionario Tupac Amaru

ONDEPJOV	Organismo Nacional de Desarrollo de Pueblos Jóvenes
PAD	Programa de Apoyo Directo
PAIT	Programa de Apoyo de Ingreso Temporal
PC	Partido Comunista (Prado's party)
PDC	Partido Democrático Cristiano (Chile)
PEM	Programa de Empleo Mínimo (Chile)
PLN	Partido de Liberación Nacional (Costa Rica)
PPC	Partido Popular Cristiano
PRI	Partido Revolucionario Institucional (Mexico)
PROEM	Programa de Empleo
PSR	Partido Socialista Revolucionario
PUM	Partido Unificado Mariáteguista
SINAMOS	Sistema Nacional de Apoyo a la Movilización Social
SUTEP	Sindicato Único de Trabajadores en la Educación Peruana
UDP	Unión Democrática y Popular
UNIR	Unión Nacional de la Izquierda Revolucionaria
UNO	Unión Nacional Odriista

MAPA POLITICO
DEL
PERU
ESCALA

LEYENDA
Capital de Republica
Capital de Departamento
Capital de Provincia
Limite Departamental
Limite Internacional

AUTORIZADO POR RESOLUCION MINISTERIAL No. 1505
DEL MINISTERIO DE RELACIONES EXTERIORES

Source: Ministerio de Relaciones Exteriores, Lima

X

1

Marginalized Society, Parties, and Democratic Consolidation: APRA in Comparative Perspective

Alianza Popular Revolucionaria Americana (APRA) in Peru is one of the oldest mass-based reform-oriented parties in Latin America, where the record of both democracy and reform is checkered. Most Latin American democracies evolved from formal electoral systems dominated by powerful oligarchies—the "vieja democracia verbal," as APRA's Haya de la Torre labeled them—into electoral systems that incorporate, at least at election time, large percentages of the population. In many cases suffrage now includes illiterates. Marxist parties, often banned in the past, now have representation in some legislatures. Yet in some countries, and particularly in Peru, there exist a host of loosely organized popular organizations, which function outside the realm of government or political parties and which are concurrent with large numbers of people who earn their living outside the formal economy—the so-called marginalized population. This phenomenon, in conjunction with the sectors of the population involved in armed insurrection, demonstrates vividly a breach between state and society, and thus a lack of national integration in many developing democracies. In this context substantive social and economic reform is a prerequisite to democratic consolidation.

The incorporation of the marginalized into the formal political and economic systems, making them citizens as well as vote-casters, is necessary for democratic consolidation. The role of political parties in this process is to serve as bridge between state and society. As most developing democracies lack strong political institutions, this role takes on increased and indeed critical importance. "For significant progress to be made toward political stability and the gradual removal of restrictions on democratic practices, two conditions [are] crucial: the emergence of a party system that [can] reassure economic elites that their interests [will] be adequately protected, and the growth in the strength of civil society."[1]

In this study of Peru's APRA in power I examine the role of the political party in democratic reform and seek to further our understanding of the role of parties in democratic consolidation. The study entails an analysis of party-government relations as well as the party's role in economic policymaking. APRA's relations with the opposition are also considered. Finally, an examination of the implementation of programs for

1

the urban poor provides insights into the party's relations with the marginalized. I posit that democratic reform is integral to democratic consolidation, and the role of the political party is a critical one in that process. In the case of Peru, APRA's nature—its effects on economic policymaking, the fragility of the coalition it built both within and outside the government, and its relations with the marginalized—was a determining factor in the dramatic failure of democratic reform. While the APRA government has received a great deal of attention, there has been no comprehensive evaluation of the *political* factors underlying its debacle. I attempt such an evaluation within a framework that focuses on the role of the governing party. The book contributes to the sparse literature on parties in developing democracies, and more generally to the literature on democratic consolidation in Latin America.

MARGINALIZED SOCIETIES AND POLITICAL PARTIES

Democratic consolidation is an elusive goal; it becomes even more so in a context where fragile political institutions are faced with economic and social demands that far outpace institutions' ability to respond. Before discussing democratic consolidation, it is necessary to briefly consider how this context creates obstacles additional to an already formidable undertaking.

In Peru, as in many other developing nations, large numbers of people earn their living outside the formal economy and are often marginalized from formal legal and political institutions. The terms *informal sector* and *marginalized* are often used interchangeably. Both attempt to describe, although neither does adequately, the complex relationship that the poor have with formal political, economic, and legal institutions. The term *marginalized* implies exclusion from civil society: "marginality is a total condition; it does not apply merely to employment but to all aspects of political, social, and interest participation." [2] The term *informal sector* is used to describe various kinds of extralegal economic activity: illegal means to achieve illegal ends, such as drug trafficking; and illegal means to achieve legal ends, such as building a house or running a small enterprise. The focus here is on the latter, on the poor's response to lack of access to basic legal services because of inadequate resources or daunting bureaucratic barriers.

That a large percentage of the population lives in a precarious legal as well as economic situation has substantial impact on society and polities. Francisco Thoumi asserts that, because values adapt in part to past experiences, individuals' respect for the law depends on other citizens. "What occurs, simply, is that in a society where there is a great amount of dishonesty and corruption, it becomes increasingly costly to behave honestly." [3] Nowhere is this more evident than in Peru, where by the end of the decade society could increasingly be described as praetorian: social forces conflicting directly with each other, with a lack of agreement on a legitimate means of conflict resolution.[4]

In such societies, as both national integration and basic consensus on societal values—what sociologist Ralf Dahrendorf labels homeostatic equilibrium—are often lacking, more often than not, the politics of reform becomes the politics of polarization. As significant sectors of society are not meaningfully incorporated into the political system—despite the fact that these people cast votes—they have limited incentive to support the established system; this can rapidly translate into polarization. Polarized polities are characterized by, among other traits, the relevance of anti-system parties, opposition from both sides of the political spectrum, and a lack of agreement on the legitimacy of the system itself.[5] In such scenarios competing political forces are involved in a winner-take-all debate—any sort of cooperation or compromise is impossible. The outcome is usually policy stagnation, a surge of reaction from extremes of the right or the left, and at times the collapse of the entire political system, as in Chile in 1973. In such a context societal demands escalate far beyond the capacity of state institutions to satisfy them. As political parties are often among the few established institutions with any mass-based legitimacy, their role in preventing or exacerbating polarization is critical, as the Peruvian case demonstrates.

Despite political parties' potentially influential position, their relations with the marginalized sectors of society are by no means simple or clear-cut. The host of community self-help organizations and group productive enterprises that exist among the urban poor—and that have increased in importance with the growth in the relative size of the informal sector in recent years—usually originate outside the realm of political parties. Party relations with these organizations often aim to monopolize or at least elicit their support. "The existence of widespread social organizations that escape party control is threatening to parties that are used to monopolizing such institutions."[6] In his recent work on popular organizations in Chile, Philip Oxhorn notes that these groups are often wary and resentful of the challenges to their autonomy that political parties may pose.[7] The relationship that these social sectors have with the state in general is divided between the desire for further integration into society and a feeling—and a reality—of exclusion or marginalization.[8]

In general the urban poor tend to vote pragmatically,[9] often lending political support as readily to dictators or populists as to democrats, and as readily withdrawing that support if it does not produce tangible results. Robert Gay, in his work on the political behavior of the urban poor in Brazil, posits that clientelism—the exchange of votes for promised public or private resources—is a relatively cheap and effective way for the marginalized to obtain desperately needed services. "Decisions about whether or not to support a particular individual depend solely on the candidate's ability to deliver, irrespective of past record, ideology, or political party. . . . Given the . . . poor living conditions of much of the population, clientelism represents a rational strategy."[10] Yet Gay also notes that clientelism is not the sole determinant of the political behavior of the urban poor. Particularly in communities where local organizations effectively provide immediate material needs, such as water and electrical service, then electoral politics may cease to be associated with the provision of community benefits. In this context "support for political parties . . . is determined by broader political issues."[11] The role of parties may increase in importance relative to that of individuals whose power is based primarily on clientelism. The nature of community organizations, and the level of development of the communities themselves, has significant effects on the political behavior of the urban poor and their relationships with political parties.

Despite their eclectic and diverse characteristics—or perhaps because of them—local grassroots organizations are increasingly recognized as important actors in democratization. They are usually autonomous and democratic in their origins and structure, and play an important role in strengthening the concept of civil society among the marginalized. The interplay between the three realms—state, parties, and popular organizations—is a complex one that is integral to democratic consolidation at the most basic and, in terms of the breach between state and society, most important level. The behavior of political parties in this arena is critical to building a lasting consensus for reform and thus to preventing the polarization that so often occurs.

POLITICAL PARTIES AND DEMOCRATIC CONSOLIDATION

"What becomes increasingly obvious . . . is how far social scientists are from achieving a widely accepted, theoretically well-grounded, and empirically well-supported explanation of the (re)-emergence and consolidation of democratic regimes in general and in Latin America in particular."[12] There is a comprehensive body of literature analyzing transitions to democracy in Latin America. There is no comparable body of literature on democratic consolidation,[13] perhaps no surprise given that many Latin nations have held only one or perhaps two rounds of open elections since the transfer from military rule. Indeed, there are few, if any, conclusive definitions of the consolidation of democracy. Cynthia McClintock, describing Peru as an unlikely but probable case for democratic consolidation, uses a working definition of holding three consecutive rounds of open elections.[14] Yet while Peru was one of the first in the

wave of Latin countries that transferred from military to civilian government in the early 1980s and has held three rounds of elections, one could
argue that it is of Latin American countries, the furthest from democratic
consolidation. Within a conception of democracy that includes civic values
and progress toward socioeconomic equality as well as constitutional
norms, consolidation seems virtually impossible in a society as violent and
poverty-stricken as Peru's.

Most of the literature on transitions to democracy in Latin America
uses a limited definition of democracy, with the holding of free and fair
elections as the defining criterion. Samuel Valenzuela expands upon this
criterion, adding three other requirements: that suffrage be wide enough
to represent all of the fundamental political tendencies in society; that
those who win elections hold important decisionmaking positions in the
state; and that elections be the only way to achieve power.[15] Yet this
definition still does not address the more nebulous socioeconomic aspects
of democracy. "Significant increases in popular participation and in the
spheres of democratic decision are bound to raise issues of distribution
and socioeconomic structural change."[16]

Samuel Huntington argues quite convincingly that democracy is not
expected to *solve* such problems; rather, it is expected to protect the
populace from the mistakes of their leaders and to provide them with a
mechanism to remove and replace them.[17] Yet Alexander de Toqueville,
one of the oldest theorists of democracy, would disagree with such a
limited definition, as he posited that once democracy is introduced issues
of socioeconomic equality cannot be separated from the political sphere.[18]
James Petras, in his critique of the current state of Latin American
democracies, also seeks a broader definition. "The euphoria accompanying electoral fronts is giving way to sharp class cleavages and new popular
movements. . . . The populace is awaiting a new conception of democracy,
one that combines changes in regime with transformation of the state and
accumulation models."[19]

The cleavages and movements that Petras refers to—the breach
between states and societies in much of Latin America—point to a need
to define democracy so that it encompasses socioeconomic as well as
institutional political criteria. The key to defining democratic consolidation in Latin America lies precisely in the cloudy relationship between
formal democratic institutions and socioeconomic progress. "One must
accept the argument that a relationship exists between the level of socioeconomic development and consolidation of democratic regimes because
too many cross-national statistical studies . . . have come up with this result.
Yet [none] provides a convincing explanation of the mechanisms that
mediate this relationship."[20] While the relationship between socioeconomic progress and democratic consolidation is difficult to define, socioeconomic reform in a democratic context is more tangible. The extent to

which a polity succeeds in implementing democratic reform can serve as a gauge of its progress toward democratic consolidation.

In the current Latin American context, in which resources are severely constrained by debt burdens and protracted economic crisis, implementing socioeconomic reform is no easy task. It entails, first and foremost, the building of consensus for a viable macroeconomic strategy. Stephan Haggard and Robert Kaufman's recent work on the political economy of inflation and stabilization in a crosscutting sample of developing countries points to the crucial role of parties and the party system in the formulation and execution of viable macroeconomic policy. "Macroeconomic stability is most precarious when the party system is fragmented or polarized, thereby reinforcing social and economic cleavages among 'conflicting groups.'"[21] Systems dominated by one or two strong, multiclass parties provide less scope for "populist" economic policies and appear more conducive to stable policy outcomes. In such systems unions as well as other interest groups must operate within cross-class organizations.[22]

Particularly in the absence of foreign and public sector resources, the cooperation and support of the private sector is critical to the maintenance of a viable macroeconomic strategy. Atul Kohli lists the prerequisites for reform in the context of a private or pluralist economy: coherent leadership; an ideological and organizational commitment to reform; and a pragmatic attitude to facilitating a nonthreatening and predictable atmosphere for the propertied entrepreneurial classes. He examines successful democratic reform implemented by the Communist party in India. "The CPM clarified the limits of its redistributive intent. All democratically elected parties in a private enterprise economy, even if communist in name, must set these limits."[23] This experience contrasts sharply with the Allende years in Chile. "Allende headed a precarious multiparty coalition lacking both internal cohesiveness and underlying agreement on the pace and character change to be implemented. . . . As coherent ideology did not exist, the revolutionary utterances, whether sincere or not, created a climate of considerable uncertainty. . . . As economic problems got worse, again in the absence of an organized, ideologically based core of support, short-term problems became impossible to handle."[24]

In the current Latin American context—weak state institutions and highly mobilized societies—meeting the requirements that Kohli points to is difficult at best. Yet in most Latin countries there exist political parties, or party systems, many of which predate military interludes, whose legitimacy is based on pursuing an agenda of social reform. These parties are uniquely positioned in society to establish the conditions necessary for reform: leadership; an organized base of support; and a platform or program that provides a predictable climate for the private sector. At the same time their multiclass organizational base places them in a unique position to bridge the breach between democratically elected states and the marginalized sectors of society.

Vicky Randall, in her work on parties in the Third World, argues that parties link civil society to the modern state.[25] In Latin America, where most states have adopted formal democratic institutions, parties are thus positioned to provide the institutional basis for incorporating society into the democratic process. There are many different kinds of parties, however, and not all of them are suited to this task. The focus here is mass-based reformist parties, as opposed to either Marxist revolutionary parties or electoral fronts based on elite alliances or charismatic personalities, with the assumption that it is precisely mass-based parties that can play a vital role in democratic consolidation.

REFORMIST PARTIES IN LATIN AMERICA

Huntington sees parties as a means for containing pressures for participation and as the only form of modern organization that can become a source of authority based on representation.[26] Maurice Duverger, in his authoritative work, assigns to parties the ultimate representative role: the creation of new elites for the purpose of representation.[27] Ironically, Duverger discounts the relevance of his work to parties in Latin America because of the frequent turnover of government. Yet Randall points to the viability of parties despite the threat of frequent overthrow, and indeed the often critical role they play in the transition back to civilian government. "While party regimes have regularly been overturned by military coups, these same military regimes have almost as regularly . . . either reinstated some form of party politics or actually restored government to party politicians."[28]

This is precisely what occurred in Peru, where the military turned to APRA in the late 1970s to play the central role in the transition to civilian politics. APRA was "the strongest, most disciplined organized political force and thus the most capable of ensuring that agreements reached with the party leadership would be honored."[29] In most other transitions in Latin America parties played a critical role as well, with Brazil being the most significant exception.

Parties not only play an important role during the transition, but in the regime that results. Randall notes that while parties' ideological role or appeal may be limited to election time, they clearly play a vital role in government—in particular in guaranteeing certain kinds of economic performance. In the current Latin American context economic performance is often critical to regime survival. Parties first of all endow the regime in power with greater legitimacy through elections. They also provide stability to the regime by lending it a structured base of support,

and insure that a coalition of political interests powerful enough to maintain a government is secured. They may also enhance regime stability by
assisting the political integration of different regions, communities, or
social groups. In this integration, while parties are usually instruments of
the government, demands do not flow solely from the top down.[30] Parties
may be one of the only means for relatively weak or isolated local actors
to make demands within the political system.

To be successful, parties need organizational effectiveness, autonomy, and political support. Yet particularly in the Third World, where
government resources are extremely scarce, parties often rely excessively
on patronage to achieve these goals. The use of patronage is not necessarily incompatible with ideological conviction. Even if the practice of patronage interferes with coordinated supervision of policy implementation,
parties can still effect social and economic change by maintaining a
ruling-interest coalition.[31] Yet there are longer-term negative effects of
patronage, as Joel Migdal posits. The predominance of nonmerit appointments weakens the coherence of the state,[32] and thus ultimately the party's
potential to serve as a link between society and the state.

It seems, therefore, that there is an inherent tension between the
widespread use of patronage as a means to build a base of political support
on the one hand, and the party's role in implementing comprehensive
reform as a means to achieve democratic consolidation on the other. As
the case of APRA demonstrates, this tension can have dire consequences.
It also reflects a more fundamental contradiction between the often
short-term concerns of party politicians and a longer-term vision of the
party's role in the process of socioeconomic reform. Leaders and parties
without a longer-term commitment to reform and, perhaps more important, the capacity to implement a viable reformist strategy are much more
likely to be guided by short-term criteria and abuse their access to resources for patronage purposes. It is in this unclear realm of contradiction
that the nature of the party in power becomes critical, and may determine
the course that a government takes.

Latin America provides good testing ground for comparing political
parties, as there have been and are a number of political parties with some
or all of the same traits: a mass based, antisystem origin; and populist
characteristics. In discussing the nature of parties, and their capacity to
implement viable long-term economic strategies and socioeconomic reform, several key distinctions can be made that help to distinguish reformist political parties from their closely related counterparts with whom they
may share several traits. It is also possible to distinguish between their
records of reform and thus ultimately the extent to which they succeed as
reformist parties rather than as short-term populist experiments.

All of the parties that could potentially be called reformist are mass
rather than cadre parties. Cadre parties are usually the result of a group

of elites forming and financing an electoral coalition. Mass parties, on the other hand, are more likely to be institutionalized. Their aim is the political education of the masses, and the members form the substance as well as provide the finances for the party. As the financial burden is distributed among as many members as possible, the party is not dependent on any one group or donor. Mass parties such as Communist or Fascist parties are highly disciplined; they are centralized, vertically structured, organized into cells, and have autocratic leaders. They also have an important ideological component, and thus "the faith of a church is combined with the discipline of an army."[33]

Parties are also affected by their origins. Those formed outside of parliament or congress tend to be more centralized and hierarchical than those formed as electoral or parliamentary arrangements, and in general place less value on the constitutional system per se. Mass parties are usually formed outside parliament.[34] Highly ideological mass parties, particularly if they have been proscribed for a long time and therefore have or perceive that they have little chance of getting into power, tend to be much less realistic in their demands on the system and attribute less inherent value to it. "The less likely a party is to get into power, the less likely it is to have realistic proposals for governing."[35] The highly centralized and hierarchical structure of such parties also profoundly influences how they interact with society. "Homogenous, centralized, and totalitarian parties introduce into public opinion irreducible cleavages which are not found in real life."[36] These sectarian and authoritarian tendencies may be reduced by the need to remain competitive electorally; electoral defeat will often spur the internal democratization of a party.[37]

In Latin America there have been relatively few, if any, Communist or Fascist parties that have been able to achieve majority status. Yet there have been a great many mass-based, reform-oriented parties—APRA being one of the first and most influential—that display some of the characteristics of highly centralized and ideological parties; at the same time, with the exception of the Partido Revolucionaria Institucional (PRI) in Mexico, they have been unable to unilaterally dominate the political system. They have either been tempered by the need to remain electorally competitive, as were Acción Democrática (AD) in Venezuela and the Partido de Liberación Nacional (PLN) in Costa Rica, or else have had their extremist tendencies exacerbated by proscription, as happened to the Peronists in Argentina and APRA in Peru. As all of these parties have significant differences, it is difficult to accurately place them in one category.

The category most often used, or perhaps misused, is "populist," Paul Drake defines populism as using political mobilization and recurrent rhetoric and symbols to inspire people; having a heterogenous class structure with significant support from middle and upper as well as working classes; and having a reformist set of policies designed to promote development without explosive class conflict.[38] Robert Dix distinguishes between authoritarian and democratic populists. Authoritarian populists, such as the Peronists, focus more on the personality of the leader, are much less likely to have a coherent program, and rely much less on an organized or developed party mechanism or structure. Democratic populists, according to Dix, such as APRA and the AD, place less importance on one leader, have a more coherent party program, and are in general more international in their orientation. The latter are more likely to implement lasting structural reform as opposed to short-term redistributive measures.[39] Dix's distinctions are a useful gauge for distinguishing purely populist from reformist parties—although reformist parties may still have some populist characteristics. The most critical difference is the existence of a program and an organized political base, two of Kohli's prerequisites for reform.

Orthodox economists tend to define populists as those who follow economic strategies that seek redistribution as a primary goal, while denying the existence of fiscal and monetary constraints.[40] Yet such a limited definition overlooks important differences in the kind of support base established for such measures; the overall strategy they may, or may not, be a part of; the tactics used to achieve goals; and the final results achieved. While both populists and reformers aim to redistribute, reformers aim to make longer-term structural changes. "Populism is more likely to be effective at mobilizing protests by the underprivileged than at securing organized participation in national decisionmaking or at delivering substantial benefits to them."[41] Populists often have a rather tentative commitment to the constitutional system and in general lack a structured program. Reformers, meanwhile, must have a certain degree of ideological coherence. This does not imply rigid attachment to doctrine, rather it implies agreement on basic principles, such as whether the party is going to use reformist tactics; working within the established constitutional system; or revolutionary ones; circumventing the system. Reformist tactics can achieve revolutionary objectives; as Kohli notes, providing a reassuring atmosphere for the private sector is often critical. For reform to succeed in an electoral democracy with a private enterprise economy, the rules of the game—that is, the extent of the reformist intent—must be made clear in order to maintain confidence and consensus. As most developing democracies lack strong state institutions with an established pattern of reputable policymaking, the governing party's platform is the primary means to establish such rules.

Revolutionaries and populists coincide in that they have little respect for the constitutional system. They differ, however, in that revolutionaries openly challenge the system, while populists may seek concurrently to work within the system and to undermine it. As they often lack a coherent program, their policies are best characterized not by Marxist or other ideological bents, but by "provocativeness, abruptness, and lack of planning."[42] Their policies ultimately prove economically inviable. When they confront economic bottlenecks, populists tend to rely on an increase in the public sector, leftist rhetoric, and confrontation to mobilize workers in "adamant opposition of a private business sector that feared massive expropriation."[43] Ironically private business is often the very sector populists depend on to finance their economic strategy.

Beyond the distinctions between populists, reformers, and revolutionaries, there are also differences between reformist parties. Many reformist or revolutionary parties are sectarian in nature and often have utopian philosophies that imply that they alone are capable of saving their nation. These exclusionary tendencies make such parties less capable of generating the cooperation among diverse interests needed for successful reform; the debate is phrased in confrontational terms and becomes polarized. Communist parties in their militant stages typically display these tendencies, but so also can such ideologically diverse reformist parties as the Christian Democrats in Chile and APRA in Peru. As Duverger notes, parties with such characteristics tend to introduce artificial cleavages into society. This clearly interferes with their ability to act as a link between society and state and is often evident in their relations with popular organizations, as our study of APRA illustrates. "Rigid, hierarchically organized political party structures, with an insulated party elite managing party affairs in a highly centralized fashion, are most likely to generate conflicts between parties and territorially-based popular organizations."[44]

A major factor leading to the breakdown in Chile during the Allende years was the loss of a coherent center coalition in the Christian Democrats, whose sense of mission and sectarian behavior at the time played a major role. The increasing polarization that occurred at the end of the Partido Democrático Cristiano (PDC) government opened the way for the Allende regime and its ill-fated coalition. The loss of a pragmatic center coalition and the existence in its stead of a sectarian center party greatly aggravated polarization.

> Even so, for such a multi-class party with such divisions over policy, the degree of party unity was surprisingly high. . . . This was in part due to a common sense of ideological purpose, not unlike the other relatively united ideological force in Chilean politics, the Communist party. . . . There is little doubt that many members of the party felt that they had become the natural governing party of Chile which gave rise to a degree of sectarianism many Christian Democrats came later to regret.[45]

The extent to which society is polarized into right and left camps is also a determining factor in a reformist party's ability to act as a strong center. Sartori notes that the position of the center party in polarized systems is often untenable, particularly if the party attempts to use extremist tactics to outdo its rivals on either the left or the right.[46]

The subtle differences between reformist and populist approaches, as well as specific traits that such parties may have, are crucial to successful reform and ultimately to democratic consolidation. In Latin America the success of Venezuela's AD and Costa Rica's PLN in implementing a limited degree of structural reform and consolidating democracy contrasts sharply with the dramatic failure of Argentina's Peronists in the mid-1970s and with Peru's APRA in the 1980s. While success or failure was in part determined by the specific conditions and structural barriers in each case, the approach taken and the ultimate success were determined largely by the nature of the party in power. All four were mass-based parties; three of them were inspired, at least in part, by APRA. Yet differences in party structure, leadership, tactics, and ultimately commitment to the constitutional system were critical in determining the party's successes or failures. A brief comparison of APRA with the AD and the Peronists provides a useful framework for the examination of APRA in greater detail.

THE APRA PARTY IN COMPARATIVE PERSPECTIVE

APRA, since its inception, aroused more emotions and animosities than any other political force in Peru, and consequently was barred from power for decades. Once it attained power, APRA managed, at least initially, to build a consensus that was unique to reformist efforts in Peru, yet that consensus broke down into extreme polarization and a dramatic increase of insurgent violence. (Clearly the party's role cannot be discussed without consideration of the difficult context in which it had to operate: an underdeveloped and crisis-ridden economy; a vast employment problem; and growing insurgent violence. That context will be discussed in detail in the next chapter.)

After sixty years of exclusion by the entrenched opposition of both the military and the conservative elites, APRA finally achieved national power in 1985. The party that took power that July was virtually an unknown entity. It was not the radical and violence-prone group of revolutionaries of the 1930s and 1940s; nor was it the ideologically compromised party of the 1950s and 1960s *convivencia* with the conservative elites; and finally it was distinct from the nascent and increasingly strong forces of the Marxist left. APRA maintained several characteristics—many of them undemocratic in nature—that were to prove barriers to its ability to govern effectively. While at first APRA seemed well positioned to implement substantive reform, it subsequently made the mistakes, and displayed the characteristics, of both populist and highly ideological sectarian parties.

APRA maintained a unique position in Peruvian politics and its own form of political culture: *mística*. This culture was an outgrowth of the mystique of the personality of Víctor Raúl Haya de la Torre, and of the years of persecution experienced by many *apristas*. Haya's persona and the emotional bonds that were formed by a shared willingness to suffer for the cause of social reform took on a familial or religious nature rather than a political one. This cultural *aprismo* was concurrently linked with and independent of APRA in government. It served to provide a sense of hope based in the legacy of a leader and an eclectic ideology that were both distinctly Peruvian. At the same time APRA culture also entailed a pervasive opposition mentality—which grew out of many years of proscription—that was a barrier to its ability to govern. As we noted earlier, the less likely a party is to get power, the less likely it is to have realistic proposals for governing.

In July 1985, despite Peru's difficulties and traditional fears about the party, there were high hopes because APRA had renovated its image, had an unprecedented popular mandate, and had a strong and charismatic leader, Alan García. By mid-1988 it was clear, after a positive start that raised expectations both within and outside Peru, that APRA could not fulfill its reformist mission; that Peru was more polarized than when the party took power; that insurgency had made substantial headway; and that the marginalized, after receiving brief attention from a variety of government programs that faded out or were discontinued, were even worse off than before. APRA's long-sought power yielded, in García's words, an "impossible revolution."

The party had taken power in the face of formidable challenges, but also at a time when consensus on the need for reform in Peru was unprecedented. At the same time the military's revolution had made Peruvian elites highly suspicious of state expropriation of property, and most observers highly skeptical about its utility. APRA initially avoided debate on the structure of property relations and focused instead on innovative reform, with particular attention to the informal sector. A clear turning point was the July 1987 surprise nationalization of the nation's banks, which also included a shift to confrontational rhetoric. The implicit rules of the game were broken; the right cried "foul," the left cried "bluff," and APRA's lack of agreement on what the rules actually were was exposed. Consensus gave way to polarization, government initiative faded, and economic crisis rapidly set in. The speed and severity of the deterioration can be explained in part by the behavior and traits of the party and its authoritarian and erratic leader García (clearly determining factors); and in part by the extent to which Peruvian society could be described as praetorian.

APRA's sectarianism, its authoritarian internal structure, and the religious or ideological nature of its commitment made it less able to build a support base in society outside the party and contributed to the polarization of opinion: the artificial cleavages that Duverger attributes to highly ideological parties. The party's position as a pragmatic center was difficult to maintain; as with the PDC in Chile, this difficulty was aggravated by APRA's sectarian traits. Finally, APRA lacked a coherent program or doctrinal clarity, which added to the sense of uncertainty once polarization began.

It is instructive to look at two similar parties that were inspired in part by APRA. One, Venezuela's AD, succeeded in implementing democratic reform; and the other, Argentina's Peronists, failed dramatically. The Peronists' tenure in power from 1973 to 1976 resulted in political polarization and violence analogous to the situation in Peru in the late 1980s.

Acción Democrática has been an integral part of Venezuela's political stability since the transition to democracy in 1958. Its founder and leader, Rómulo Betancourt, was a colleague of Haya de la Torre and shared Haya's antiimperialist bent; Betancourt was also influenced by Marxist thought. The AD began as a revolutionary party, with a program similar to APRA's: agrarian reform; national control of the oil industry; and redistribution of wealth. The AD also shares APRA's strong party discipline and loyalty to its founder and leader. Yet Betancourt did not have the deified stature that Haya had, and this was in the long run to the AD's benefit; the AD did not suffer a leadership crisis in the post-Betancourt era, as APRA did after Haya, and was thus able to develop a leadership structure that was less authoritarian, religious, and personalist in nature.

There are other critical differences between the parties: the AD achieved power by 1958 and implemented land reform early on; in 1976 it nationalized the oil industry; the AD alternated tenure in power with another strong party, the Comité de Organización Política Electoral Independiente (COPEI). And Venezuela is much wealthier than Peru and does not have the rift between Andean and coastal cultures. Finally, and perhaps most important, the AD is committed to the democratic system, since "the system is fundamentally [its] creation."[47] The AD's Political Thesis, updated in 1964, commits the party to working through democratic means, without violence.[48] It formally recognizes that it is a reformist and not a revolutionary party, which dictates certain behavioral norms. "Adecos [AD party members] today are not interested in transforming the system, but in managing and improving it. . . . It [the AD] is pragmatic, in the sense that the principal source of variation in policy is economic feasibility, not ideology or loyalty to any one class or sector."[49] This was a critical difference between the AD and APRA.

Both the AD and APRA attained power for the first time in 1945; APRA in an alliance with José Luis Bustamante y Rivero and the Fiente Democrático (FREDEMO), and the AD in an alliance with the military. In both cases the parties' tenure in power was cut short in 1948 by a military coup supported by entrenched elites. In both cases overly audacious reform mongering, sectarian behavior, and incoherent economic policy alienated not only the conservative private sector, but other significant societal actors, such as the Catholic church. The 1948 coup in Peru led to the eight-year Odría dictatorship; in Venezuela to the Pérez Jiménez decade.

When the AD came back to power in 1958 it did so with an explicit commitment—in the Pact of Punto Fijo—to share power with other political forces, primarily its rival party, COPEI. AD leaders accepted that the unilateral domination the party had attempted in its first tenure in power was incompatible with democratic government. A change in approach was evident even at the municipal level, as the study of party relations with the urban poor will detail. Finally, the AD's change of approach was facilitated by the extent to which all of Venezuelan society had united against the corruption of the Marcos Pérez Jiménez dictatorship and in favor of democracy. This had a major impact on the AD's decision to work within the system; there were clearly greater incentives to do so than in the Peruvian case.

Neither APRA nor the Peruvian political system experienced a similar evolution. While the AD was able to achieve power through elections in 1958, APRA was able to attain legal status only by entering into an alliance with the conservative Manuel Prado government in 1956. Party leaders maintained that this was the only means to guarantee APRA's survival. Yet much of the party, particularly its youth, saw this as a betrayal of its original ideals. Many potential young leaders left APRA at this point. While in Venezuela there was a much broader support base for democracy, due to opposition to Pérez Jiménez, in Peru the political spectrum remained much more conservative, and the power of entrenched elites was virtually unchallenged until 1968. This clearly had an impact on how radical youth sectors viewed the "democratic" system. From the time of the convivencia, APRA was tainted by cooperation with an elitist system that it had so long fought against, and it was unable to resolve the conflict within its own ranks over whether to work within the system or to attempt to overthrow it. This conflict would have profound effects on APRA's tenure in power.

Peru and Venezuela are incomparable cases in terms of social and economic characteristics. However, the AD's record of successful reform must be largely attributed to a commitment, both pragmatic and doctrinal, to working within the constitutional system and to pursuing pragmatic reform. In addition, the AD's ability to temper its earlier sectarian and authoritarian tendencies resulted in a much improved ability to effectively act as a link between state and society. This was no doubt enhanced by the presence of a viable electoral challenge from the opposition party, COPEI. Finally, unlike APRA, the AD never alienated the left wing of its own support base and was thus never caught in an inviable center position. While this clearly says something about political consensus in Venezuela, it also points to the enhanced possibilities for pragmatic reform if the governing party is not forced to outdo its rivals on the left or right, the scenario that Sartori describes.

In this light, it is useful to briefly consider the Peronists' tenure in power, 1973–1976. The political violence and economic chaos that the Peronist regime faced by 1976 are analogous to the crises of APRA's 1985–1990 regime, and so also are the centrifugal political tendencies toward polarization. In both cases pressures for extremist tactics and violence stemmed not only from the extremes of left and right, but also from within the ranks of the governing party.

> As the period of Peronist government came to an end, inflation was galloping toward world records and Argentina was approaching a cessation of debt payments. One political killing was occurring every five hours and a bomb explosion every three. In the face of a power vacuum caused by the disunity of Peronism and the ineptitude of the government, and with opposition from both labour and entrepreneurial groups mounting, a military golpe de estado was generally regarded as inevitable.[50]

This description could easily apply to Peru during the latter half of APRA's tenure, with the main difference being that the military—discredited by its recent experience in power—was reluctant to take direct control of the government.

Both APRA and the Peronists were highly nationalist parties that were supposedly the proponents of sweeping social change. The founders of the Justicialist movement (the basis for Peronism) were influenced by Haya de la Torre, among others. Both parties displayed highly sectarian characteristics and had an almost mystical or religious faith in the party leader; membership was more a question of identification than of affiliation. Being an aprista or a Peronist signified not just party membership, but a distinct vision of society and a distinct place within society. Both parties lacked a firm commitment to the constitutional system and had eclectic philosophies rather than ideological coherence. Both were multiclass in origin and reformist in doctrine, but highly authoritarian in structure, although the Peronist party was much more loosely organized than APRA. "[Peronism] was a 'movement' pivoting on a vertical axis rather than a 'party' with a horizontal class-based structure."[51]

Both parties alienated the private sector with a combination of economic mismanagement and extremist rhetoric, and ultimately also alienated much of nonparty society with sectarian behavior, creating the sorts of cleavages in political discourse and in society that Duverger attributes to totalitarian or highly ideological parties. In both cases the nature of the party was critical in precluding the formation of lasting consensus, in exacerbating existing cleavages in society, and in polarizing the political system. Leadership was also a factor in both cases; neither Isabel Perón nor Alan García were the political masters that their party founders had been. The fact that poor decisionmaking was backed by what were perceived by outsiders to be monolithic, quasi-fascist, quasi-religious parties further alienated nonparty members of society.

Despite the fact that neither of the party founders, Haya and Juan Perón, were ever fully committed to armed struggle or to Marxist revolution, they inspired armed wings or branches on the extremes of both left and right of their own parties. Perón encouraged the Montoneros' violence from his exile in Spain in the early 1970s as a means to disrupt the military government. Haya de la Torre, meanwhile, tacitly condoned APRA's involvement in armed insurrections as early as the 1920s and as late as the mid-1970s. Consensus was impossible in a situation where, for example, the left-wing Peronist-affiliated Montoneros were repressed by the government of Isabel Perón and the paramilitary squads of her right-wing interior minister, López Rega. In Peru's case the García government was challenged by an armed insurrection, the Movimiento Revolucionario Tupac Amaru (MRTA), led by former members of APRA ranks; at the same time a right-wing paramilitary squad, the Comando Rodrigo Franco, had direct links to APRA and to Interior Minister Agustín Mantilla. The resort to violence in both cases grew in part out of the past behavior of the party founders. "[The Peronist] militant's faith in Perón's revolution was absolutely sincere, rooted in his sanction of armed struggle, in [his] own youthful lack of political experience."[52]

The existence of armed wings of the governing parties exacerbated already polarized systems and severely undermined the legitimacy of both governments. Yet the armed groups reflected some of the most basic traits of both parties and portray very vividly how internal party characteristics impeded the consensus building that is necessary for reform and ultimately for coherent governance.

Despite their divergent traits, in all three cases at the time of transition to democracy (Venezuela in 1958, Argentina in 1973, and Peru in 1978) the military—or factions of the military—turned to its formal rivals. The parties became critical actors for a variety of reasons. Military rulers had very weak links to society, and the parties were the only remaining civilian groups with any institutional viability. In all three cases popular mobilization was heightened, in part because of opposition to military rule, to the point that a return to the political status quo ante military government was impossible. These multiclass parties with eclectic party doctrines were much more acceptable to the military than were more-radical groups to the left. Mass-based parties were uniquely situated to play this transitional role. In 1973 Peronism was seen as the only movement having the power and political clout to curb the influence of leftist groups both within and outside the Peronist movement.[53] The situation in Peru in 1978 was analogous, as the military, partly in response to widespread popular protest, turned to APRA to lead the transition but also to limit the role of the nascent forces of the Marxist left.

The basic role of political parties—providing a link between society and state—was a particularly critical one at a time when highly mobilized societies were attempting to make the transition from military dictatorship to civilian government. Yet the context in which parties had to fulfill their role was challenging, marked by a preexisting breach between state institutions and society exacerbated by lengthy periods of military rule. At the same time the traits of these parties, traits that were deepened by persecution or proscription during military rule, made them ill suited to fulfill their difficult obligations. Indeed, while weak institutions, heightened political mobilization, and the need for socioeconomic reform pointed to a critical role for reformist parties in the transition to and the consolidation of democracy, the parties' machinery and complex ideological baggage made them incapable of building the consensus necessary to pursue viable economic strategies concurrent with social reform. Nowhere in Latin America is this failure more evident than in Peru in the present day. A closer examination of APRA's experience in power lends strength to the thesis that the nature of political parties, particularly in the context of weak institutions, can be a determining factor in the difficult process of democratic consolidation.

In this study of APRA in power I examine the party's role in the context of its own history, of its dominance by the autocratic and erratic Alan García, and of the substantial existing constraints to reform when the party took power in 1985. In the first part—Chapters 2–4—I describe the Peruvian socioeconomic and political contexts, and the party's origins and evolution up until 1985. Chapter 2 covers the party's history from the 1920s until the 1968 military revolution. In Chapter 3, I examine APRA's development from 1968 to 1980—a period during which Peru underwent substantial social, economic, and political change. The relationship of APRA to these changes is crucial to the understanding of the current party and its program, and the regime that evolved. Chapter 4 looks at APRA in the post-Haya years, the rise of Alan García, and the renovation that the party underwent for the 1985 presidential campaign. The second part—Chapters 5–8—analyzes the party in power: its macroeconomic strategy (Chapter 5); the party-government relationship (Chapter 6); its relations with the opposition (Chapter 7); and its relations with the urban poor (Chapter 8). The analysis of how the party operated among the marginalized of society, as well as at the municipal level, demonstrates how the traits that are barriers to reform at the macropolitical level affected APRA's relations with society as well.

The analysis in Chapter 9 of APRA's evolution from 1968 to the present, and of its performance in government, will help determine what sort of party APRA is and provide insight into why it was not able to maintain the consensus that it initially constructed, and that was so necessary to reform in Peru. Such an analysis adds to the understanding not only of APRA's, but also of any party's role in the difficult process of democratic consolidation.

1
APRA as Opposition

2

APRA 1924–1968: Confrontation, Compromise, and Counterreform

The formation of Peru's APRA, one of Latin America's oldest mass-based political parties, fundamentally changed the nature of politics in a nation where the system had consistently been monopolized by caudillo-like dictators and by a small but powerful elite. The bulk of the population had very little access to and virtually no influence on the nation's politics. "Unlike previous efforts to reform the country . . . no well-organized, mass political party had, prior to 1931 dared to directly challenge and confront the traditional power structure. The year 1931, then, was in many aspects a true watershed in Peruvian history, for from that date forward the possibility of translating individual or group satisfaction into political channels increasingly became a part of everyday life."[1]

APRA brought the issues of social justice, structural change, and national integration to the fore of the nation's politics. The bulk of the population had, for the first time, a vehicle through which to directly challenge the existing system. APRA was to remain the majority political force until the 1960s when it faced competition for the first time; even then it was still considered the major force in Peruvian politics and remained the only truly institutionalized political party. Power constantly eluded APRA, however, both because of its own flawed tactics and because of the entrenched opposition of the Peruvian elites, aided intermittently by direct military intervention. Despite APRA's existence for three decades, and the widespread support it kept, Peru remained strikingly backward in terms of political development, economic structure, and social welfare. As late as 1977 Peru was described as a country "which has been 'underdeveloping' rather than 'developing' over the long run."[2]

Several questions are raised by the paradox of this dismal record of reform in the face of a lasting and popular reform-oriented party. What makes the implementation of reform so difficult in Peru, and why did APRA in particular fail? Why, at the same time, was APRA able, despite its failure to attain power and implement reform, to maintain a substantial support base and mass appeal? The party's origins and its nature, and the socioeconomic context in which it operated; its ideology, organizational structure, bases of support, and almost "messianic" appeal; and finally the personality of its charismatic leader and founder, Víctor Raúl Haya de la

Torre, are crucial to the explanation of APRA's ability to survive and also of its dramatic failure when it finally held the reins of government. While APRA's origins and early years (prior to 1968) have been well documented elsewhere,[3] it is worth noting some of the particular traits that resulted from those experiences.

ORIGINS AND IDEOLOGY OF APRA

APRA was formed in 1924 by a Peruvian student leader from Trujillo, Víctor Raúl Haya de la Torre, while he was in exile in Mexico during the Augusto Leguía dictatorship. APRA was conceived as a mass-based, reform-oriented, antioligarchic, and antiimperialist party. The party had a "maximum" program, based on the ideal of a pan-American and not solely Peruvian party. Coining the term *Indo-America*, Haya de la Torre called for the unity of the continent and its peoples against US imperialism; for the political unity of Indo-America; for the nationalization of the Panama Canal; and for the solidarity of all oppressed peoples and classes, particularly the Indians of the New World.[4] The "minimum" program applied specifically to Peru and focused on the need to end the traditional exploitation of the indigenous population by the oligarchy, which had dominated Peru's polity, society, and economy since colonial times. APRA also stressed the need to develop a dynamic national economic capacity to free Peru from its extreme dependence on external trade and foreign capital. The state had a vital role to play in national economic planning, which included regulating foreign capital and increasing the purchasing power of the working class, thus creating a dynamic internal market. While APRA professed to be revolutionary, its official program implied that the party would come to power through "peaceful, constitutional means."[5]

The tension between reformist and, for Peru at the time, revolutionary goals and the attempt to achieve power through a constitutional system manipulated, if not totally controlled, by the oligarchy became evident early on. APRA's own commitment to the constitutional system was dubious. Several violent uprisings were either instigated or supported by APRA, including one in 1932 in Trujillo that culminated in the military's massacre of approximately a thousand apristas; the details of this affair remain obscure. The result was a deeply entrenched and enduring hatred between APRA and the military. The armed forces feared APRA's mass appeal and organizational capacity. The party, meanwhile, gained a reputation for violence with which it must still contend today. APRA's sporadic involvement in insurgencies served to legitimate, in the eyes of the repressors, violent and extralegal means to curb its activities. APRA's last involvement in such an insurgency was in October 1948, and the effects of subsequent repression and the leaders' response were to last for decades. In the 1950s the party tempered its rhetoric and colluded with the oligarchy, losing whatever ideological clarity it had, as well as much popular appeal; it was not rejuvenated until the 1980s.

APRA's origins and ideology must be seen in light of Peru's economic transformation in the early twentieth century, and the social tensions that transformation created. A wide area of the Peruvian north coast, where APRA originated, changed from prosperous small and medium-sized sugar farms and the vibrant urban centers created by their commerce into two giant and self-sufficient sugar plantations. The increase in land concentration took place as downturns in the world economy bankrupted smaller exporters, and they were bought out largely by foreign interests.

APRA's very creation was a function of the socioeconomic changes affecting Peru, and the party's regional patterns of support to some extent have mirrored the country's economic trends. APRA's electoral success over the years has been tied to agricultural extension and capitalization and the marginalization of the small farmer. APRA was able to organize and appeal to the new proletariat that arose. The party was traditionally weaker in Lima, which is the most industrialized region of the country and in relative terms was able to provide opportunity and mobility. APRA's support base consists primarily of the middle classes, workers, and certain groups of campesinos: all those who could not compete with the intrusion of big foreign capital.[6] Because the dislocation caused by the intrusion of big capital in Peruvian society affected a large and multiclass sector of the population, APRA was able to cross both class and rural-urban boundaries, and is often labeled a "populist multiclass party."[7] Yet because it also had a detailed program, an organized support base, and a long-term commitment to structural reform, APRA also fits into the category of reformist parties.

The party has its roots in Haya de la Torre's organizational activities among students and labor groups in the early 1920s. Haya undoubtedly capitalized on opposition to the Leguía dictatorship, which had been substantially increased by Leguía's unilateral decision in 1923 to consecrate the nation to the Sacred Heart of Jesus. On May 23, 1923, Haya led a student protest against that decision. The protest was repressed, and Haya exiled from Peru until 1931. Yet with his exile, the powerful legend "of the eternally persecuted Haya was born. . . . The 'martyr' image has constituted a vital element of Haya's political style."[8] Haya and APRA entered the national limelight through a speech he gave, upon his return to Lima in 1931, that outlined APRA's program and goals. Haya's oratorical prowess and the novelty in Peru of his revolutionary and confrontational rhetoric enabled him to elicit a strong and favorable popular response.

Haya de la Torre's personality had significant effects on the party's success. The other major Peruvian political thinker of the time, José Carlos Mariátegui, whose followers formed the Peruvian Communist party, was perhaps a superior intellectual, theoretician, and writer. Haya de la Torre, however, possessed unique oratorical skills and a strong penchant for organization and action.[9] Haya's oft-criticized manipulation of ideology led to a pragmatically oriented reformist party that was uniquely Peruvian. While both Haya and Mariátegui were influenced by Marxist thought, Haya was much more willing to mold ideas to fit Latin American realities and his own needs. His approach was inclusionary in nature and avoided the terms of class conflict. Even in his most radical work, *El antimperialismo y el APRA,* he made a point of the need to include the middle classes: because in Latin America the proletariat was still in feudal conditions, the middle classes, who were displaced by imperialist penetration, should lead the revolutionary struggle.[10]

While Haya wrote and spoke prolifically, APRA's appeal was not confined to its ideology; to some extent it rested on the personality of Haya himself, who had a mystique that gave him "a stature in national politics not shared by anyone."[11] This mystique began with his 1923 exile and ended only with his death in 1979. The persona has traditionally been extremely important and remains so even today. It was particularly important at the time when APRA surfaced, a time when the political system was increasingly open to mass participation, yet there were no institutions or organizations to channel that participation.

Haya had traveled extensively, including going to Germany at the time of the rise of the National Socialists and to the Soviet Union shortly after the revolution, and he was deeply affected by the potential power that he saw in these mass movements. He was also attuned to how to mobilize the discomfited and discontented of Peruvian society during a period of economic and social dislocation. Most important, he and his followers backed rhetoric with organizational and political action. The combination of charisma and impatience that characterized Haya also applied to the image of the party as a whole; his followers responded with an almost blind loyalty. APRA was more than a political party and aprismo more than party loyalty: it was analogous to a religion.

The loyalty that APRA aroused among its followers was matched by an intense fear or hatred on the part of its opponents. APRA offered to Peruvians, or threatened them with, the fundamental transformation of their society. It directly addressed issues of cultural integration, economic dualism, foreign domination, inequitable structures of wealth and power. Even more frightening than APRA's rhetoric was APRA's capacity to organize and to act. Haya's personality and experiences, and the many years of repression, clandestine activity, and exile suffered by the party, resulted in a hierarchical structure that was in part responsible for the APRA's exceptional capacity to organize and to mobilize, which rivaled that of the army. This, coupled with its emotional appeal, reinforced the dominant classes' fear of APRA.[12]

The shared experiences of persecution, imprisonment, and social isolation that the apristas suffered created a clanlike mentality—an "us versus them" attitude in the party in general—that affected not only its politics but its interpretation of history and society. "For the apristas [this] implied something biblical: 'he who is not with me is against me,' and for anti-apristas a system of recognition through opposition."[13]

Hatred of APRA was not restricted to the elite and the military. The Peruvian left, from the time of the 1929 split between Haya and Mariátegui, and Mariátegui's death, faced a crisis of identity of sorts. A prominent leftist leader of the 1960s, Hugo Blanco, explained the left's constant dilemma with APRA. "[APRA] is the oldest party in Peru, and the best organized. It has the longest tradition of struggle and has suffered the most murders, the most deportation and the most torture victims. . . . The Communist party has always called the APRA fascist and has always had a very sectarian attitude. But on many occasions the Communist party has actually stood to the right of APRA. . . . So this has something to do with the Communist party's great hatred towards the APRA."[14]

The image of ideological fervor and discipline that APRA projected was reminiscent of Communist and Fascist parties. This, combined with the fact that one could not be neutral about the party, created the "artificial political cleavages" in society that Duverger attributes to highly ideological parties. The direct challenge posed by APRA and its 1931 introduction into Peruvian politics very soon led to its repression. Haya de la Torre lost to the caudillo-like Luis Sánchez Cerro in presidential elections that APRA to this day claims were fraudulent[15] (see Table 2.1). In August 1932 a military revolt in Trujillo, instigated by local apristas, resulted in the brutal repression of the nascent party by the military and in the exile of its leaders. The party's appeal was strong enough, however, that it was able to survive the many years of exile. In fact, its tradition of suffering increased its appeal and decreased the legitimacy of the regimes that repressed it. "We are the exemplary citizens of an exemplary party. And if we are so it is because we have suffered and we have known how to suffer."[16]

In a short time APRA was able to rise to national renown, arouse and organize a great many Peruvians, and sufficiently threaten the dominant classes' political monopoly that the fears behind the "antiaprismo" movement became almost as strong and certainly more violent than the movement itself. The constant and often violent resistance to APRA's inroads into the political scene raised tensions within APRA between its commitments to a revolutionary program and to the achievement of that program by constitutional means. Repression of legitimate political gains resulted in an increased willingness by many apristas to resort to violence as a

Table 2.1 Elections 1931–1980: National Totals (Percentages)

1931

Sánchez Cerro	49.1
Haya de la Torre	34.2
Others	16.7
Total votes:	309,580

1945

Bustamante	69.8
Ureta	30.2
Total votes:	455,104

1956

Prado	45.4
Belaúnde	36.6
Lavalle	17.8
Total votes:	1,249,866

1963

Belaúnde	39.1
Haya de la Torre	34.4
Odria	25.5
UPP	1.1
Total votes:	1,814,568

1978

Left[a]	36.25
APRA	35.34
PPC	23.78
Others	4.0
Total votes:	4,173,571

1980

Acción Popular	45.4
APRA	27.4
Left[a]	16.7
PPC	10.2
MDP/UNO	0.6

Sources: David Scott Palmer, *Peru: The Authoritarian Tradition* (New York: Praeger, 1980); Sandra Woy-Hazelton, "The Return to Partisan Politics in Peru," in *Post-Revolutionary Peru: The Politics of Transformation,* ed. Stephen Gorman (Boulder, CO: Westview Press, 1982).
Note: a. The left was a loose front composed of the PDC, the Partido Socialista Revolucionario (PSR), the Partido Comunista del Perú, and others in 1978; in 1980 it consisted of Unida Izquierda, the Unión Nacional de la Izquierda Revolucionaria (UNIR), and others.

means—a tendency that still exists. APRA-led revolts in Trujillo in 1932 and Callao in 1948 intensified the cycle of violence and repression. Elites in the mid-twentieth century were clearly unwilling to accept APRA's reformist program, despite its popular mandate. In the context of Peru's sociopolitical structure at the time, APRA's ideology was revolutionary. Haya's call for the replacement of the *vieja democracia verbal*[17] was definitely unacceptable to the dominant classes, and exposed their democracy as exactly what Haya called it: a democracy in name alone. From the time of the party's formation, whether legal or in exile, whether radical or modified in its stance, APRA's presence as a challenge to the existing social and political structures permanently changed the nature of politics in Peru.

THE CONTEXT FOR FRUSTRATED REFORM

By the mid-twentieth century, when many Latin American countries had made a great deal of progress toward industrialization and economic diversification, Peru lagged far behind. Peru entered the 1960s with an extremely dependent economy, an extraordinarily high level of foreign penetration, a lack of domestic technological capability, and an export-dominated growth pattern. Even after the military's "revolution" of the 1970s, Peru's social indicators displayed preposterously poor conditions for the many at the bottom of the income ladder and an extremely skewed income distribution, even in relation to its Latin neighbors (see Tables 2.2, 2.3, 2.4).

The nation's economic underdevelopment was matched by a political system based on manipulation and co-optation of the majority of the population by a small elite, with the frequent aid of the military. The elite's control of the political system was not total, however, and was eroding with the increase of urbanization and popular mobilization that accompanied industrialization. "The failure or inability of the elite to concern itself with the generation of popular support is shown by the rise of the APRA party. There was little attempt to mobilize that important stratum of society which found its political home in the APRA."[18]

While the elite did not have total control, it did have a de facto monopoly due to the fragmentation of the new upwardly mobile sectors. "By themselves neither the industrial sector, the middle class, the working class nor the peasantry could have devised and implemented a strategy commanding the majority support of the population."[19] This fragmentation was due to the diversity of economic base, level of income, and regional affiliation that characterizes Peruvian society. These fragmented social sectors had little power vis-à-vis the centralized control of government in Lima. APRA, which had mobilized the support of some of these

Table 2.2 Peru: Basic Indicators

Land and People	
Area (square kilometers)	1,280,219
Population[a]	21,256,000
Annual growth rate	2.6%
Birth rate	36.7%
Mortality per 1,000 inhabitants	10.7%
Infant Mortality	79.0%
Life expectancy	58.6%
Literacy	86.0%

Labor force by sector	
Agriculture	35.2%
Mining	1.8%
Manufacturing	12.8%
Construction	3.7%
Others	46.5%

Economy	1984	1985	1986	1987	1988	1989
GDP growth rate	4.8	2.4	11.3	7.8	-8.9	-10.4
Agricultural sector		11.8	3.7	6.2	5.0	5.7
Mining sector	4.8	4.3	-4.5	-2.9	-18.7	
Manufacturing sector		5.5	4.9	16.8	13.7	-14.3
Construction sector		0.8	-10.5	21.3	15.5	-5.4
Real wages	-8.9	-12.4	14.4	8.7	-23.2	
Terms of trade[b]	94.0	90.0	87.0	9.0	108.0	

Balance of Payments (in millions of dollars)					
Current account	418.2	667.1	-520.9	-1,069.4	-1,046.0
Capital account	1,031.2	337.1	733.2	897.4	723.0

Total external debt (in millions of dollars)					
Disbursed debt	13,189	14,136	15,925	17,983	19,000
Debt service paid	1,015	990	623	464	196

Source: *Economic and Social Progress in Latin America.* Inter-American Development Bank, *Annual Report—1989* (Washington, DC: IADB, 1990).
Notes: a. Of the total population, 68.9 percent lived in urban centers.
b. Index 1980=100.

Table 2.3 Selective Socioeconomic Indicators: Peru and Her Neighbors

	Chile	Peru	Ecuador	Bolivia	Colombia	Brazil	Mexico
			Population				
Total (millions)	12.7	21.2	10.2	6.9	30.5	144.4	84.8
Growth rate (1981–1988)	1.7	2.6	2.9	2.7	2.1	2.2	2.4
			National Accounts				
GDP per capita[a]	2,518	1,503	1,477	724	1,739	2,449	2,588
Per capita growth[b]	5.6	-11.1	5.0	0.0	1.6	-2.3	-1.1
		Employment and Wages (percentage of labor force)					
In agriculture	20.3	35.2	36.0	49.0	34.3	25.9	37.6
Urban unemployment[c]	10.2	—[d]	13.0	5.5[e]	11.4	4.0	3.6
Real minimum wage changes[f]	57.6	60.8	68.8	—	113.9	57.6	57.7
			Urbanization[g]				
Percentage of urban population	83.4	68.9	54.2	50.4	71.5	72.9	70.3
Urban growth rate	-0.5	0.8	1.1	1.4	0.0	-0.2	0.4
			Education[h]				
Literacy (percent)	92.5	86.0	85.2	63.2	82.1	68.7	87.9
Enrollment (primary)	109	122	114	91	114	103	114
Enrollment (secondary)	16	24	33	20	13	11	16

Sources: Inter-American Development Bank, *Economic and Social Progress in Latin America* (Washington, DC: 1989); Carlos Amat y León, *Niveles de vida y grupos sociales en el peru* (Lima: Universidad del Pacífico, 1983).

Notes: a. All figures are in 1988 US dollars.

b. Growth rates for 1988.

c. Open urban unemployment, 1988 rates.

d. Exact figures are not available for comparable dates. Estimates for open unemployment at the end of 1989 were 10 percent, and for underemployment 70 percent.

e. This is the 1987 figure; the 1988 figure was not available.

f. 1980=100.

g. Percentage urban is for 1988; growth rate percentage is for 1981–1988.

h. Enrollment is the percentage of the relevant age population enrolled in primary (5–10 years old) and higher (20–24 years old) education. The figure may be greater than 100, as it includes adult students outside the respective age groups.

Table 2.4 Macroeconomic Indicators 1980–1989

	1980–1984	1985	1986	1987	1988	1989
Real GDP growth	-1.0	2.4	9.5	7.8	-8.8	-10.4
Per capita	-3.6	-0.2	6.9	5.2	-11.4	-13.0
Consumption growth	-0.4	2.3	13.3	8.3	-11.5	-7.5
Inflation rate	87.0	158.3	62.9	114.5	1,722.3	2,775.3
Money supply growth	94.0	122.4	64.4	113.0	585.1	2,775.3
Public sector borrowing as percentage of GDP	7.8	5.7	9.0	11.6	10.6	6.2
Tax revenue/GDP	13.5	12.4	10.8	8.2	7.3	4.4
Current account deficit/GDP	3.9	0.3	6.0	7.2	7.4	1.0
Gross international reserves (in millions of dollars)	—	2,283	1,861	1,130	1,125	1,512
Foreign debt/GDP	51.0	76.8	67.8	62.4	77.0	75.3
Accrued debt service ratio	61.1	69.8	77.9	77.0	79.3	64.0
Paid debt service ratio	53.7	32.3	23.3	18.7	12.2	11.4
Real exchange rate[a]	77.1	99.6	86.8	74.9	91.2	59.0
Terms of trade	118.4	90.6	66.4	66.9	72.8	68.9
Real wage[b]	95	64	83	90	71	38
Employment growth (percentage)	2.2	-0.5	4.3	5.7	-0.8	-3.7
Utilized capacity (percentage)	56	45	61	69	59	46

Sources: Ricardo Lago Gallego, "The Illusion of Pursuing Redistribution Through Macro-economics," in *Macropolitics and Income Distribution in Latin America,* ed. R. Dornbusch and S. Edwards, (Chicago: University of Chicago Press, forthcoming); and Ricardo Lago Gallego, *Peru: Policies to Stop Inflation and Initiate Economic Recovery* (Washington, DC: The World Bank, 1989).
Notes: a. December 1978=100.
b. 1979=100.

sectors, was fundamentally weakened by its lack of substantive peasant backing, by its inability to dominate in Lima, and by the virulent opposition of the military.[20] Thus the political game in Peru was one of default, of manipulation, and of co-optation: a game most skillfully played by an elite whose primary objective was to maintain its status free of state interference. The resulting situation was one of relatively high levels of economic growth yielding benefits for a small and privileged stratum of the population. "Success of the Peruvian oligarchy can be attributed to its capacity to employ modern technology, its success in legitimizing itself as the only agent able to guarantee expansion of economic production, and its acceptance of wealth as a measure of power while still maintaining other traditional values."[21]

"Although the major challenge to the domination of export capital in Peruvian politics came initially through the formation of APRA,"[22] the bulk of APRA's supporters, who initially were those of the middle class who were disaffected with the system, increasingly came to have an interest in the system, whether through the ownership of a small farm, union membership, or a stake in a small business. APRA's base expanded from its initial focus on the sugar workers of the North both socially and territorially to include the mining centers, and the factory workers and employees, particularly in the textile industry, in Lima and provincial towns. APRA also gained support among small traders and entrepreneurs. Many of these supporters fit into the ambiguous category of the middle class, but they were not necessarily united in their interests. In part as a response to the divergence of interests and stakes, Haya's ideology was inclusive and eclectic rather than confrontational, preventing the party's taking a coherent stance against the system in favor of the masses.

APRA's base among the peasants has never been particularly strong, yet its composition reflects the diversity within the socioeconomic structure of Peru's highland peasants. In the sierra APRA was primarily a class party, representing the interests of the richer, smallholding peasants and of the miners, shopkeepers, and transport and textile workers. The eclectic nature of its commitments prevented the party from becoming committed to particular forms of either urban industrial or rural agricultural development. It made it possible for APRA to dominate the politics of many regions in the sierra and also to play a key role in the politics of migrants, but not to take a coherent stance against the system. While the party had no ties with the business class in the region, and periodically supported peasants in their clashes with hacendados,[23] it was unable to represent the interests of all the peasantry, as those interests were so diverse and often tied to the existing economic structure. APRA never, for example, was able to take a definitive position on the agrarian reform issue.[24]

The labor movement in Peru has traditionally been weak, and its fate, until 1968, was inextricably linked to APRA's. The Confederación de Trabajadores Peruanos (CTP), begun in 1944 and officially recognized in 1964, was founded by and dominated by APRA. The major labor dispute has traditionally been between the CTP and the military governments; there is a direct correlation between union activity and the legality or illegality of APRA, which was usually banned by military governments, such as the Manuel Odría regime.[25] After 1968 the Communist labor movement, the Confederación General de Trabajadores Peruanos (CGTP), was legalized and began to erode APRA's monopoly on union support, in part because APRA had relinquished its radical stance. The characteristics that were held typical of APRA support—marginal, socially ambitious, socially frustrated—began to be typical of the Maoist left in the 1970s.[26] Until 1968, however, organized labor and APRA were virtually synonymous, and APRA was more concerned with using the labor movement for its own political ends than with enhancing labor's objectives. APRA curtailed strike activity, for example, during its years of collaboration with the Prado government and strongly promoted a collective bargaining strategy to avoid confrontation.[27] Labor was weak and fragmented; its nature reflected Peru's economic development in general: it was very much affected by the enclave-like nature of enterprises and by the rural or community background of many of its members. Consequently, labor suffered from the same problem that classes in general had in articulating a coherent set of interests. While APRA did not substantially improve the fate of the labor movement, the party's organizational capacity and popular following did appeal to the movement[28] and served as a mobilizational force, particularly in the absence of other alternatives.

The context in which APRA, or any reformist element, had to operate was not conducive to the implementation of coherent policy. Neither the forces in power nor those in opposition seemed able to undertake a unified political strategy, and in light of this general fragmentation, the status quo was preserved. The elite sought to preserve their world as it was through leaders either from their own ranks, such as Manuel Prado, or through caudillo-like protectors of their interests, such as Manuel Odría; and to prevent APRA from taking power through co-optation or outright banning of the party. The diverse groups in Peru that had an interest in structural reform, while lending support to APRA, were unable to develop a successful strategy, as is demonstrated by APRA's constant shifting of tactics and ideological stances. Finally, intermittent periods of persecution also diminished apristas' ability to construct a consistent strategy and led to splits within the party between those who sought more-radical, violent action against their oppressors and those who chose to compromise with the elites in power in order to have legal status and some influence in national policymaking. These tensions were vividly demonstrated by the outcome of the periods when APRA was accorded legal status and allowed to participate and even hold the majority in the legislature.[29] Each of these experiences culminated in either military coups or the party's making major tactical and ideological concessions. APRA's heavy-handed reform mongering and resort to violent tactics during the 1945–1948 Bustamante government resulted in a military coup and the eight-year Odría dictatorship. (This is analogous to the AD's experience in Venezuela in the same years, which ushered in the Pérez Jiménez dictatorship.)

APRA's convivencia, or cohabitation accord, with the Prado government in exchange for legal status in 1956 was at the expense of a major ideological shift to the right and the disaffection of some of the best and brightest young ranks of the party. During the Fernando Belaúnde Terry regime (1963–1968) the party adopted a policy of blocking all reforms in conjunction with Odría's backers in the legislature in order to improve its electoral position in 1969. Yet APRA's stubborn stance led to political stalemate in the face of increasing economic stagnation, rural unrest, and urban poverty. While APRA was not solely to blame—Belaúnde's political leadership was largely responsible—this culminated in the military's total frustration with civilian politics and the "revolution" of 1968. Throughout these experiences APRA clearly failed to provide a viable strategy for reform, yet it was still able to hold a strong popular following and remain the primary party in Peruvian politics.

Thus context is important to the explanation of APRA's political behavior and evolution from 1931 to 1968. In 1931 APRA was a radical party with a confrontational approach. By 1968 it had made several alliances with conservative forces, including one with the very dictator who had outlawed and persecuted APRA from 1948 to 1956. Its ideology and reformist platform lost coherence, and it had acted as a counterforce to reform through its refusal to cooperate with other emerging reformist forces. Its leaders were divided, and many of its younger and more radical members had splintered off, disillusioned with the party's evolution. There was still enough coherence and popular support for APRA, however, to ensure its survival during the military years, its predominance in the transition back to civilian rule in the late 1970s, and its rejuvenation and eventual rise to national power in the 1980s.

Reform is clearly not easy to implement in Peru. The fate of the country's first reform-oriented party demonstrates this. Even bare survival proved difficult at times for APRA. The persecution and exile suffered by APRA leaders, coupled with Haya de la Torre's dominance and his ideological ambiguity, led to the party's compromises and tactics in 1956–1968. The party's hierarchical and tight organization may have served to decrease its capacity to adapt to new social realities and use different tactics to take advantage of new political opportunities as well as to appeal to nonparty members of society. The opposition of the military also proved an unconquerable obstacle for APRA, and probably fed the resentment that lay behind the party's disruptive political behavior from 1963 to 1968. What remains ironic, however, is that by the late 1960s—at the time when Peruvian society was clearly changing; clashes over social issues and development had finally become central to the political debate; and there was no longer any party that overtly resisted change—APRA was unable to adapt its outdated tactics or rejuvenate its compromised ideological position in order to capitalize on the situation. Because the party had faced entrenched elite opposition for so long, it maintained a pervasive opposition mentality and was woefully inexperienced with both reform mongering and democratic government, a problem that had surfaced in 1945 and 1963, and would again become apparent during APRA's 1980s tenure in power.

Despite the failures of 1931 to 1968, the party did manage to survive and hold on to its traditional third of the electorate, no small achievement. Despite its compromises and mistakes, APRA maintained its core base of support and the mystique that was key to its appeal. By the time of the 1979 transition to civilian rule, APRA was able to play a leading role and demonstrate that it was still a major, if not the major, force in Peruvian politics.

APRA also had international influence. Haya's writings and the party's struggles attracted the attention of other Latin leaders and had a formative impact on movements ranging from Venezuela's AD to Costa Rica's PLN to Sandino's rebellion in Nicaragua.[30] APRA was the first political party to call not only for the transformation of its own society, but for a united and uniquely Latin approach to the continent's problems.

Finally, and most difficult to define in concrete terms, one of the main reasons for APRA's survival was the sense of exceptionality and mission, which grew out of its history of suffering, that its core members felt. In many ways, this elusive sense of mission is responsible for the party's persistence through its times of persecution and compromise, and for its eventual rejuvenation. Yet unfortunately the same sense of mission that guaranteed APRA's survival was one of the traits that were to prove barriers to its ability to govern. "How to explain such resistance. The courage, the determination of clandestine apristas all have their part. But to appreciate more exactly these qualities, a hypothesis is necessary: if APRA was able to stay alive between 1933 and 1945, and again between 1948 and 1956, it is because at that time, for an aprista, by which I mean an active militant, there was no road conceivable other than APRA."[31]

3

APRA and the Military Docenio: The Stolen Revolution, 1968–1980

Deliberately, I do not accept that the revolution began on October 3, 1968; one has to distinguish between revolutionary process and government. The revolutionary process began over fifty years ago, with the generation of Haya de la Torre and Mariátegui.
—Armando Villanueva, member of APRA's Secretaría Colegial, in *Caretas* (Lima), September 30, 1974, p. 26

Because of oligarchic inspiration, we also were trained with an antiaprista bias.... The ideological factor appears in 1968 when, from a revolutionary perspective, we rejected APRA and its old and weary leaders who were responsible for a sinister trajectory of pacts and transgressions... totally abandoning the revolutionary flags.
—General Jorge Fernández Maldonado, cabinet member, 1968–1976, in an interview with the author

APRA AND THE MILITARY'S REVOLUTION

When the armed forces took power on October 3, 1968, it was not immediately clear that it was not another typical military coup, and that APRA would not once again be the subject of persecution. It soon became evident, however, that the regime was progressive rather than reactionary in nature, and that there would be no widespread repression. As the regime took concrete actions—the expropriation of the International Petroleum Company (IPC), the Agrarian Reform Law, the formation of Industrial Communities—APRA was left as a stunned onlooker. The military, the age-old persecutors of the party, implemented what apristas considered their revolution. As apristas were neither the proponents of reform nor the martyrs of repression, the party faced what Luis Alberto Sánchez—one of the original and highest ranking party members—called its most critical moment.[1] Yet the military regime met its demise in the late 1970s and ironically turned to APRA to orchestrate the transition back to civilian rule, precisely the scenario described in the first chapter.

The military, while not openly repressing political parties, and in fact not even outlawing them, had no respect for the existing parties and saw them as part of the traditional societal structure it was trying to overthrow. Military leaders were aware of the need to incorporate popular demands, and particularly of the challenge posed by the well-organized and extensive party machinery controlled by APRA. They also aimed to undermine APRA's long-term domination of organized labor by sponsoring alternate union movements to APRA's CTP: the Communist-controlled CGTP and the government-affiliated Confederación de Trajabadores Revolucionarios del Perú (CTRP). Until 1968 "the working class [had] been insulated from more radical mobilization by its loyalty to APRA."[2]

The Velasco regime, advised by a dissident aprista, Carlos Delgado, set up an elaborate mechanism—the Sistema Nacional de Apoyo a la Movilización Social (SINAMOS)—to channel popular demands. SINAMOS was designed to cope with public demands that in part were fueled by the military government's own rhetoric, and also to undermine the virtual monopoly that APRA had had for forty years on grassroots political organization and activity. "SINAMOS is of particular importance . . . because there are striking parallels and contrasts between the tactics which Odría used to undermine APRA and the approach taken by SINAMOS to weaken political opposition."[3]

While there was no overt conflict between the military and APRA, there was clearly rivalry, at both the ideological and practical levels. The military, having taken both the revolutionary initiative and control of the state, clearly had an advantage in the early stages of the game. As the regime met greater obstacles, however, and eventually had to return control of the nation to civilian hands, the tables turned to some extent, as was demonstrated by the pivotal role played by Haya de la Torre in the Constituent Assembly. The military's revolution indeed caused an internal crisis in APRA and resulted in a renovation of ideology and leadership—sponsored by Haya—within the party. It is from this renovation that the current APRA leaders, Alan García in particular, emerged.

The military's borrowing and use of aprista ideas and doctrines forced the party leaders to come to terms with the vacillations and compromises that had caused the disaffection of a great deal of its youth in the 1950s and 1960s. In the past, electoral losses and paucity of new leaders were always blamed on persecution or the *veto militar*. "No one looked to the interior of APRA in search of the mistakes committed. They blamed the military, the oligarchy, ignorance. . . . The logic of the persecuted was used: all against me and me against the world; only aprismo will save Peru; the more they defeat us, the stronger we will be; discipline, comrades, the next time we will triumph."[4]

In the absence of outward repression, the party was forced to look inward and revamp. There was some subtle harassment of APRA leaders, and the theory that the coup had occurred to prevent Haya's victory in the 1969 elections may have some validity. However, the military was careful not to make martyrs of the apristas, as it had in the past. Thus rather than being persecuted for attempting to implement its revolution, APRA stood by while the revolution took place without it—ironically under the auspices of the very institution that had persecuted the party in the past. As Haya himself said, "Why did they do what they tortured APRA for trying to do?"[5]

Many observers agree that despite its intent, the military's revolution was not successful, and that many of the reforms, such as the land and industrial reforms, reached a privileged group of workers rather than addressing the more serious underlying problems of the landless and the unemployed.[6] The attempt to use SINAMOS and the government-controlled labor federation, the CTRP, to control popular participation was a total failure, as was exemplified by the 1975 looting and burning of SINAMOS headquarters in the February 5 protests, and the 1977 and 1978 general strikes. The main criticism is that the very nature of the military regime, which excluded genuine popular participation and attempted to impose a "revolution from above," doomed it to failure. It is relevant that not only did the military's Inca Plan draw heavily from Haya's early writings, but the model implemented strongly resembled that envisioned by Haya. The early Haya was impatient and lacked faith in the individual's ability to function as a political subject. The political movement that he envisioned was hierarchical and authoritarian—assigning the state the role of building the nation[7]—and he favored taking power by insurrection. This same choice of strategy led Haya to break with Mariátegui in 1928, and also led to APRA's history of conflict with the military. "APRA mistakenly used violence. It seems that it had the goal of forming its own army. They assumed that the official army was the tool of the oligarchy and that it should disappear with it. This is the principle sin APRA committed against the army."[8]

Haya never succeeded in attaining power through armed rising, and by the mid-1940s abandoned insurrection as a strategy, although it was never totally discounted as an option by the party rank and file and at times was tacitly condoned by Haya. Ironically, in the convivencia, he engineered political arrangements with the very groups whose power he had sought to overthrow. The military, meanwhile, which had been the traditional watchdog of the oligarchy, virtually switched roles with APRA and challenged the existing power structures. Upon taking power by insurrection, the military tried and failed to impose a hierarchical vision of popular organization through SINAMOS. As its failure became evident, it turned, ironically, to Haya and APRA as the bridge with civil society.

When the Peruvian military seized power in October 1968, one of the guiding motives was to deny Haya de la Torre the possibility of gaining the presidency.... By the mid-1970's, Haya was coming to be recognized as the military's shrewdest and perhaps most constructive critic, as the kind of patient statesman who could be most effective in facilitating the return of the officers to the barracks ... with dignity.... After fifty years Haya completed the cure of what had originally been a serious case of extremist exclusivism, whose initiating germ was the conviction that through some sort of Armageddon, Apristas must definitively crush their foes.[9]

Haya had clearly evolved from the radical revolutionary of the 1920s to the crafty politician and statesman of international stature in the 1970s. The Constituent Assembly of 1979 was in many ways his finest hour, as he played the critical role of mediator and conciliator between the divergent forces of the right, the military, and the nascent and fragmented left. Haya's death prior to the 1980 elections left his party leaderless and divided. The ensuing debacle of APRA in the 1980 elections as well as the reelection of Fernando Belaúnde temporarily obscured the extent to which both Peru and APRA had changed during the military *docenio*. A brief analysis of the military's major reforms, of the initial reaction of APRA and of the ensuing change in attitude and strategy of Haya himself, and of the role played by APRA during the transition to civilian rule sheds some light on those changes, and also demonstrates how they were critical in APRA's renovation and rise to power in 1985.

Revolution from Above

The October 1968 coup in Peru was largely a result of the military's frustration with civilian politics—hardly a novelty in Peruvian history. What was different, however, was that this time the military's frustration was with the slow progress toward what it saw as urgently needed reforms. The military announced that it was going to implement a "revolution from above." The officer corps had in the mid-1960s experienced the poverty of the sierra while combatting a guerrilla uprising led primarily by ex-apristas. This was coupled with the military's vision of national security, expanded in the 1950s and 1960s to incorporate the need for social reform. This vision was expounded by both the Centro de Altos Estudios Militares (CAEM)—the National Intelligence Service—from which Velasco emerged. The disintegration of the Belaúnde regime, coupled with the likelihood of an APRA victory in 1969, spurred a group of officers, led by Juan Velasco Alvarado, to take power.

The junta had no coherent government plan prior to takeover, however. A written plan, the Inca Plan, did not appear until 1974. A key participant, General Fernández Maldonado, remarked, "Listen, our revolution in reality is not born with a program. It is a group of individuals with good faith and good intentions, with set points that signal a transformation . . . but whose practical application has to be studied."[10] The different nature of the regime was indicated early on, however, by the immediate takeover of IPC operations in Peru. At this point the true nature of the regime was still not totally clear, as there had in the past been populist nationalist dictators, such as Sánchez Cerro. The turning point for most observers, and certainly the most significant for APRA, was the June 1969 announcement of DL 17716, the Agrarian Reform Law.

The law had its basis in the bill that had been proposed and debated during the Belaúnde administration, and, according to Luis Alberto Sánchez, the text was similar to that of an act proposed by the apristas in the Congress.[11] There were crucial differences, however. The first was that the military boldly and swiftly implemented the law, without any public debate. The second was that the first properties expropriated were the prosperous sugar haciendas of the north coast, a region to which the APRA proposal had given low priority both because of the high productivity of the lands and because of the high degree of organization and standard of living—among the best in the country—of the hacienda workers. The reform was much less effective in the sierra region, where the plight of the landless was far worse. "The reforms begun in 1969 have continued to the present, but there is a general consensus that the takeover of the north coast sugar haciendas has been a failure. Sugar workers . . . who prior to 1969 were the highest paid agricultural workers in Peru, have seen a severe decline in their pay since."[12]

The most plausible explanation for the regime's focus on the sugar plantations was the extent of support that APRA had among the coastal workers. APRA's political activity began among these workers, and until the time of the coup, the party was virtually guaranteed at least 75 percent of their votes.[13] At the same time the owners of the sugar haciendas— Grace and Company, the Gildemeisters, the Larcos, for example—were the agroindustrial export elite that had for a long time controlled Peru's economy and polity. Thus, regardless of its effectiveness in terms of redistribution, the reform struck at the backbone of both the oligarchy and APRA. During the reform debates from 1963 to 1968 the coalition of apristas and *odriistas* had always prevented reform from taking that tack, and there was even collaboration between the apristas and the landowners, as they both had a stake in upstaging Communist and other influences in the sugar unions. Interestingly enough, even after the agrarian reform the aprista union leaders maintained their influence, as the leaders of the former sugar workers' confederation became the leaders of the cooperative system, including the National Center of Sugar Cooperatives.[14] This occurred largely because APRA put pressure on the government to allow the cooperatives to choose their own leaders through elections. Given the government's commitment to cooperatives, it could hardly refuse. However, "in several cases, government administrators simply voided elections in which anti-Velasco workers were named to the new administrative committees."[15]

The implementation of the Agrarian Reform Law thus did not benefit the poorest peasants, but rather affected a privileged few. About one-fifth of the country's rural population was to receive three-fourths of the land, leaving little for the rest. Crucial credit and technical support was also lacking. The 1970 General Industries Law followed a similar pattern: it affected the privileged 5 percent of the labor force that worked in the manufacturing sector.[16] In part because of the structural dualism of the Peruvian economy, and in part because of the ad hoc way in which the military's revolution was carried out, the reforms barely scratched the surface of Peru's problems, and in some senses exacerbated existing inequalities.[17]

The enclave-like nature of Peruvian economic development, and extensive repression, had kept the labor movement weak and fragmented before the 1968 coup. Until that time the movement had been virtually dominated by APRA. At least three-fourths of all union members—between 200,000 and 400,000 workers—belonged to APRA-dominated CTP. As Andrés Townsend, a prominent party leader, stated, this was the party's most effective weapon in times of crisis. In fact, APRA's strategy of defending particularistic union interests may have been a factor in its loss of mass and youth appeal.[18] At the same time the party did not use the labor movement to push for broader social reform, but rather as a tool of opportunistic politics.[19] The Communist-led CGTP achieved recognition from the military government in 1971. The CGTP was much more active in supporting labor unrest than was the CTP. Unlike the CTP, whose power was dependent on APRA, the CGTP was a force in its own right, with links with, but without dependence on, the Communist party, whose political influence was far more limited than APRA's. As APRA had been gradually discredited among emerging and more radical labor groups, the CGTP rapidly gained support, and labor was, for the first time, given a choice. The CTP remained strongest in those sectors of the economy that developed early in Peru: sugar; copper mines; textiles; banks; and among teachers and *chóferes*.[20]

The military clearly wanted to draw labor away from APRA, and the rise of the CGTP was, at least initially, not totally to its detriment. As the CGTP became more active in labor unrest, particularly after 1972, and as the military government's CTRP was unable to compete for support with the CGTP, it became a major rival and ultimately one of the military regime's most active opponents. The undermining of APRA's control, on the other hand, may have occurred on the labor front, but this did not directly transfer to political support, as, eventually, the 1978 elections demonstrated.

> Although many unions have deserted Apra, this does not mean ... that the populist or paternalistic attractions of Apra are irrelevant. On the contrary, the move of Apra back into the center of the political stage might well coincide with a revival of the fortunes of the party in the union movement. ... Apra remains the most popular single party in Peru. It is quite possible that in union elections workers vote for the left wing candidates while in national political elections they will cast their vote for Apra. Apra's strength does not, therefore, lie in its union base as is the case with the Communist party. Its popular following and powerful machine do provide resources, however, that the party can mobilize to maximize its appeal to the labor movement.[21]

The issue of union support became crucial in the latter phase of the military regime, as the CGTP was responsible for the sponsorship of two highly successful general strikes that were extremely damaging to the regime. The strikes were the spark for a great deal of pent-up popular frustration. "Strikes in Peru show a high degree of communal solidarity; popular protest movements involve trade unions ... as the cause of strikes reflect issues of deep concern to the urban and rural poor."[22] In keeping with the thesis that union support does not necessarily translate into electoral support, it is interesting to note that APRA's CTP did not participate in the general strikes, yet APRA still obtained a plurality in the Constituent Assembly elections. While the military was able to undermine APRA's support in the unions, it was not able to on the political front. A relevant factor in this development was the failure of SINAMOS.

SINAMOS was a response to the need to incorporate popular participation and, in part, an attempt to duplicate or undermine APRA's "popular following and political machine." The military began by placing a strong emphasis on building a support base in the *pueblos jóvenes*. The Velasco government began to use the term *young town* or pueblo joven, for what had before been called *barriadas*, or slums. Only one week after taking office, President Velasco announced the founding of the Organismo Nacional de Desarrollo de Pueblos Jóvenes (ONDEPJOV) to sponsor self-help efforts and deal with new settlements.[23] Carlos Delgado, an ex-aprista, who was to be key in the design and direction of SINAMOS, was deeply involved in early settlement policy. Delgado, who had been an ardent party member and extremely close to Haya, now had strong negative feelings against APRA. His experience in the party, and his animosity against it, were crucial in both the designs of these programs and the attitude that the Velasco regime in general had toward APRA.

An April 29, 1971, land invasion in the Pamplona section of Lima, involving tens of thousands of people, coupled with a rise in strike activity in the sugar cooperatives and in the southern sierra mines, "made it clear that the government needed to increase its ability to deal with the sectors of society capable of mass political action."[24] The government founded SINAMOS in June 1971 to serve as a link between the government and the people, and purportedly to make the bureaucracy more responsive to the people. SINAMOS incorporated ONDEPJOV and also dealt with cooperatives, agrarian reform, and other activities, although the settlements were its main focus. The combination of the strikes and the massive Pamplona invasion had left the government without a mechanism of social control and communication; political activity would normally have filled, and SINAMOS was supposed to fill, this gap. Carlos Delgado's thesis— that of the "nonparty"—was crucial to this design.

> These strikes, and ... the Pamplona invasion, had support from opposition parties, including the left as well as APRA. The government is naturally interested in limiting the power of these parties and in competing with them for support at the local level. . . . The overall purpose is to create alternative organizations in all sectors of Peruvian society that will fill political space that ... might be occupied by these parties. The concern with the role of political opposition in squatter settlements [was] particularly intense.[25]

SINAMOS was designed to guarantee local participation in the planning of development actions, and created a complex system of state-run offices that were to be responsible for the distribution of land titles, water, electricity, and other such services. SINAMOS could only promote, not enact, these projects, however—which gave it no more of a function than an ordinary political party, except that it had ties to the government. Under SINAMOS applications for land titles were subordinated to the organization's approval and therefore extended the government's domination to the internal neighborhood structures.[26] The poor usually agreed to use SINAMOS's organizational structure, as it was their only means to obtain necessary services. They saw SINAMOS as a threat, however, as it attempted to close their informal but highly useful avenues of demand making, deprive them of their separate identities, and rob them of effective, independent leadership.[27] Finally, because SINAMOS was unable to actually provide the services, making participation an empty exercise—a means without ends—SINAMOS was a failure.

"The poor, of course, were aware of the co-optative nature of SINAMOS."[28] In some cases it aroused violent opposition; for example, the 1972 storming and burning of SINAMOS headquarters along the Rímac River. After 1975, as public funds ran short, SINAMOS became increasingly a system to repress the demands of the poor. Ironically, SINAMOS was one of the many factors that served to politicize the urban poor, in opposition to the government, after 1975. It is of particular importance, however, not only because of the high degree of publicity that it achieved, but because of its origins in the desire to replace political parties in general and APRA in particular. The personality of Carlos Delgado and his relation to APRA are critical to this analysis.

Carlos Delgado had been very active in the APRA youth movement, and came from an aprista family. He was elected national youth secretary in 1948 and served in Haya's secretariat at age twenty. Delgado even served two years in prison during the Odría years because of his affiliation with the party. Despite witnessing the disaffection of a whole generation of APRA youth, Delgado remained with the party until the early 1960s, when he left Peru disillusioned with APRA's conservative bent. He returned to work for the party's 1962 campaign, but finally broke with APRA in 1963, after a conversation with Haya in Cologne revealed irreconcilable differences.[29] The breach with the party affected Delgado deeply, not only in his own behavior, but in the policies of the Velasco regime.

> I do not know at what point I ceased to be and to feel that I was an aprista. ... I think that what occurred was similar to what a Catholic, a Communist, or whatever man possessed by a total faith [experiences] when that faith ceases to drive his conscience and his heart. . . . And while the conservative tendencies of the aprista leadership did not escape my eyes, this perception was clearly neutralized by the elements of emotional attachment that apristas always had for their party . . . something more than a simple political organization, a sort of lay religion . . . the exercise of a total commitment to the ideal of a fight for social justice . . . which explained the phenomenon that APRA was the only political movement of this century that profoundly pierced the soul of our nation.[30]

Delgado was well aware of the strength of APRA as a phenomenon in Peru, regardless of its electoral fate. His disaffection resulted in intense feelings about the party, which were soon to translate into government policy. Delgado returned to Peru in 1968 and worked in the government planning office, Plandemet, where an article of his on self-help in the pueblos jóvenes attracted the attention of members of the junta.[31]

Delgado was an important member of the ONDEPJOV efforts and later the principal designer and organizer of SINAMOS.[32] In his thesis of the nonparty he criticized the existing parties for their oligarchic nature and redefined political parties during the military years as a new social form. He blamed the existing parties, primarily APRA, for being counter-revolutionary forces. He explained that the need for a revolution from above stemmed from the inability of the old parties, with their links to the traditional structure of power, to participate in the ideals and activities of the revolution. At the same time Delgado noted that no Marxist-Leninist regime had effectively solved the problem of popular participation with a party. Thus emerged his nonparty thesis and the design of SINAMOS as an instrument to incorporate popular participation.[33]

SINAMOS grew out of the military's obvious need to deal with growing popular mobilization and politicization. Delgado, who had become "the most important civilian advisor of the military government,"[34] and who had a great deal of experience with party organizational work and in the pueblos jóvenes through ONDEPJOV and Plandemet, was the main force behind SINAMOS. Velasco personally was extremely supportive of both Delgado and SINAMOS, and the agency lost a great deal of support from within the regime with the transition to leadership by Francisco Morales Bermúdez.[35] Many of the leaders of the second phase disapproved of the infiltration of Communists in the agency, and as the organization had become odious to the urban poor, its dissolution became inevitable.

SINAMOS clearly had impact and also symbolic importance. With the fall of SINAMOS came the reincorporation of political parties into the system, and the reliance on their participation, particularly APRA's, in the transition to civilian rule. The idea behind SINAMOS's original formation had been an attempt to take over the role traditionally played, if not always effectively, by APRA in mobilizing people and channeling that social mobilization. SINAMOS's failure, interestingly enough, is often attributed to its hierarchical structure and unresponsive nature. APRA is clearly a hierarchical organization; its survival and effectiveness must thus be attributed to other qualities that SINAMOS did not have. First, APRA was not imposed by a dictatorial regime as an order on top of existing ones. Second, APRA had years of experience in political organization, unlike the military officers who often headed SINAMOS offices. Finally, APRA had its age-old and unquantifiable mística, by which it had always managed to maintain loyal supporters even when the party lost its revolutionary vigor; Delgado's persistent support throughout the 1950s is a good example. A similar comparison can be drawn between the regime itself and APRA. One of the major criticisms of the military regime was of its authoritarian and exclusionary nature; this nature made it impossible for SINAMOS, or any other such organization, to bridge the gap between the regime and the population, and exposed the inherent flaws in Delgado's nonparty thesis. He could not replace the role played by APRA with an organization imposed from above; although APRA was hierarchically structured, participation in its ranks was voluntary. SINAMOS, on the other hand, was seen as a requirement and a bureaucratic barrier to desired ends rather than an effective means.

The August 29, 1975, overthrow of Velasco by Morales Bermúdez not only signified the end of SINAMOS, but a new phase of the military regime that was to emphasize economic austerity and an end to reforms.

The huge and largely unaccounted debt piled up by the Velasco regime had become an issue of concern, as had rising inflation and growing labor unrest.[36] The private investment that the Velasco regime had hoped for never occurred, largely because of the regime's antiimperialist and revolutionary rhetoric. While claiming that the revolution would continue its course, the Morales Bermúdez regime was clearly committed to a change of tack, in part because of the need for foreign credit and the conditions imposed by the International Monetary Fund (IMF), and in part because of the desire for a rapprochement with the domestic business sector. Yet even with its switch to procapitalist policies, the military was not able to appeal to parties on either end of the spectrum; it had alienated all parties through its vision of society without them. In the meantime the switch to a probusiness, austerity-oriented approach released a flood of discontent among the workers.[37]

The military government was discredited among all sectors of society, to some extent because of the increase of repressive activities at the end of the Velasco years as the regime lost coherence in the face of rising opposition and Velasco's illness. The military was aware of this, and in Morales Bermúdez's first speech—where he indicated that the course of the revolution would not change ideologically but that its political management must[38]—it became clear that the military was considering returning to the barracks. In 1977 the government announced that there would be elections for a Constituent Assembly. The new regime's attitude to the parties was a much more conciliatory one, in part because of the government's failure to channel popular participation through SINAMOS, and in part because of its need for the parties' cooperation for the transition. "It seems not unlikely that the government calculated that the 30 month transition period would help diffuse political opposition to unpopular economic policies by absorbing the political parties in the process of designing the country's future constitutional parameters."[39]

APRA's role was to be crucial in this transition, as the first contacts with civilians were made with APRA leaders, and the party, particularly Haya, served as a mediator between the military and political parties of the right and left. The party's central role in the transition process is ironic in light of the extent to which it was perceived to be, and actually was, in a state of crisis and disarray when the Velasco government implemented what APRA had considered its revolution. The fact that the military turned to APRA despite its state of crisis points to the unique position that parties have in society. This position allows them to bridge the gap between civil society and state in a way that no other organization can, as was proved by the failure of SINAMOS.

The Velasco revolution created an internal crisis within APRA, but that crisis led to the eventual revamping of the party's platform and to the training of a new generation of leaders—that of Alan García—by Haya de la Torre. The relationship between García and Haya at the time also points to the extent to which Haya, although refusing to make a public choice, had found his handpicked successor. APRA's reaction to the Velasco reforms, and its public stance as well as internal changes, were critical to both the transition to civilian rule and to APRA's final attainment of power in 1985.

Crisis in APRA

The irony of APRA's traditional rival—the military—taking power and then implementing what was deemed to be APRA's revolution created shock, surprise, and finally great bitterness in the party. The Velasco regime's antiimperialist and reformist rhetoric virtually mirrored APRA's original doctrine, both in terms of ideology and in terms of the reforms that were implemented. In the words of one of the highest-ranking party members at the time, "they want to do in five or six years . . . what they prevented from being done for forty. First, they turned back the clock. Now they speed it up with a furor capable of breaking the chronometer."[40] There was the feeling that the military had stolen the very soul of APRA. APRA had been the first party in Peru to call for social reform, for land reform, for an antiimperialist stance, for the nationalization of key industries, for rights for the Indian; now the same institution that had persecuted the party for forty years had once again preempted it from power and had taken its program to boot. Even more damaging was that APRA was seen as more conservative than the military, and was even accused by the military of being counterrevolutionary.

The effect of the military's revolution on the behavior and the doctrine of the party was far-reaching, and as late as 1987, when Alan García was contemplating the nationalization of the nation's banks (in his attack on the famous *circuitos de poder* [circuits of power], the perception that APRA had been upstaged by the military may have been a factor. "People say that Velasco stole our grand flag, the agrarian reform. The agrarian world was the expression of something much more important. . . . I am going to finish with the 'latifundios' of money."[41] The land reform, for all its failures in implementation, was symbolically extremely important: the Velasco regime had challenged—and broken—the power of the export oligarchy in Peru, as APRA, from its very origins, had proposed doing.

The psychological and symbolic impact of the first revolution in Peru being implemented by a group other than APRA, and even worse, by its traditional enemies, was tremendous. Although the party had clearly undergone hard times and had lost a great number of youths during and after the compromises of the convivencia, there had never been such an ideological challenge. While APRA was challenged to some extent by the reformist rhetoric of Acción Popular (AP), it could always blame its 1963 defeat on the 1962 coup. The AP was clearly not the institution that APRA was, and was based more on the personality of Fernando Belaúnde. APRA depended on Haya, but APRA was in and of itself much more; it was one of the three principal institutions—the church, the armed forces, and APRA—in Peru, a status that the AP could not attain when fundamentally it was an imitator of APRA. The left, meanwhile, was not a unified force. Thus the most formidable challenges to APRA had always come from reactionary forces—the oligarchy and the army—and the party could always justify defeat by pointing to the actions of its persecutors. There had been no need for internal criticism.

The fact that there was no outright persecution, that APRA was not outlawed, that the party was indeed not even directly mentioned by the military government placed it in a tenuous position. APRA was not being oppressed, yet its revolution was being carried out by its former oppressors. Yet how could apristas criticize their main rivals when they had adopted APRA's own ideology? Both parties played a delicate game. Velasco, aided by Carlos Delgado, knew that persecuting APRA would harm the regime more than APRA, and Haya knew that criticizing the military would harm APRA more than it would the military.

The day after the coup, APRA issued a protest that called for the restoration of civil liberties. (At the time it was not immediately clear what sort of regime would emerge. There had certainly been nationalist and populist military leaders, such as Sánchez Cerro, who had also persecuted APRA.) The day of the coup had seen some student unrest and a clash with the police in the center of Lima, in which one APRA student was killed; there were also some clashes between APRA and Communist student factions at APRA-affiliated Villareal University in November,[42] but there was no military-inspired campaign of repression.

The military seemed to want to avoid a repressive image. On October 5, Andrés Townsend, a party leader and president of the Senate until the coup, received a direct message from Velasco saying that the coup was not against either APRA or its leaders.[43] There were other contacts between party leaders and the military; Luis Alberto Sánchez, for example, early on met with the economics minister, General Valdivia Morriberón.[44] Members of the AP were actually treated far less well by the military, and most of them spent the entire period in forced or self-imposed exile.

At the time of the coup a small group of aprista youths, led by Armando Villanueva and Luis Felipe de las Casas—older-generation leaders both of whom had been imprisoned during the Odría years—organized what they thought would be a clandestine action group. Originally the group numbered two hundred university students, including Alan García; after the military's nationalization of IPC installations six days after the coup, the group's numbers diminished by one-half; as the government was institutionalized, the group diminished to fifty, then twenty, and eventually dissolved.[45] Ironically, de las Casas later served as ambassador to Colombia for the military government. While apristas did not necessarily participate in the military government on a widespread scale, there was some desertion from APRA to its ranks, which was hardly appreciated by the party leaders. While the rank and file in large part remained loyal to the party, the disaffection occurred more on the *dirigente* level,[46] thus depriving the party of some of its more talented members.

As the reformist nature of the Velasco government became clearer, APRA's own position became more tenuous. Haya de la Torre was abroad at the time and did not return until February 1969. Prior to his return the party leaders recognized the need to come to grips with APRA's situation in light of the nature of this military regime, and to determine what the party's approach to the regime should be. Contacts were made with Haya.[47] When Haya returned and addressed APRA's traditional Día de Fraternidad rally, he limited his criticisms to the lack of civil liberties and electoral rights, and did not address the nature of the regime, except to agree with its antiimperialist stance. As the reforms progressed, the party maintained a position of constructive criticism, always praising the direction of the reforms and always criticizing the lack of electoral freedom. At times specific criticisms yielded results, as when Haya called for internal elections in the sugar cooperatives in February 1972; elections were held and apristas on the whole were the victors, although in many cases results were annulled.[48] The military was not opposed to retaliation if criticism appeared to be going too far. In May of the same year, Haya alluded in a discourse to the success he had had with the sugar elections and urged the government to convoke municipal elections. A few weeks later, Haya's secretary, Jorge Idiaquez, disappeared when he went out to the pharmacy; he was deported by the military a few days later.[49] This seems to have been a warning to Haya not to overstep the unspoken behavioral bounds.

While there was no overt persecution, there was subtle harassment of APRA leaders as well as attempts to discredit the party. The military wanted to create the impression that APRA was *deshaciéndose*, or falling apart, as the existence of a strong party organization would clearly challenge its own support base. The needling campaign began in 1969. The government allowed the party to hold its traditional yearly rallies but used a variety of tactics to discourage attendance. In February 1969 Interior Minister Armando Artola told Armando Villanueva that there was a plot to kill Haya, obviously hoping that the apristas would cancel their rally. The rally was held anyway, and the APRA leaders avoided publicizing the rumor; no attempt on Haya was made.[50] In 1974 there was a supposed attempt on Haya's life—this one by the Policia Investigadora Peruana (PIP), the military intelligence police, whose truck crashed into Haya's car as he was returning to his home at Villa Mercedes. Haya suffered a fractured rib.[51]

Every year on the day of the rally, the official Comité de Deportes contracted two football matches at the same time that the rally was to be held. In 1972 the government did not authorize the rally in its traditional place, the party locale, but instead authorized the party's holding it at the huge Campo de Marte fairground, which holds 300,000 people. This was probably an attempt to ridicule the size of the rally—an attempt to demonstrate the demise of the party. The grounds mysteriously flooded at 5:00 P.M.; meanwhile the government contracted the usual football matches, prohibited any crowds gathering beforehand, and said that the meeting had to end by midnight, the traditional time of Haya's speech. Finally, the rally was closed down with gunshots from a state security patrol. Despite this, the rally was the best-attended in years, according to apristas; the official press said there were 60,000 people, and APRA claimed that there were 150,000.[52]

Some individual party leaders were also the subject of substantial harassment. Luis Alberto Sánchez, one of the oldest and most respected party members, had charges pressed against him, and his building was invaded by the Judicial Police. In 1969 the Fiscal Police attempted to implicate Sánchez in a crime committed in the 1940s by an aprista youth. Sánchez was also charged with 120 fraud counts, in relation to his position as rector of the University of San Marcos, before the Tribunal de Cuentas, which all turned out to be false. The tribunal also tried, and failed, consistently to prove that Sánchez was receiving income from his training as a lawyer, although he maintains that he never practiced for profit.[53] Armando Villanueva and Luis Negreiros were both deported in 1974, and Jorge Idiaquez was deported twice during the military years—clearly an indirect stab at Haya; other party leaders were subject to different kinds of harassment.[54] This subtle persecution, however, was very different from the oppression that the party had suffered in the past, as it was aimed to discredit rather than make martyrs of party members. For the first few years of the military docenio, with the exception of some student unrest, the party did not mount any active opposition to the regime,[55] nor was there a particular strength of antiaprismo among the military leaders.

There was clearly a resentment against all parties in general, as they were seen as an integral part of the traditional power structure, and there some of the traditional rivalry between the army and APRA persisted. But this had clearly mellowed with time, and also with the changes within the military's ideology and its sympathy for and leaning on APRA's doctrine. General Javier Tantalean, the influential fisheries minister, for example, was known for his pro-APRA sympathies. Velasco clearly had sympathies for APRA's ideology, and no particular personal grudge against APRA.[56] His reliance on Carlos Delgado was seen by some as a way of obtaining "aprismo without APRA."[57] At one point in a speech,

Velasco used the phrase "we have lifted ourselves up against the shameful past," which is directly from the APRA *Marseillaise*. Andrés Townsend's response to this was that "Delgado even [had] Velasco singing the Marseillaise without even knowing it!"[58] Velasco, meanwhile, rarely even mentioned APRA by name, another way of decreasing its influence. While he accepted that his program was influenced by APRA doctrine, he also faulted APRA for failing to implement it. "It was not only a case of having good ideas, rather . . . carrying them out in practice, and one cannot deny that the revolution executed many of the works and changes that APRA considered in its politics."[59]

Military harassment of APRA grew as a response to a perceived growth in belligerency on the part of the party. By 1971 there was increased strike activity, and more-aggressive statements by leaders, such as that which provoked the Idiaquez deportation. The decision to deport Idiaquez was spurred by the ex-apristas in the government, who were surely aware of how indispensable Idiaquez was to Haya and knew that it would be an effective stab. Carlos Delgado in particular resented Haya[60] and was behind many of the attempts to discredit the party. Thus, ironically, the perceived antiaprismo of the military was more a product of the nettled sensitivities of former apristas than the result of opposition within the military itself.

Delgado's influence is key here. He had been one of Haya's favored leaders,[61] and his estrangement from the party was a bitter one. He was seen as a traitor by APRA leaders,[62] and his writings displayed his acrimony against the party leaders and Haya in particular. "The evident and profound political crisis that affects the oldest Peruvian political party is, fundamentally, a crisis of leadership. . . . The crisis that APRA is living is accentuated by the inability of its directorate to accept . . . its responsibility for the immense political disaster that today reflects the culmination of the many years of absolute control of the party."[63] Delgado was the leader of the aprista dissidents in the government, which had direct effects on various kinds of policy, SINAMOS in particular.[64] As the influence of Delgado and other dissident apristas was spread throughout the government, it is not surprising that anti-APRA sentiment pervaded different policy levels.[65]

Not all apristas who participated in the government left the party; de las Casas, for example, eventually realigned himself with APRA. However, the loss of more young talent at the dirigente level, after the dissension of the 1950s and 1960s, was clearly not welcome. This, coupled with the irony of the military's implementing APRA's own revolution, caused a crisis within the party and for Haya in particular. The party could not lash out at its oppressors the way it had in the past, and Haya did not have his martyr role. Haya had no personal animosity against Velasco, however, and in fact regarded him with a sort of tenuous respect for his courage in confronting the oligarchy.[66] When Velasco fell ill in early 1973, Haya softened APRA's criticisms—his own and those of Sánchez—at the yearly Día de Fraternidad rally.

Haya's Response

Víctor Raúl Haya de la Torre had to rethink his strategy. For the first time in many years, he looked inward at his party and noted the dearth of qualified leaders and the lack of ability to challenge the revolution that was being swept from under their feet. He returned to Peru in February 1969 at age seventy-four; his long-held ambitions for attaining the presidency had been finally shattered on October 3, 1968. At that point he decided to remain in Peru and dedicate his remaining years to the youth of the party, in order to train new leaders for the time when the party was ready to take power.[67]

Throughout the 1960s, Haya had spent only six months per year in Peru, and the rest of the time traveling abroad. During that decade he had regularly held, when in the country, Tuesday colloquia that dealt with all aspects of APRA doctrine. Among the regular attendees was young Alan García. As of 1969, Haya remained in the country full-time and began to select approximately one hundred university-age youths whom he felt were particularly bright or active in the party to form a leadership training school, or Buro de Conjunciones. By June 1969 he had chosen his group, and activities—debates, speeches, lectures several evenings a week—had begun. At this point there was a debate going on within the party—and particularly among the youths, who were much affected by the revolution happening without them—about whether Haya's *Antimperialismo y el APRA* or *Treinta años de aprismo* were the legitimate summation of APRA doctrine. The debate began in the Villareal and San Marcos universities, where a new interest and investigation of aprista doctrine was gradually beginning. In 1962, the much more radical *Antimperialismo,* the original 1930s APRA doctrine, had been excluded from Haya's collected works. *Antimperialismo*'s conclusion refutes the claim that APRA is a reformist rather than a revolutionary party. As if to tilt the debate, and clearly in a change of ideological strategy, Haya ordered a new edition— the third—of *Antimperialismo y el APRA* printed in 1970. This edition was sold out by 1972, and a new one had to be issued.[68] At the same time, apparently shaken by the writings of one aprista currently at Villareal University, whose polemics totally ignored aprista doctrine as a basis for debate and focused on Marxism-Leninism, Haya called for a university parliament. Its president was none other than Alan García. In the meantime the Buro de Conjunciones was whittled down to about fifty youths, and from these a more intense group, the Escuela de Dirigentes, was chosen. Haya began to speak of his own death in his discourses, and of the future of the party. He calculated that the military regime would last ten or fifteen years, and he spoke of training leaders for the future.[69] He emphasized the need for party unity. This sort of discourse was clearly a novelty; for the first time APRA was rethinking its future, its ideological place in Peru's political spectrum, and contemplating its direction without Haya.

The idea behind both the Buro and the Escuela was to create a sort of shadow cabinet of the party leadership structures, with each secretariat having a youth representative who was supposed to take responsibility in the secretary's absence. Carlos Roca—a prominent party leader in the 1980s—for example, was under Armando Villanueva as secretary for exterior relations, and Alan García was at the Secretariat for Organization. In reality the youths were not allowed the designated responsibility, however, and in the absence of the secretaries, decisions were usually made by the subsecretaries. Middle-generation leaders who still maintained political ambitions patently felt threatened by this group of youths in their early twenties who were receiving so much of Haya's attention. A remarkable amount of Haya's time during this period went to training this group. The Buro met with Haya Tuesday nights for the university parliament, Wednesday nights they attended Comité Ejecutivo Nacional (CEN) meetings, Thursday nights were devoted to the general colloquium at the party locale, Saturdays the Escuela de Dirigentes met, and Sundays Haya hosted a weekly reunion of youths at his home, Villa Mercedes.[70] One reason that Haya may have chosen to focus on the youngest generation of dirigentes for new leadership development was that they were still too young to challenge him in any way. Haya clearly wanted to remain the unquestioned *jefe* of the party until his death.

From the Buro emerged many of the members of the 1985 government, notably Alan García. During the early years of the Buro, and in particular before García went to study in Spain and France, he received particular attention from Haya and accompanied him during his normal weekly duties.[71] According to François Bourricaud—a personal friend of Haya who was to be García's professor at the Sorbonne—Haya contacted him and told him that he was sending him "one of our best."[72] This promotion continued when García returned, as he was appointed by Haya to the post of secretary of organization during the transition years. He was also chosen, along with Sánchez, to speak at the welcoming rally on January 6, 1978, when Haya returned from Europe to launch the Constituent Assembly electoral campaign.

In addition to the attention Haya gave to his new leaders-in-training, he was insistent that there be constant activity at the party locale, and that the lights be on late into the evenings, clearly attempting to revamp the party's image. Haya had a popular history—a historia gráfica—of the party written, under the direction of Andrés Townsend. This was an official version of the party's history, but the pamphlets were evidently intended for popular consumption; the graphic illustrations, which dominated the text and included close-up photographs of bullet-ridden apristas, gave them a kitschy quality. The history was designed to glorify APRA's past suffering and the central role that Haya de la Torre had played in Peru's political history. The account also tried to build Haya into a character of more international renown than he was in actuality. This publication was an attempt to refocus the attention of the masses on APRA's role as a martyr in the struggle for social justice, and also on the animosity of the military during this struggle. The theme in the "Historia gráfica" is the celebration of APRA as the hero in the nation's history. The hero is a victim as well, however: apristas are persecuted; Haya does not get to be president, as he deserves. Thus the revolution in the "Historia gráfica" is not the taking of power, but the celebration of the hero.[73] Haya's death is not mentioned; rather he is immortalized through the 1979 granting of the Orden del Sol and the signing of the Constitution. "There is no reference or illustration that relates to the death or the funeral: the hero lives on—eternal glory!"[74] The pamphlets demonstrate Haya's strategy in renovating the party by focusing on its finest hours and its history of heroism, rather than on the compromised moments and loss of revolutionary fervor. This seems to complement the revival of the original aprista doctrine, but was probably targeted at a less sophisticated audience.

Haya also sponsored the founding of a student magazine, *Claridad,* in 1977 as a venue for university students to expound alternative views. The magazine was purposely named after a magazine founded by Víctor Raúl thirty years earlier. The original *Claridad* was designed as an arm of the Universidades Populares, to reach those marginalized from culture and education.[75] Again Haya was trying to renovate APRA by focusing on its young and on its original concepts and doctrines.

The party renovation was not occurring in a vacuum, however. There was a flurry of activity, as, concurrent with the emergence of the political left, the number of left-affiliated think tanks and research institutes that focused on the economic and social sciences increased. Some of these received funds from *velasquistas* in the government, as well as external funds. APRA, dominated single-handedly by Haya and focused exclusively on his works, in many ways prepared a less capable and educated leadership base than did the left. While Haya's chosen few, such as Alan García and Carlos Roca, may have flourished under this strategy, the renovation did not necessarily affect the party rank and file. Throughout the Velasco years there were only two functioning APRA locales in the country.[76] Members of the Marxist left were usually educated at the more prestigious Universidad Católica, and on the whole had more funds available for training.[77] The lack of talent at the lower echelons of leadership, while not evident when the most talented of the party functioned as drafters of the Constituent Assembly or as leaders of the opposition, was later to be exposed when APRA was in power. While Haya was able to renovate the party enough to act once again as a powerful electoral machine, and to train a few capable leaders, he could not repair the damage that decades of persecution, sectarianism, and ideological vacillation had done to the party's image, nor could he recover the resulting defections of talented youths. Finally, there were splits within APRA— between the more conservative older wing and established local "bosses" and union leaders on the one hand, and the increasingly radical youths on the other—that deepened at this time.

Once new life was injected into the student movement, both by the attention paid by Haya and by the general political trends in the nation, particularly the rise of the left, it took on a momentum of its own, which was in many ways beyond the control of the aging Haya. Haya's focus on a select few in the Buro did not guarantee him total control over the youth of the party, and particularly over the more radicalized elements. Perhaps the most extreme case was that of Víctor Polay Campos, an active member of the Buro, who broke with APRA in the late 1970s while studying in Europe and returned to Peru to become one of the founders and leaders of the MRTA guerrilla movement, which launched armed struggle against the government. The student movement split between the traditional Juventud Universitaria Aprista (JUA) and the Alianza Revolucionaria Estudiantil (ARE), a more radical movement whose legitimacy was at first denied by Haya, although eventually tacitly supported as the movement became a key actor in the opposition to the military government.

The ARE movement cooperated with numerous other forces in opposing the regime; for example, during the police strike of February 5, 1975, and the teachers' strike organized by the Sindicato Único de Trabajadores en la Educación Peruana (SUTEP). The movement actively competed with Maoist groups for the control of the Secondary Students Federation, and in the process suffered the death of one of its members. Also extremely important, the ARE became highly critical of the CTP's lack of participation in popular protests, and in its 1974 Youth Congress voted to censure its "pro-patron" and "yellow" leaders and change the CTP's traditional slogan from "Free and Democratic Syndicalism" to "Syndicalism of the United Front of Exploited Classes."[78] In part because of Haya's new focus, in terms of both party personnel and doctrine, and in part because of the general political trends in the country, in particular the rise of the left, APRA youths grew more radical and more influential simultaneously. Ultimately, they were to be an important force in the rise of the new party leaders in the early 1980s. The strengthening of the student movement, as it was a function of a party renovation based on its more radical doctrine, was ultimately related to a democratizing trend in the general party organization.

With Víctor Raúl begins . . . the turn towards the "original sources."
Consequently . . . two tendencies emerge: . . . the traditional aprista
sectors and the youth sectors . . . Haya is to have a very important role
in this context, because, ultimately, he permitted these sectors to gradually have more presence in the leadership of the party. . . . The [Partido
Aprista Peruano] was to be totally revived and mobilized after various
years of virtual hibernation. This permits more participation by the rank
and file and this results in greater democratization; . . . better relations
with the provincial rank and file are then sought.[79]

The Velasco years, because of the military's reforms and the growth
of the left, clearly caused a crisis within APRA; a crisis that spurred the
party into self-examination for the first time. This was caused, in part, by
Haya's realization that the military regime would be in power for an
extended period of time and that Haya would most likely never attain the
presidency. He was thus forced to think, for the first time, of the party's
future, and of an APRA not dominated solely by Haya. Yet he refused to
choose his successor.[80] He established the Buro de Conjunciones as the
pool from which his successor would be chosen, and probably did see Alan
García as a likely candidate, but he by no means openly made the choice,
nor did he dictate the overthrowing of the older generation of leaders by
the younger. He did, however, attempt to pave the way of youth. In this
manner he avoided a leadership challenge from those in the older generations who were his logical, at least by chronological criteria, successors.
Finally, given the history of animosity between the armed forces and
APRA, it is an ironic twist that the military's revolution was the initiating
factor in APRA's preparation for being a governing party rather than
continuing its perennial role as the "impotent giant" of the opposition.

February 5, 1975

One of the turning points of the military years, and one of President Velasco's
most critical moments, was the police strike of February 1975, and the
uprisings that followed. During these events, approximately one hundred
striking Guardias Civiles were shot by army troops, the entire city of Lima
was without any police protection for over twenty-four hours, and student
protesters looted and burned the offices of the government-controlled
newspapers Correo and Ojo, the SINAMOS offices in the Centro Cívico,
and the Lima Sheraton. There was considerable damage throughout the
city, as both looting and rioting exploded the day of the fifth. The extent
of the chaos and the strength of the protest movement—in particular the
direct attack on SINAMOS—was an unmistakable expression of the
growing discontent with the Velasco regime. APRA student leaders were
clearly involved in planning and leading the protests, but were by no
means the only participants. Velasco directly blamed APRA—along with
the US Central Intelligence Agency (CIA)—for the protests—the only

time he directly attacked the party in a public speech.[81] The events of February 5 reopened the old APRA-versus-military debate, albeit temporarily. Haya, meanwhile, while not publicly endorsing the destructive actions of APRA activists, clearly gave tacit approval to their involvement.

One does not have to seek far for the cause of popular dissatisfaction with the military government. While economic growth was still high—6.9 percent for 1974—a balance of payments crisis was becoming evident, and both inflation and labor unrest were on the rise, as were criticisms of the regime's policies. Velasco had already become ill (his leg was amputated in 1973) and the lack of coherent leadership was coupled with an increase in repression. On July 24, 1974, Peru's private newspapers had been expropriated by the government, which stated that the press was leading the "counterrevolutionary campaign," and several members of the Law College were deported for criticizing the nation's oil contracts. "The labor relations climate gets more complex . . . the number of strikes grows. It is the critical point of the 'velasquista process,' its inherent limitations are exposed."[82]

The student movement, meanwhile, was increasingly mobilized. There were clashes between APRA and the growing Marxist student movement, and increased animosity against the regime on the part of both. SINAMOS was viewed as an authoritarian threat. "The strengthening of SINAMOS marks the initiation of a new phase in the military regime. The initial dispositions toward change give way to attempts at vertical control, at manipulation."[83]

The police strike primarily involved low-ranking members of the Guardia Civil, who were the worst paid of the armed forces. By the second half of 1974 the lower ranks not only agreed on the need to improve their situation, but more important, had a directorate. They staged an unsuccessful strike on December 12; the military's response was that it was an internal problem. In early January there was student unrest in a campaign against corruption in the Law Faculty at Villareal, led by apristas. Involved in this unrest was a Guardia Civil captain who was studying law at the university, who also was the head of the Guardia Civil's Comando Revolucionario at Villareal. This captain began to coordinate with a group of aprista student leaders who were led by Carlos Belapatiño and Manuel García, among others. Belapatiño became the students' main contact with the Guardia Civil leaders. This group formed a joint command, called Tupac, and the students held a strike in support of the Guardia Civil on January 18. On the morning of February 3, 1975, Lima mobilized normally, but with no police protection. By the next day it was obvious that the bulk of the Guardia Civil was on strike. Among students, support for the striking policemen grew. In the early hours of the morning of the fifth, the government—with the authorization of General Leonidas Rodríguez, the military commander for the region—ordered army tanks and troops into the barracks at Radio Patrulla, where the striking police were waiting for a response from the Interior Ministry. An undetermined number (nearly one hundred) police officers were killed. Some Guardia Civil members and their families made contact with APRA youth leaders García and Belapatiño and revealed that there had been a massacre in the police barracks; and some of the wounded Guardias Civiles went to Villareal University. Approximately four thousand students took to the streets. They marched through downtown Lima and held a rally at the Plaza San Martín. Their slogan was "Pueblo–Fuerza Armada–Unidos Venceremos." When they reached the Plaza Manco Capac, there were some shots, and on the Avenida 28 de Julio, four or five municipal buses were burned and the violence began. The students burned an army Jeep and a truck, and threw stones at the US Embassy; they then entered and burned the offices of *Ojo* and *Correo*. There were more shots, and the coherence of the Tupac movement was lost as they joined other rioting students, most of these Marxist. At this point they torched the SINAMOS offices in the Centro Cívico; on the way the group ransacked the Sheraton Hotel.[84] In the center of Lima, in the meantime, there were unrestrained robberies and lootings.[85] Eventually order was reestablished by army troops.

While the direction of the February 5 revolts was clearly not from the upper echelons of APRA leaders, it did have roots in the ARE—the more radical wing of APRA's student movement, whose legitimacy had originally been disputed by Haya. And while Haya, in an Argentine newspaper, did not condone the looting and also did not concede that the events were the party's responsibility, he did acknowledge that APRA youths had participated.[86] His tacit approval of their participation was in keeping with his desire to be more responsive to radical ideology in general, as was demonstrated by his return to the early APRA doctrine, and to youth in particular, in an effort to foster new leaders. According to Pedro Richter Prada, who held the positions of interior and prime minister during the military government, APRA's opposition to the regime grew substantially after 1974, primarily as a response to pressures from the student movement. Carlos Roca, one of Haya's favored members of the Buro, was instrumental in imposing this pressure.[87] The party's opposition to the Velasco regime also increased as the government's behavior grew more dictatorial, a trend exemplified by the June 1974 takeover of the nation's press.

The events of February 5 are important here for two reasons: they signified the Velasco regime's loss of control, the beginning of the end for the first phase of military government; and they placed APRA once again at the center of active opposition and radical action against the armed forces. APRA was using its traditional strategy of trying to build support among the lower ranks of the armed forces—those most likely to be sympathetic—to spur an antiregime movement; a tactic very much resented by the army. As he had in October 1948, Haya gave tacit support to APRA involvement in such a movement. Also analogous to the events of 1948, the uprising spurred a reaction among military leaders and was a factor leading to a coup by more-conservative elements. However, unlike the 1948 Odría coup, the Morales Bermúdez coup resulted in a lengthy transition to civilian rule rather than a period of persecution of APRA. Almost all members of the military cabinet blamed APRA for having led the February 5 events. There was increased repression of political opposition during Velasco's final months: on August 5 several journalists, the heads of SUTEP and of the Movimiento de la Izquierda Revolucionaria (MIR), and a large group of APRA leaders—Negreiros, Roca, Villanueva, and Carlos Enrique Fereyros (an APRA CEN member and the head of the Law College)—were deported; that same day the left-wing newspaper *Marka* was shut down.[88] However, as soon as the Morales Bermúdez coup occurred, APRA was treated much better, and constitutional guarantees were maintained—at least in the case of apristas.[89] This was probably in part a function of the regime's realization, once it decided that it would dissolve the military government, that it very much needed the party, both to implement the transition as sort of a middle voice between the military and the more radical opposition, and to absorb increasingly hostile and powerful popular pressure.

APRA AND THE TRANSITION

The August 29, 1975, *tacnazo,* as the Morales Bermúdez coup was called, was clearly a surprise both within and outside the military, especially as there was an implicit agreement between Velasco and Morales Bermúdez that Morales would be the successor. While Morales Bermúdez had the support of a key group of leaders, he was clearly opposed by several velasquistas in the junta, most of whom—including Generals Tantalean, Rodríguez Figueroa, de la Flor, and Fernández Maldonado—resigned by mid-1976. In their stead rose a more conservative group of generals: Arbulu; Bobbio; and Cisneros Vizquerra.[90] Early on it was clear that there was to be a change in tactics, beginning with Morales's August 29 speech in which he stated that "none of this [the reforms in place] will change one single millimeter. . . . But this process will have to, necessarily, have important changes not in its programs or in its ideopolitical bases, but rather in its political procedures; in the management and political conduct of the revolutionary process."[91]

The Morales Bermúdez government christened its regime the "second phase," stating that no new reforms would be undertaken; rather the existing ones would be institutionalized. It soon became clear that the new junta had two goals: to cope with the nation's economic crisis and burgeoning external debt, the exact amount of which had not even been recorded by the Velasco government;[92] and slowly to devolve the armed forces from responsibility for government in order to preserve their unity as an institution. Not immediately willing to call direct elections, the military reached out to the political parties, through the Constituent Assembly, as the mechanism through which to deal with the civilian population. One of the Morales Bermúdez government's first acts, for example, was to revive the independent status of the government-expropriated newspapers.[93]

The Constituent Assembly played a unique role in the nation's politics and altered the traditional role played by parties. Because the political parties became involved in the constituent process, the widespread popular opposition to the regime and its austere economic policies had to be channeled through other venues, primarily organized labor. The labor movement reached the height of its strength during the second phase, staging two successful general strikes, in 1977 and 1978. The union movement in some ways took over the traditional party role of opposition to the regime. The overall current of discontent with the military government, which was particularly strong among the low-income sectors who were hardest hit by the regime's austerity policies, latched onto the activities of the unions in order to express itself. The political parties, while opposing the regime, were thrown into a position of collaborating with it in order to be allowed eventually to attain power through elections. The unions, meanwhile, provided an effective enough opposition to act as a catalyst for the transition to civilian government.[94] APRA was the leader in the parties' role in the process, associating it most closely with the Morales Bermúdez regime. APRA's dominance was due to its electoral mandate in the Constituent Assembly; to its ability to survive the military years—despite its ideological crisis—as an organized party machine that continued its nonelectoral activities throughout the docenio; and finally to the legacy of the persona of Haya de la Torre.

The party's move back onto the center stage of political activity had both positive and negative consequences: although Haya received credit for the successful conduct of the Constituent Assembly, by playing the role of mediator between the military and the other elements of the population, APRA also was associated with the regime in a way that Belaúnde and the AP (who abstained from the Assembly) managed to avoid. The process that culminated in the military's bestowing upon Haya the Orden del Sol, the nation's highest honor, seemed to end, once and for all, the traditional animosity between APRA and the armed forces, clearly a positive result. This honor, however, was soon followed by Haya's death, and APRA was left with a leadership vacuum that, at least in the short term, no one could fill.

Initial Contacts with the Military

It was not obvious in the beginning that the Morales Bermúdez regime
would signify a total shift in strategy, in its attitude to reform and to
political parties. There was concern among some apristas that Morales
Bermúdez was an adamant antiaprista (his father had been killed by an
aprista in 1939) and that he would launch an anti-APRA or anti-Haya
campaign. There were several rumors to that effect in the France Presse
news agency. However, Morales Bermúdez seemed to have lost any
resentment he might initially have had. He served, for example, along with
apristas as minister of hacienda in one of the final Belaúnde cabinets.
Morales Bermúdez seems to have had a mercurial nature: he went from
being one of Velasco's most ardent supporters and a backer of the initial
reforms to staging a coup against Velasco and virtually dismantling the
reforms. In the same way, he dropped the strong antiaprismo rhetoric of
his younger years, and by early 1976 the Morales Bermúdez regime had
made the initial contacts with APRA.

In his memoirs Luis Alberto Sánchez recounts what he considers to
be the first contacts between APRA and the Morales Bermúdez regime.[95]
In early 1976 Sánchez received word through Carlos Olivera—an ex-cap-
tain and current customs agent at the Lima airport and an intimate friend
of General Cisneros—that Luis Cisneros Vizquerra was interested in
meeting with him. Thus Sánchez, Cisneros, his brother Jaime who had
been appointed head of *La Prensa,* and Olivera all dined together at
Sánchez's son-in-law's house. At the time, the France Presse agent who
wrote for *La Prensa* was reporting that there could be no positive discussion between the military and APRA, and that the military old guard
would never forgive the apristas' assault in Trujillo. Cisneros and Sánchez,
meanwhile, did have a productive discussion during which, among other
things, Cisneros revealed to Sánchez that Morales Bermúdez was to
announce the next day—in Trujillo, no less—that the army and the *pueblo*
must drop their mutual animosity. True to his word, on April 30, 1976, in
Trujillo, Morales Bermúdez made a speech along those very lines. "President Morales Bermúdez announced today that it is now time to forget
events that occurred forty-five years ago in Trujillo, 'because this Revolution fights in accordance with its principles for the unity and fraternity
of all Peruvians.'"[96] In the same speech he declared amnesty for political
exiles and political prisoners. Cisneros and Sánchez had also spoken about
the military's plans to cancel its traditional ceremony honoring those
killed in Trujillo, and Sánchez said that APRA would reconsider holding
its annual commemoration of the July 7 revolution.[97] Haya was apparently
very pleased at the results of the Sánchez-Cisneros meeting. A few days
later the first meeting between Haya and members of the military junta
was held at Sánchez's son-in-law's, this time entailing the original group

with the addition of Haya, his secretary Idiaquez, and Armando Villanueva. The conversation lasted six hours and was purportedly relatively frank and animated.[98] When it came to publicly responding to Morales Bermúdez's peace proposition, however, Haya was much less certain, and in his discourse on the May 7 anniversary of APRA's founding, Haya's response was lukewarm. Among other things he affirmed that "we ourselves do not want either dictatorship by a proletariat that practically does not exist with the capacity for political direction . . . or a dictatorship by the oligarchs or by the military"[99]

Cisneros in particular was upset at this response and publicly blamed it on Haya's advanced age. Haya was outraged by the insult and refused even to speak of Cisneros for several months. Not all sectors of the military were totally content with events either, as was demonstrated by the attempts of some of the velasquista wing, purportedly led by General Maldonado, to hold the traditional July 9 ceremony for the Trujillo dead. The reconciliation continued, however. Other meetings between apristas and the military were held at the home of César Garrido Lecca, a former army officer who had joined APRA in the 1950s.[100] Morales Bermúdez publicly invited conversations with party leaders and called for the formation, through elections, of a Constituent Assembly on July 28, 1977. This coincided with Haya's consistent calls for dialog between the armed forces and civilians, and for a Constituent Assembly to serve as a bridge between the dictatorship and civil society. The members of Acción Popular—although some of them had discussed the idea with apristas in Spain the year before—rejected this mechanism totally. While not all APRA members agreed on the need for a new constitution, APRA saw the Assembly as the best way out of the dictatorship, as the military clearly would not accept immediate direct elections.[101]

Conversations began with all political parties, and, according to Sánchez, APRA was not the first party to be convened. Their official delegation, which was composed of Sánchez, Ramiro Priale, Andrés Townsend, Carlos Enrique Melgar, Luis Negreiros, Carlos Roca, and Alfonso Ramos Alva (the latter two of the new generation), met with Morales Bermúdez on the same day and immediately after the delegation from the Partido Popular Cristiano (PPC). Morales Bermúdez had also met with the head of the CGTP—which was responsible for most of the labor unrest—and with the Communist party directorate.[102]

Despite military contacts with other actors, APRA was to maintain a central role. Working conversations on how to run the transition were carried out between the new prime minister, Molina Palocchia, and APRA leaders—usually Villanueva, Townsend, Priale, Julio Cruzado of the CTP, and León de Vivero. After APRA dominated in the elections, relations between government and party improved, and APRA took on a more central role.[103] As the Assembly proceeded, it became evident that

Haya was acting as the nation's preeminent politician and as a mediator between all the political forces and the military. He inspired the respect of both left and right; Hugo Blanco, one of the leaders of the extreme left who had most severely criticized Haya in the 1960s, purportedly called him "Don Víctor."[104]

Haya became increasingly ill, however, and was finally unable to carry out his charge as president of the Assembly. It is indicative of the extent to which the relationship between APRA and the military had changed that the president and the then prime minister, Pedro Richter Prada, visited Haya at Armando Villanueva's house the evening before Haya's departure for cancer treatment in Houston on March 11, 1979.[105] Finally, just days before his death in August 1979, the Morales Bermúdez regime bestowed the Orden del Sol on Haya. Relations between APRA and the military clearly had come full circle since the early years of the revolution and the 1932 Trujillo revolt. The Constituent Assembly may have been Haya's finest hour; yet after he signed the Constitution the party was left with a vacuum in leadership and strategy.

After almost twelve years of military rule—which had combined initial revolutionary rhetoric and institutional reforms, and raised expectations and higher wage levels with a period of harsh economic austerity and real wage repression—the Peruvian population was much more politicized than it had been in 1968. This was reflected by the growth in strength of leftist parties. In the same way that it had been ill equipped in 1968 to deal with the challenge from the Velasco government, APRA, now without Haya, was left divided and without a coherent strategy for the 1980 elections. The leaders that Haya had trained were still too young to take over, and the older generations were split by both ideology and personality.

The Constituent Assembly

> Although it can be argued that the 1978 election is not comparable to the others ... and that the writing of the old Constitution essentially endorsed the old system, the experience was a crucial one. ... First, the Constituent Assembly was the vehicle for the rise and fall of the Peruvian Aprista Party. Second, it initiated the popular left into the game of electoral democracy. Finally, it served firm warning to the political center and right that the ideological bases of partisan competition had taken a substantial step toward the left, with greater representation of the more populous urban areas and the emergence of the popular sectors as a politically relevant force.[106]

The Morales Bermúdez government made a calculated and cautious decision to reopen the political process in 1978 in an atmosphere of growing economic crisis and social unrest, as well as persistent demands for political participation. The decision to hold elections clearly served as a tool to defuse criticism by occupying the political opposition without letting them wield any real power. Haya, as president of the Assembly, called the Assembly the "primary power of the state," yet he was unwilling, as some of his fellow constituents demanded, to call for immediate resignation of the military government. Indeed, it would be difficult to speculate which political party—the fragmented left, an APRA led by an increasingly unwell Haya, or the beleaguered right—would have had the strength to cope with the unrest created by the economic stabilization and adjustment measures that were required at the time. In some ways the Assembly bought time not only for the Morales government, but for the political parties as well. Regardless of the benefits that the decision to hold elections provided the military by containing social unrest, the opening of the political process offered benefits to society as a whole.

The fact that during the docenio political parties had not been repressed, although they were not allowed to perform their representative functions, meant that they had at least been able to survive intact. Those parties that were best able to survive in the nonelectoral game were those with good organization; with a significant popular base that rested on nonelectoral activities such as unions, adult education, and the like; or those with strong and charismatic leaders. APRA was in the best position in this sense. The atmosphere created by revolutionary change and then retrenchment, meanwhile, served to stimulate political activism, whether in support of or in opposition to the military.[107] As is demonstrated in APRA's case, the "revolutionary" atmosphere resulted in the party's renovating its ideology and leadership structure.

The union movement had increased in size and audacity, stimulated by both the military's reforms and the emergence of other confederations to compete with APRA's CTP. Labor's role also took on an increased significance as the political parties, absorbed in the transition, did not actively incorporate popular opinion in opposition to the government. The urban and rural poor, in part as a function of the union movement, had become politicized to an unprecedented extent. The general strikes of July 1977 and May 1978 showed the extent of the union's strength. The CTP did not participate in either strike, in part because of APRA's desire to cooperate with the Morales Bermúdez regime. This was damaging to the party's image at a time when both the labor movement and the political spectrum were shifting to the left, and further tainted it as a collaborator with the regime, although Haya purportedly gave tacit support to the participation of the party's student movement in the strikes[108]—as he had to apristas' unofficial part in the riots of February 5.

The changes in the Peruvian political spectrum were reflected in the results of the 1978 elections. The number of political parties that registered for the 1978 elections increased dramatically over the last election in 1963

Table 3.1   Registration and Results for 1978 Constituent Assembly

	Registration	Percentage	Votes	Percentage	Seats
		Right			
Movimiento Democrático					
Peruano	57,104	6.0	68,619	1.95	2
Unión Nacional Odrista	68,001	7.2	74,134	2.11	2
Partido Democrática					
Reformista Peruano	50,876	5.4	19,594	0.55	0
Partido Popular Cristiano	154,850	16.3	835,294	23.78	25
Total right	330,831	34.9	997,641	28.39	29
		Center			
Acción Popular	137,000	14.5	—	—	—
APRA	77,777	8.2	1,241,174	35.34	37
Total center	214,777	22.7	1,241,174	35.34	37
		Left			
Frente Nacional de					
Trabajadores y Campesinos	86,000	9.1	135,552	3.86	4
Partido Democrático Cristiano	70,000	7.4	83,075	2.37	2
Partido Socialista					
Revolucionario	54,479	5.8	232,520	6.62	6
Acción Revolucionaria					
Socialista	41,130	4.3	20,164	0.57	0
Partido Comunista Peruano	50,000	5.5	207,612	5.91	6
Frente Obrero Campesino					
Estudiantil y Popular	47,194	4.9	433,413	12.34	12
Unión Democratica Popular	53,004	5.6	160,741	4.58	4
Total left	401,807	42.6	1,273,077	36.25	34
All parties	947,475	100.2	3,511,892	99.98	100

Source: Sandra Woy-Hazelton, "The Return to Partisan Politics in Peru," in *Post-Revolutionary Peru: The Politics of Transformation*, ed. Stephan Gorman (Boulder, CO: Westview Press, 1982). Reprinted with permission.

(see Table 3.1). Nonelectoral participation in social and economic activities at local and regional levels provided greater participatory experience for groups such as peasants and illiterates, through the workplace and neighborhood organizations. These groups had been marginal in previous elections. Their heightened awareness served to increase politicization and resulted in an expanded electorate with regard to age, as well as increased pressure for the inclusion of illiterates in national suffrage.[109] Finally, perhaps as an outgrowth of these trends, the ideological center of the political system shifted substantially to the left.

The three most salient features of the 1978 assembly elections, which were to affect future trends, were the absence of ex-president Belaúnde's Acción Popular, APRA's prominence, and the size of the left. The elections gave APRA 35.3 percent of the vote, diverse groups of the left together got 36.2 percent, and the center-right 23.7 percent. Belaúnde's abstention from the elections proved to be an extremely well-calculated move. "By keeping aloof from the military's shows, AP retained the status of democratic opposition to the revolution, a role that APRA had now relinquished."[110] APRA's prominent role in the Assembly had the effect of painting the party as a collaborator with the military regime, ironic in light of APRA's traditional animosity to the Peruvian armed forces. This image was to play directly into Belaúnde's hands in 1980.

APRA had clearly suffered a loss of support during the Velasco years. By 1974 the military's policy of undermining traditional party support had affected APRA in terms of membership in labor confederations, student involvement, and migration of talented apristas into the "revolutionary" camp. Although Haya did indeed make a major attempt to revamp the party ideology and structure, and established the Buro as a training school for new leaders, there was still a flight of youths, at least in the early years when the Velasco regime was at the height of its popularity. During the unpopular Morales Bermúdez government, although the APRA student movement actively opposed the regime, the upper echelons of leadership did not. By the mid-1970s, the leaders were divided, with a majority favoring coexistence with the military. Ironically, this coincided with the military's shift to the right. The emergence of the left as a force, meanwhile, made APRA all the more acceptable to the military. "The party offered the new leadership support from the only noncommunist political entity with mass organizations acceptable to the patron sector."[111] The approval of the military helped APRA during the Constituent elections and in the Assembly, but put a weapon in the hands of the opposition in the 1980 elections.

While many elements of the left suffered repression or exile, APRA was allowed relative freedom prior to the 1978 elections. This coincided with the AP's absence and the left's inability to form a coherent front. APRA, meanwhile, conducted a significant effort to renovate its rank and file. Haya appointed Alan García, just returned from five years of studies in Europe, as secretary of organization—a post he had experience with through the Buro de Conjunciones—to head the renovation. Haya was well aware of the need for energetic younger elements to participate in the campaign. At the time the campaign got under way, Haya's illness began, and he even temporarily considered not participating in the Assembly. Upon his return from a trip to Venezuela and then to a Houston hospital, Haya arranged a rally on February 6, 1978, and had García as one of the speakers along with him. The press began to mention Alan García as the new *cachorro* (little pup) of APRA, a nickname previously given to the now deceased right-hand man to Haya, Manuel Seoane. As secretary of organization, García was one of the apristas closest to the rank and file, and the first to experience the growth of the left among them.[112]

At age eighty-three and in the early stages of his cancer, Haya de la Torre managed an impressive electoral campaign.[113] He traveled tirelessly over a great part of the country. He even broke with tradition and held the yearly Día de Fraternidad rally in Arequipa rather than in Trujillo that year. For the elections, each party was to present a list of one hundred candidates in preferential order. There were to be no provincial or departmental elections—all were elected nationally. People were to vote for a party, and then mark one preferred candidate, in order to break the monopoly on choice held by the party lists. For APRA, Haya was the number-one candidate, Priale was second, Sánchez third, Carlos Manuel Cox fourth, and Andrés Townsend fifth. Villanueva did not participate in the elections and remained in the post of general secretary. The APRA campaign focused on marking Haya as the preferential vote, in order to attain presidency of the Assembly. This was a practice copied by Bedoya of the PPC and Jorge del Prado of the Communists. As a result Haya won the most votes nationwide, followed by Luis Bedoya. APRA won the majority in the elections. Thirty-seven of the one hundred Assembly delegates were apristas; twenty-five seats went to the PPC, and most of the rest to diverse groups of the left, with the Frente Obrero Campesino Estudiantil y Popular reflecting the most strength. Within APRA, Sánchez replaced Priale as number-two candidate, given the results of the preferential voting, and subsequently became vice-president of the Assembly. Most of the aprista old guard was elected to the Assembly as well. Of the members of the young generation promoted by Haya, Carlos Roca Caceres and Alan García were elected to the Assembly and thus initiated their political careers there. Carlos Roca was number eighteen by preferential voting, and García number twenty-eight.[114]

After APRA easily attained a plurality in the 1978 elections, it seemed that the party was finally positioned for a rise to national power. Instead a variety of factors—its role as leader of the Constituent Assembly included—interacted to promote victory in 1980 for the same man the military had overthrown in 1968. APRA's role as leader in the Assembly burdened the party with responsibility for the solution of several touchy issues. The leaders of the Assembly had to establish a relationship between the Assembly and the military, create an alliance to draft the

Constitution, and establish the bases of electoral competition for 1980. There was an inherent tension between maintaining the military's support and gaining that of a population increasingly adamant in its opposition to the military, as was demonstrated by APRA's position vis-à-vis the general strikes. The left, meanwhile, pressed consistently for the Constituent Assembly to declare itself sovereign, thus rendering the military regime null and void. While Haya declared the Assembly the "'main power of the state,' thus proclaiming its autonomous existence, separate and equal to the military regime,"[115] he was not willing to call for the regime's resignation and for the Assembly's sovereignty. His main goal was to guarantee the writing of a Constitution and the 1980 elections. He was also reluctant to take control of and therefore responsibility for the nation's deepening economic crisis and to give up the free rein to organize and campaign given APRA by the military. Thus APRA often broke with the left and allied with the PPC in the Assembly.[116]

After years of involvement in antagonistic political activity, Haya displayed a concern for national unity in the Assembly. He managed to play the moderating role between left and right well, a role that rarely yields political rewards. However, he was nearly debilitated by lung cancer at the time, a condition that was noted by the opposition. Once, when Haya called for an early close to one session because of his illness, Luis Bedoya tried to play up the issue in the press.[117] The party, meanwhile, refused to publicly acknowledge that Haya was sick, and up to his death proclaimed him as presidential candidate. Haya spent the last few months of the Assembly in the hospital in Houston, and was replaced in the Constituency by Sánchez. He signed the Constitution virtually on his deathbed; he was so ill that he had to practice his signature several times prior to signing.

Haya's illness caused those closest to him to begin to play more-prominent leadership roles: of the older generation, Sánchez and Townsend in the Congress and Villanueva in party activities; of the younger generation, García and Carlos Roca in the Assembly and Luis Alva Castro in party activities. Luis Alva Castro was given the job of organizing the Twelfth Party Congress of 1979 by Haya from his hospital bed in Houston. While the old guard and the Sánchez-Priale-Townsend wing of the party prevailed in the Assembly, the more left-wing Villanueva group prevailed at the party congress, where there was more contact with the rank and file.[118] This split was to become an increasingly debilitating factor and was largely responsible for the party's debacle in the 1980 elections; the party formally split in 1981.

Haya was able to provide the Assembly with enough initial leadership—as did Sánchez after him—to merge the divergent forces of right and left and draft a Constitution: a remarkable deed in an Assembly composed of both freewheeling capitalists and Maoists and Trotskyites.

The Constitution ushered in a much more presidential style of government, which gave the executive a great deal of policymaking freedom,
particularly in the economic arena. The opposition's charge that APRA
designed the Constitution with an eye on the presidency was at least
partially true.[119]

APRA's image, tainted by perceived and actual collaboration with
the military and the right, was devastated by the passing away of its
charismatic founder and leader on August 2, 1979. The eventual result was
an irreconcilable split between the younger, more progressive wing of the
party led by Armando Villanueva and the older wing, associated with the
party's drift right, led by Andrés Townsend Escurra. The compromise that
resulted—Villanueva as presidential candidate and Townsend as vice-
presidential candidate—neither ended the internal division nor provided
a unified, organized party image, which was the party's traditional
strength. Finally, not only was APRA divided and without leadership, but
it also lacked a coherent program. The Velasco regime had already
implemented the key points of APRA's traditional program. APRA,
meanwhile, had vacillated all too often: after its initially strong antioligarchic stance, its "domestication" of the 1950s and 1960s cost it a great
deal of credibility; finally it attempted to ally with both the military and
the right in the late 1970s, neither of which ever fully trusted the party.

The left-leaning Villanueva wing of the party did have some influence
on APRA's program: support for turning the newspapers over to workers'
organizations; support for the SUTEP-led teacher's strike; a change in
union leadership; ratification of the antiimperialist doctrine; rejection of
transnational influence, totalitarian communism, and the reactionary
right.[120] The party remained associated with the conservative old guard,
however, which without the charisma and stature of Haya de la Torre had
little popular appeal. In the same way that the Velasco revolution spurred
Haya in the 1970s to change his strategy and focus on a new generation of
leaders and the future of the party, the debacle of the 1980 election was
to spur the young leaders, primarily through the personality of Alan
García in the 1980s, to rise up and take control. As is noted in Chapter 1,
an electoral defeat often provides the impetus for the internal democratization of parties.

The military years were clearly difficult ones for APRA. Even the
eventual recognition that Haya attained after the Constituent Assembly
was marred by his illness and death, and the final acceptance of defeat:
that the great Haya de la Torre would never become president. The old
guard of leadership, too long dominated by the single hand of Haya, was
neither emotionally prepared nor able to adapt the party to Peru's new
realities. It was to take a virtual revolution within the party ranks to do
this; a revamping that was carried out, at least superficially, by Alan
García. Even García, however, never attained the acceptance and stature

held by Haya—both within and outside the party. The death of Haya, in many ways, opened a new era in Peruvian politics. The Belaúnde regime may have been a step back and temporary pause, but even that regime was marked by breaks with the past, such as the election of Alfonso Barrantes, a Marxist, as mayor of Lima. The left had entered Peruvian politics, and this, more than any other political issue, was something APRA would have to contend with. APRA no longer had a monopoly on a revolutionary platform; it now had to share political space with the left. The social pressures and economic problems of the next decade were to be much more daunting than any that past generations of civilian politicians had had to deal with. It would take a new generation of APRA leaders to adapt to these changes and challenges, and to be open to new ideas and strategies.

While the military docenio signified an end to APRA's monopoly of the political space on the left, the period did provide the party with the opportunity to serve as the institutional basis for the transition to democracy. As a party in the center of the political spectrum, led by a renowned national leader, APRA provided a guarantee of stability that was key to maintaining the necessary cooperation of the military and conservative political forces throughout the transition. (An analogous role was played by Patricio Aylwin and the Christian Democrats in the recent Chilean transition.) Yet while APRA successfully fulfilled its role in the transition and was finally able to attain power in 1985, the implementation of socioeconomic reform and the consolidation of democracy were to prove far more elusive goals, as the evaluation of APRA in power in Part 2 demonstrates.

4
APRA 1980–1985:
Renovation and Results

"[Nor] would Peruvianists in 1979 or 1980 have expected that Belaúnde would hand over power to an Aprista leader in 1985. Few commentators had any confidence that civilian government would persist into the second half of the decade. Nobody . . . forecast the resurgence of APRA. . . . One well-known observer dismissed the APRA as 'a collection of tired old men and their memories.'"[1]

Peru in 1979 was poised for transition to civilian rule after twelve years of military dictatorship. The Constituent Assembly had been, in many ways, Haya de la Torre's, and his party's, finest hour. Yet in 1980 APRA was proved an impotent giant by its electoral debacle.[2] The party was debilitated by the death of its founder and leader and by its perception of itself as a perennial opposition party. Racked by internecine strife, it was clearly unable to cope with the complex political, social, and economic challenges facing the nation as it made its transition to civilian rule. As is noted in the first chapter, the longer a party is in opposition, the less likely it is to have realistic proposals for governing. Peru had undergone substantive socioeconomic change during the military docenio, and required innovative and coherent leadership. APRA in 1980 was led by an old guard that was ill fit to govern the nation: they were both inexperienced—the result of Haya's singlehanded dominance for almost fifty years—and obsessed with internal power struggles rather than with issues of national concern. The inadequacy of the apristas coupled with the fragmentation of the left led to the electorate's opting for the known persona of its past, Fernando Belaúnde.

Peruvian society, because of the military's "revolutionary" rhetoric and the politicization that it caused; economic structural and demographic changes; and the crucial role that popular opposition—led by the unions—played in toppling the military government, had changed substantially since 1968. By late 1978 the number of trade unions, for example, had doubled. The unions were also able to tap the massive force of the unorganized workers in the pueblos jóvenes,[3] whose numbers had increased dramatically during that decade, in their launching of three successive and highly successful national strikes. The success of spontaneous protest movements demonstrated a crucial characteristic of Peru in the late 1970s, which persists today: the breach between state and society. This was a challenge looming over all political parties, and one APRA, for a variety of reasons, was not in the least prepared to face; nor was the nascent and fragmented left. Belaúnde, in part because of the advantage of having been the last civilian president, was temporarily able to fill a leadership vacuum, but failed in any way to provide the institutional base for narrowing the gap between state and society.

The Belaúnde government's inability to steer the country away from the deep socioeconomic crisis that it was heading for was to the nation's detriment, but it did serve to provide the Peruvian aprista party with a historic opportunity to implement its decades-old reformist platform. What APRA was not prepared to do in 1980, it clearly seemed to be in 1985. The evolution that occurred within the party is crucial to explaining this change. As is also noted in Chapter 1, an electoral defeat will often spur the internal democratization of a party; this is precisely what happened in APRA, providing an opening for Alan García's rise to power.

In some ways, APRA was a totally different party in 1985, with new leaders, led by Alan García, and a renovated platform. Other aspects of the party remained unchanged, however, and APRA was unable to shake off many of its regional, sectarian, and cultlike characteristics, or its tradition of incontrovertible faith in the party leader. These aspects were to resurface and present obstacles to APRA's ability to function as a governing party. The party's initial blind faith in García was to the severe detriment of both the party and the nation. The examination of the changes that occurred within APRA from 1980 to 1985 and of the traits that remained is critical to the analysis of APRA in power. The context in which these changes occurred—the second Belaúnde regime—must first be discussed, as the failures of that regime provided APRA with both unique opportunities and formidable obstacles.

THE SECOND BELAÚNDE REGIME

With the virtual disintegration of the opposition, Fernando Belaúnde Terry won the 1980 presidential election riding on his old—and perhaps questionable—laurels. It was immediately evident, however, that they could not carry him through the challenges he was to face in his second term. Peru had undergone dramatic demographic, political, and economic changes since Belaúnde's first tenure of power. There were highly visible manifestations of these changes, such as the huge growth of squatter settlements in and around Lima; there was clearly a need for a government capable of responding to the growth of popular pressure in the face of half a decade of dramatically decreasing living standards. This need was demonstrated by the speed with which the Morales Bermúdez regime was discredited by widespread strike activity in the late 1970s. By 1980 the Peruvian population was mobilized and politicized in a way that it had never been before; at the same time it was weary of the sharp and steady decrease in the standard of living it had experienced during the Morales Bermúdez years of recession and austerity. Belaúnde's electoral platform may have been vague, but there was certainly a mandate for change and initiative—a mandate Belaúnde proved unable to fulfill.

The surge in popular mobilization that took place in Peru was in part a function of the opening to civilian politics, and in part a function of the socioeconomic trends that had been a cause of the military's revolution in the late 1960s, and were then accelerated by its rhetoric. Accompanying this surge was an economic base that was ill equipped to provide for the rapidly growing population and the vast influx into the cities of migrants who sought opportunity and employment. Until the late 1960s the economy had suffered from excess dependence on exports and foreign capital and a concurrent lack of domestic entrepreneurial capacity. The economy then was almost crippled by the military's mismanaged attempts at industrial and agrarian reform, which resulted in widespread capital flight, decreased agricultural productivity, and excessive growth of the state bureaucracy and of public sector debt. The second phase of the military docenio was an attempt to stabilize the inflation-ridden and debt-strapped economy with an IMF–inspired austerity program, which aimed to dismantle many of the policies implemented in the first phase. The reforms and the expectations raised by the reformist rhetoric, and then the drastic shift to austerity measures, with their negative impact on real wage levels, had significant effects in terms of popular mobilization.

The union movement's strength had grown substantially with the attempts at state-led industrialization and the failure of industrial reform to create harmonious worker-management communities, and it grew increasingly willing to wield that strength with the dramatic deterioration in real wage levels that occurred in the mid- and late 1970s. There had been a demographic explosion in Peru in the 1960s and 1970s. The population had tripled from 1941 to 1981 and had become increasingly urban: 47 percent lived in cities in 1961 as opposed to 65 percent in 1981. By the 1980s over 30 percent of the nation's population lived in Lima. The industrial and agrarian reforms of the early 1970s had, in general, primarily affected privileged sectors of urban labor and of the peasantry, leaving large sectors of the population with raised expectations but in the same state of poverty and marginalization. Meanwhile, although the reforms had undermined the power of the old hacienda and mining elites, a new dominant class had emerged, composed primarily of private capital associated with the state and transnational capital.[4] Control of the key economic sectors was concentrated either in the hands of a small number of private interests or in state monopolies or associated industries. The burgeoning informal sector was the visible manifestation of the economic structure's inadequacy. Political power, on the other hand, had become more disperse, as was demonstrated by the growth of the left and the election of Alfonso Barrantes—a Marxist—as mayor of Lima in 1983.

Peru in 1980 was by no means a stable society. The coalition that supported Belaúnde was an uncertain one, and the vote that elected him one of desperation rather than of positive choice. Increasingly evident was the *desborde popular*—the overflow of demands created by demographic, political, and economic changes—that the state was incapable of addressing. The result was the broadening of the already existing gap between state and society,[5] which was demonstrated on the economic front by the vast growth of the informal sector, and on the social front in its most extreme form by the emergence in 1980 of Sendero Luminoso.

The government of Fernando Belaúnde Terry and his Acción Popular party proved unable to bridge this gap between Peruvian society and its state. Instead the government increasingly projected an image of detachment and, unintentionally, of grandiose and irrelevant vision in the face of deepening social and economic crisis. The Belaúnde government lacked a concept of national development. Its economic strategy was an attempt to return to the nation's pre-1968 model of economic liberalism. On the political front, the government's approach was paternalistic and devoid of grassroots organization and activity—a void that was gradually filled up by the left and APRA—at a time when political mobilization was on the rise. The result of the lack of government attention to and contact with the masses, particularly the urban poor, as the country entered the worst economic crisis in its modern history, was the widespread radicalization of the working class and the inhabitants of the pueblos jóvenes. This was demonstrated in November 1983 by the victory of Izquierda Unida in Lima, and by the emergence of support for Sendero Luminoso and the MRTA in some pueblos jóvenes. The government's continued inability to respond to popular sentiments led to the disastrous electoral performance of Acción Popular in the 1985 elections.

The Belaúnde government had inherited substantial constraints. In addition to the fragile economy and the demands of the newly mobilized sectors of the population, the government had to cope with the age-old yet ever-present threat of military intervention and the very new and complex threat posed by the rise of Sendero. In 1980 the military left power discredited, yet it had a desire to maintain some control over the political process. This was evidenced by a warning that Morales Bermúdez privately made to a group of APRA leaders, as their internal struggles came increasingly into the public eye prior to the 1980 elections. "One of the conditions for returning to civilian life in the eyes of the armed forces was the emergence of a strong and united party the way APRA had been."[6] It is significant that despite the fact that APRA's image was tainted as a collaborator with the armed forces, the military's tacit support prior to the elections seems to have shifted to Belaúnde.[7]

As in the case of several transitions to democracy in Latin America, the military took precautions to protect its institutional viability and to increase its strength vis-à-vis the new civilian government before surrendering power. Nineteen days before the Belaúnde regime took over, the military passed the so-called Mobilization Law. This law, passed with no publicity in order to avoid civilian reaction, enabled the military to expropriate or requisition companies, services, labor, and materials from all Peruvians or foreigners in the country at times of national emergency. These times included cases of "internal subversion and internal disasters."[8] The military maintained autonomy over its budget and arms transfers. Interventionist tendencies continued to exist among many officers, and the military continued to exercise influence in all matters of national security and domestic order.[9] This influence was primarily evident in the counterterrorism arena, where the government had no coherent policy to fend off an increasingly potent challenge from Sendero, which left no alternative other than default to the military, with the consequence of unconstrained human rights violations in the emergency zones.

Economic Policy: Crisis and Controversy

The government's economic strategy generated increasing opposition among the population, in Congress, and within Acción Popular itself. Congressional opposition, despite the impressive gains made in November 1983 by opposition parties in the municipal elections, had very little effect on government policy, as the executive had a great deal of freedom, especially in the economics sphere. The 1979 Constitution significantly strengthened the power of the executive, and in particular allowed it to enact legislation without recourse to Congress on all decisions involving changes in government expenditure. "At a stroke this gave the executive almost complete autonomy in the enacting of government policy."[10] Belaúnde and his cabinet were able, largely by decree, to impose controversial economic policies for five years, causing a great deal of popular unrest and deteriorating standards of living as well as rifts within his own party and the Congress. The split within Acción Popular over economic policy mirrored the dispute that factionalized Congress between hard-line Acción Popular personnel and PPC conservatives on the one hand, and the progressive wing of the AP, apristas, and Izquierda Unida deputies on the other. Belaúnde's drop in popularity was reflected in the results of the 1983 municipal elections. The AP came in fifth-place nationwide, with 15 percent of the vote, as opposed to the 35 percent it obtained in the 1980 municipal elections.[11] The opposition to Belaúnde's policies, at least as of 1983, was led in large part by none other than Alan García.

The neoliberal, export-based strategy met its nemesis in 1982 as the world prices for Peru's revenue-producing mineral exports fell dramatically with world recession, and the Niño current damaged another of Peru's main exports—the anchovy. The current also produced a series of devastating disasters in 1983; floods in the North and drought in the South combined to severely curtail Peru's food production, necessitating substantial funds for food imports and disaster relief. Meeting foreign creditors' conditions assumed a more crucial importance. At the same time successive devaluations fueled an inflation rate in the triple digits from 1982 to 1985. As the adverse economic trends continued through 1983, the real growth rate fell to negative 12 percent. While there was a slight recovery in 1984, with 4 percent growth, by the middle of the next year the economy remained in deep crisis.[12] The high inflation rate, coupled with the phasing out of most food subsidies in order to reduce the public sector deficit, understandably created havoc for consumers, as even the prices of the cheapest available staple goods soared out of reach of the lowest-income groups, and a promised food stamp program was never implemented. The executive branch remained adamant in its adherence to its strategy despite any prospects for recovery in the short term, and seemed virtually blind to criticism, even that which came from within its own ranks, such as from Central Bank President Richard Webb. This intransigent adherence to a flawed economic policy fueled the support that García and APRA were to elicit for a heterodox economic model and a strong stance on the foreign debt issue.

The Belaúnde government did, to its credit, achieve some positive results in the social welfare arena, in education in particular. In both his terms Belaúnde placed a great deal of emphasis on education, and in the years 1980–1983 increased school enrollment by 1 million.[13] Yet this also led to an increase in social mobilization at a time when economic crisis was closing off opportunities.

Mucho Ruido y Pocas Nueces

The policies of the Belaúnde administration could be described by the Latin expression *mucho ruido y pocas nueces* (lots of cracking but very few nuts). There was no effort to buffer low-income groups from the impact of severe economic crisis. As the prices of basic commodities led the inflationary surge and there was an absence or cutting of social welfare policies, low-income groups—particularly the urban poor, who spend the highest proportion of their budgets on food—fared the worst of all. Rising food prices, meanwhile, did not stimulate peasant agriculture, as there was no attempt to guide pricing policy in favor of the products traditionally grown in the sierra. Instead the market was dominated by imported food, which substantially increased with the administration's trade liberalization. The bulk of the peasantry of the southern sierra, already living at the bare subsistence level, was threatened with near or total starvation by the devastating drought caused by the Niño current.[14] It is hardly surprising that Sendero, which launched its activity in the southern sierra region, increased its violent activities significantly by the middle of Belaúnde's term.

The fact that the economic crisis was brought on by world recession and the Niño current is not sufficient excuse for the poor record of the Belaúnde government; nor is the burden of external debt payments, as the regime, more often than not, was out of compliance with its creditors. There was both congressional and popular support for change and for policies to buffer the poorest groups from bearing the brunt of the effects of the economic debacle, as the results of the 1983 municipal elections demonstrated.

The Belaúnde era clearly created the political conditions for a reformist consensus. By thoroughly discrediting the center-right as a political option and neoliberalism as an economic one, the Belaúnde regime gave the García campaign the opportunity to gain support for a relatively radical reformist program. It also placed APRA in the position of being for the center and right the *mal menor* (lesser evil), as the only other option was the more radical Izquierda Unida. In the short term, APRA had much to gain politically from the failures of the AP government. APRA's task in government, however, was made much more difficult by the extent to which economic degradation had created crisis in Peruvian society. In economic terms, although APRA inherited a depressed economy, it also received some advantages. It inherited a stabilized economy with acceptable levels of international reserves and a great deal of existing excess capacity, which facilitated the economic reactivation that APRA implemented. Finally, there is one major point to Belaúnde's credit: he was able, despite the severity of the crisis and the challenges confronting him, to hand over the reins of government to an elected successor; a phenomenon that had not occurred in Peru for over forty years.

THE EVOLUTION OF THE APRA AND THE RISE OF ALAN GARCÍA

It is impossible to separate the 1985 victory of the APRA party from the role played by its charismatic leader, Alan García Pérez. Under the leadership of García the party attained the presidency for the first time in its sixty-year history, and a working majority in the Congress as well. This outcome was the result of a decade of political, economic, and social trends, but was also inextricably linked to the emergence of García as the party's leader in late 1982. García's rise to power reflected changes both within the APRA party, and in Peru's socioeconomic and political structure in general. García's rapid rise demonstrates the increased strength of the social and political forces that supported him. At the same time the success of yet another charismatic leader with a populist orientation also exposed age-old continuities in the nation's political culture. The thirty-six-year-old president's meteoric progression from virtual anonymity in 1982 to overwhelming victory on a national scale in 1985—when he won more votes than all the other candidates together—was indeed astounding. This victory was a function of García's own personality, of the renewed image that APRA was able to present, and of the absence of political alternatives acceptable to the center and right.

The evolution that the APRA party underwent in the early 1980s had its roots in the ideological challenges posed by the military's revolution, and the ensuing renovation of the party. While the APRA old guard squandered the party's political opportunities in 1980 because of internecine struggles, the generation of young leaders that had been fostered by Haya during the docenio began to plan its rise to power and the revamping of the party's image. The 1980 electoral debacle provided this generation with the impetus to assert itself in the leadership of APRA.

The phenomenon of *velasquismo*—the reformist rhetoric, the institutional change, and most important the increased politicization and raised expectations—posed an ideological challenge to all parties. In the face of this challenge and Haya's death in 1979, APRA's weaknesses became evident. By 1980, despite its prominent role in the Constituent Assembly, and in part because of it—its cooperation with the military and perceived collusion with the right—APRA had a jaded image. The party's image had been damaged in the 1950s and 1960s by the convivencia. APRA was then forced to acknowledge its internal crisis when the military implemented a program virtually identical to the original APRA one. At the time the party lost some key young technocrats who left to join the planning staff of the military government. Finally Haya's illness and the leaders' involvement in the Constituent Assembly resulted in the neglect of the party's program and its relation to changed political, economic, and social realities. In the interim, Haya's efforts to renovate the party had focused on a select group of young leaders but had done little to forge the party's links with the rest of society. These trends led to reduced influence in unions and universities. The party functioned in the 1980 elections as an electoral machine that was devoid of substance.[15]

At the Twelfth Party Congress in August 1979, just weeks after Haya's death, there was no debate about APRA's program. The party was totally involved in deciding on a candidate, as Haya had remained the official choice until his death.[16] The two obvious choices were Andrés Townsend and Armando Villanueva, the party leaders who had received the most publicity (other than Haya) in the past three years.[17] Townsend was the superior intellectual and orator, but his conservative bent made him less attractive to the party youth. Villanueva, who had been in charge of party affairs during the Constituent Assembly, leaned more toward the left, but his violent, *búfalo* reputation made him less acceptable to those outside the party. The contest between the two, who had been intimate,[18] was a highly personalistic one, acerbic, bitter, and often violent. In part this was a function of Haya's failure to prepare for his successor, or at least establish procedural rules. As Townsend admitted, the rules were not clear and neither side paid them much attention.[19] After much controversy Villanueva emerged as presidential candidate, and Townsend, after initially refusing the post, as vice-presidential candidate. The party had little to offer the electorate other than the campaign song *El APRA es el camino.*

After the elections the party split irreconcilably into an "armandista wing," which was younger and more progressive, and was led by León de Vivero, Carlos Enrique Melgar, and Luis Negreiros, and an "andresista wing," supported by the key old-guard members Luis Alberto Sánchez and Ramiro Priale. Symbolic of APRA's predicament at the time was that the traditional celebration of Haya's birthday in February 1981, the Día de Fraternidad, was celebrated in two competing rallies—Townsend's in the Plaza San Martín and Villanueva's in party headquarters—and dubbed the "Noche del Fratricidio."[20] Townsend had been expelled from the party in January 1981. This split was so deep that it continues to play a role among the provincial militants today.[21] When Townsend formed his Bases Hayistas party he lost key supporters such as Sánchez, for whom an alternative to APRA was unthinkable.[22] The split had two results. The first was to disrupt the party from top to bottom and expose the absence of leadership since Haya's death. The second was to open a space for the rise of the young generation that was determined to renovate the party's image and focus its attention on issues of national importance. Although the subsequent meteoric rise of Alan García to party and national prominence seemed unexpected, the basis had been laid by Haya in the 1970s, as Chapter 3 demonstrates.

The exodus of young militants and leaders during the convivencia had left practically an entire generation missing in APRA leadership. There was a split between the first and generally more conservative generation, then in their mid-fifties or older, and the next group, in their twenties and early thirties.[23] It was this latter group that was sympathetic to the reformist attempts of the Velasco government and to whom Haya turned to build a foundation for new leadership, in part as a means to avoid a challenge to his own predominance from the older group.

Haya had handpicked protégés in this generation, as is demonstrated by his choosing García to speak at the January 1978 rally and appointing him secretary of organization, a post key to power in the party.[24] He gave Luis Alva Castro responsibility in party matters, such as organizing the

Twelfth Party Congress in Trujillo.[25] Competition for Haya's attention may have been one of the roots of the intense rivalry that later surfaced between García and Alva Castro.

Thus the new generation of APRA leaders did not rise out of nowhere, and the Andrés/Armando split, although it temporarily debilitated the party, gave youth the opportunity to assert itself. The split eliminated the older generation of leaders: after Villanueva's electoral debacle, he was tainted politically, and Townsend would have been the logical candidate for 1985.[26] Prior to the 1982 Fourteenth Party Congress, in which a new secretary-general was to be elected, there was quite a bit of subversive planning. Several meetings were held at the home of César Garrido Lecca that involved Sánchez, García, and Alva Castro, and from which Villanueva was explicitly excluded. At these meetings the plans for García, then a deputy from Lima, to vie for the post of secretary-general and then as candidate for the presidency purportedly were cemented.[27] Villanueva, who spent several months in Europe in a sort of self-imposed exile, resented this, although he did grudgingly support García once he was chosen.[28] At the time of the party congress these plans came to fruition through the combined support of a few key old-guard members and of the rank and file, who had been influenced by the reformist rhetoric of the Velasco years and were tired of an inactive CEN and internal squabbles still smoldering after the Villanueva-Townsend split. García's rise was also facilitated by the commitment of Fernando León de Vivero, then secretary-general, to the party's emerging intact from the transition.[29]

While these trends seem clearer with the benefit of hindsight, at the time of the congress the likely victor was thought to be either Guillermo Larco Cox or Carlos Enrique Melgar, younger members of the old guard. Both were of the forties and fifties generation that was logically the next phase of APRA leadership. Larco Cox fell ill, and thus Carlos Melgar was heavily favored at the start of the congress. He had the backing of many of the key dirigentes of the party: the Aprista Parliamentary Cell in private lent its support, as did the secretary-general, León de Vivero; the bulk of the Villanueva wing and the left wing or *izquierda aprista* of Luis Negreiros, Carlos Roca, and Javier Valle Riestra also backed him. Alan García was not considered a major challenge by the bulk of the Melgar supporters.[30]

García, meanwhile, had two formidable factors in his favor that led to his attaining the post. The first was a product of his background and of negotiating skill. He had the support of one of the oldest and most respected apristas, Luis Alberto Sánchez, who also happened to be his godfather. He was able to elicit the support of the influential mayor of Trujillo, Jorge Torres Vallejo, and of Luis Felipe de las Casas, a renowned party member who had constantly questioned Haya's dubious pacts and alliances. García also had the guarded support of Luis Alva Castro, who had united the party's public administration technicians and the nonleftist progressives around a lengthy and well-accepted project: the Comision de Plan de Gobierno (CONAPLAN). Alva Castro was well respected as a *técnico* (technocrat) within the party. García promised, and delivered, prestigious posts: to de las Casas the secretariat of organization; to Torres Vallejo the subsecretary-generalship; to Sánchez the presidency of a new political commission that was to wield a great deal of power in the party's future planning.[31]

Finally, García had excellent credentials. His career had been totally devoted to APRA. He was born into the party in May 1949. Both his parents were apristas, and his father, who had worked with de las Casas in clandestine organizational activities, was imprisoned for political reasons for the first five years of Alan's life. Alan García joined the APRA youth at age eleven. In 1972 he went to Europe to study in Spain with, among others, Franco's former minister, Fraga, whose neocorporatist theory of society apparently impressed García. Haya had arranged for him to study with a prominent Peruvianist at the Sorbonne, François Bourricaud. His former professor described him as not an intellectual, but clever and very astute, and determined to succeed in politics.[32] He came back to work for the party in 1977. Haya appointed him secretary of organization and right-hand man during the Constituent Assembly years and pushed him into the public eye. He supported Villanueva's candidacy in 1980, and had remained aloof from internal party squabbles since then. He was also totally free of links to the drug traffic, unlike many other high-level apristas at the time, who had been implicated in the highly publicized "Caso Langberg." García developed, from the late 1970s onward, from an "introvert"[33] and *cualquier joven del APRA* (typical APRA youth)[34] into a gifted orator and skilled politician. He was determined early on to be president.[35]

García's own record, and the backing he had from the best and the brightest of the aprista leaders—those whose backgrounds were free of corruption or violence—led to the second and most important factor in his favor: the wide degree of support he had among the aprista delegates, the rank and file of the party, the majority of whom were younger and much more progressive than the Melgar and Cox generation. This *masa aprista* and the weight of its vote was overlooked by many of the directors of the party. This younger generation sought a united party, without links to external forces or other parties. They resented much of the older leaders' record of collusion and alliances with the right as well as the Villanueva and Roca wing's courting of the left, and in particular the implications of some of the leaders' links with the drug traffic.[36] They were interested in starting anew and breaking with APRA's past history of violence and fanaticism—its reputation as " 'matones' [thugs] or instigators of 'golpes.' "[37]

Alan García fit in well with this new generation. Since the Villanueva-Townsend split, he had strategically refrained from taking sides in internal party politics; an alternative to *andresismo* or *armandismo* was emerging: *alanismo*.[38] García made a definitive effort to distance himself from the left as well as the right. The creation of a new party image was central to García's aims and campaign, as it was to the new generation that he represented. Soon after his election at the congress as secretary-general, García was elected presidential candidate with 96 percent of internal votes.[39] He announced his candidacy in Ayacucho in August 1983.[40]

Campaign 1983–1985

"The emergence of a new generation of aprista leaders was necessary before the party could shed its decades-old image of violence and fanaticism. García's talent was to exorcise this past."[41] García's and the party's strategy was to open up APRA to new sectors and regions and to tone down the party's sectarian image. Their primary focus was the nonaprista middle-class sectors: those who wanted social change but feared the Marxist left in general. On the economic front they focused on pragmatism and technical capacity to dispel their image of mediocrity, while still presenting an image of social conscience. Alva Castro's group was instrumental in this arena. The party recognized and attempted to capitalize on the emergence of a new, young working class that had a higher level of education and was primarily concentrated in the dynamic industrial sectors—those who were not a part of the traditional aprista trade unions.[42]

García had learned from Villanueva's failures and from Belaúnde's effective campaign style.[43] His opening up of the party even involved public criticism of the old guard and the dropping of traditional APRA symbolism. The left-handed salute—labelled by opponents as reminiscent of fascism—was dropped, and the aprista Marseillaise was replaced as a campaign song with the nationally known waltz "Mi Perú." For the first time the party was not insisting that "solo el APRA salvara el Perú" (only APRA can save Peru)[44] and instead promising that García's "compromiso es con todos los peruanos" (commitment is to all Peruvians). Yet the removal of traditional symbols was not without substantial resentment by many in the party.[45]

The strategy was highly successful. The November 1983 municipal elections proved a major turnaround for APRA, which was the overwhelming winner nationwide (see Table 4.1), followed by Izquierda Unida, which won the mayoralty of Lima. The governing Acción Popular party suffered a resounding defeat. The November 1983 results were first and foremost an overwhelming rejection of the AP's economic policies. The left and APRA together took 63 percent of Lima's vote versus the 32 percent obtained by the AP together with its coalition partner the PPC.

Table 4.1 Elections 1980–1990

	Municipal Elections			
	Total Votes in Lima (percentage)			
	November 1980	November 1983	November 1986	November 1989
AP	34.9	11.9	—	—
PPC	20.6	21.2	26.9	—
APRA	16.3	27.2	37.6	11.53
IU	28.3	36.5	34.8	11.54
ASI	—	—	—	2.15
FREDEMO	—	—	—	26.79
Obras	—	—	—	45.15

	Nationwide (percentage)[a]			
AP	35.8	15.0	—	—
PPC	10.9	10.0	9.0	—
APRA	22.6	34.0	42.0	17.0
IU	23.9	30.0	32.0	15.0
ASI	—	—	—	0.7
FREDEMO	—	—	—	30.0
Other	—	—	—	25.0

Percentages in Major Cities, November 1986, by Party

	APRA	IU	PPC	Others
Lima	34.5	31.6	26.7	—
Trujillo	60.0	19.0	8.0	22.0
Chiclayo	45.0	36.0	—	13.0
Ayacucho	28.0	32.0	—	—[b]
Puno[c]	48.0	32.0	—	—

Percentages of Votes for APRA in Lima, by Year

1978	25.5
1980(presidential)	22.95
1980(municipal)	17.0
1983	28.0
1985	50.6
1986	37.6
1989	11.53

(continues)

Table 4.1 continued

Percentages in the 1985 National Elections
By Party and Candidate

APRA (García)	47.8
IU (Barrantes)	22.2
PPC (Bedoya)	12.2
AP (Alva)	6.4
Others	2.8
Null and blank[d]	8.6

Seats Won in the Senate

APRA	32
IU	15
CODE[e]	8
Izquierda Nacionalista	1

Percentages in the 1990 National Elections
Presidential Race, First Round

FREDEMO (Vargas Llosa)	28.19
Cambio 90 (Fujimori)	24.32
APRA (Alva Castro)	19.57
IU (Pease)	7.12
ASI (Barrantes)	4.16
Frenatraca (Caceres)	1.00
Others	1.26
Null and blank	14.38

Second Round

Cambio 90	56.53
FREDEMO	33.92
Null and blank	9.55

Senate Seats

FREDEMO	22
Cambio 90	15
APRA	14
IU	5
ASI	3
Frenatraca	1

(continues)

Table 4.1 continued

	Chamber Seats
FREDEMO	64
Cambio 90	49
APRA	33
IU	18
ASI	4
Frente Tacneno	1

Percentage of Total Electorate,[f] by Candidate and Year

Belaúnde (1980)	28.4
García (1985)	43.9
Fujimori (1990)	56.53[g]

Sources: For municipal elections, see Fernando Tuesta Soldevilla, "Pobreza urbana y participación política" (unpublished manuscript, DESCO, Lima, 1988); *Qué Hacer* 62 (1990); *Sí* (Lima), November 20, 1990; and *Andean Reports.* For results by party in major cities, see *Andean Report* (November 1986). For percentages in Lima for APRA, see Sandra Woy-Hazelton, "The Return to Partisan Politics in Peru," in *Post-Revolutionary Peru,* ed. S. Gorman (Boulder, CO: Westview Press, 1982); *Latin American Weekly Report,* November 18, 1983; Tuesta Soldevilla, "Pobreza urbana;" and *Qué Hacer* 62. For percentages in the 1985 elections, see *Andean Report* (May 1985). Results of the 1990 presidential race were provided by the Peruvian Embassy, Washington, DC, summary of JNE final results. For Senate and Chamber of Deputies seats, see *Caretas* (Lima), April 16, 1990.

Notes: a. Figures for 1989 are preliminary. Release of official returns was long delayed.

b. Null and blank votes were 20 percent.

c. In 1983 Puno.

d. The number of null and blank votes in this election was half the average number in the first four elections.

e. CODE is the PPC and Townsend's Movimiento de Bases Hayistas.

f. These percentages account for null and blank votes.

g. Fujimori's percentage is taken from the second round.

This contrasts sharply with the 34.9 percent won by the AP alone in 1980. The AP won only one provincial city—Tarma—while APRA dominated the country. Alfonso Barrantes of the Izquierda Unida, meanwhile, with 36 percent of the vote, became the first elected Marxist mayor in a South American capital.[46]

García quickly cultivated the role of leader of the opposition. When Barrantes defeated APRA's 1983 Lima candidate Alfredo Barnechea, García retook the initiative the next month with a highly publicized "open letter" to Belaúnde, protesting the social costs of his economic policies.[47] In April of that year García had personally delivered CONAPLAN's criticisms of the regime's political economy to the presidential palace.[48]

García easily captured the party's presidential nomination and by 1984 the thirty-five-year-old, whose experience was limited to only one term in Congress, had become by far the most favored candidate.[49] García's performance in Congress had not been particularly noteworthy;[50] in 1984 he took a leave of absence in order to pursue the campaign.[51]

While APRA no doubt capitalized on the misfortune and ineptitude of the second Belaúnde administration, its appeal to nontraditional bases of support was also clearly working. The party made substantive efforts in nontraditional regions, which were reflected in the 1983 and 1985 electoral results. García and his team placed special emphasis on getting the support of nonparty sympathizers, particularly from the middle class. They aimed to dispel APRA's image as a closed, sectarian, and violent organization. Key to the party's strategy of opening up was the recruiting of nonapristas in forming the party's government plan and in setting up, outside the traditional party structure, Civic Communities to support the García candidacy.[52] This included what Alva Castro called a "national consensus" with other political forces, including the armed forces and the church,[53] to confront such pressing national problems as Sendero. As early as March 1982 CONAPLAN held meetings with representatives of the armed forces, including former velasquistas such as Mercado Jarrín, and other outside experts such as Central Bank President Webb.[54]

On the economic front García's team tried to display a pragmatic and technical capacity. They called for cuts in defense spending and a halt to the giant investment projects of the Belaúnde government, and instead suggested smaller, short-term, labor-intensive projects. The focus on the technical was intended to dispel a reputation for mediocrity among the APRA ranks due to Haya's single-handed dominance of the party's ideology and program, and to the detriment to leadership development caused by past persecution of apristas. APRA was not able to overcome that image totally, yet it did have "a certain social consciousness that Manuel Ulloa's intellectually much more brilliant team didn't have."[55]

Alan García's personality and beliefs had a definite influence on his campaign and its successful outcome. He seemed to be, above and beyond his charisma, a pragmatist. As early as 1980 he was determined to solve the leadership crisis afflicting his party, and soon began tactically planning for 1985. His book *Un futuro diferente*, published in 1982, combined the influence of Haya de la Torre and aprismo with a pragmatic appeal to the emerging middle sectors whose support he and the younger aprista generation were trying to garner. His focus was clearly on maintaining a serious and capable image without losing ties to APRA's traditional revolutionary vision. "Revolution is therefore a collective science. Aprismo, like all schools of thought, found its inspiration in the same alternative. Utopia in conjunction with ideas, or the essence of the concrete, the reality of the possible. It chose the second without abandoning the first."[56]

The cultivation of image was critical to García's political behavior. According to François Bourricaud, García believed that in Peru people have difficulty differentiating between good and bad governments—they are easily swayed by the image projected.[57] García's future behavior in office, as when he nationalized the banks, supports this interpretation. His training, which was rich in philosophy and theory, and devoid of practical economics, accentuated that perspective. During the campaign he stated, "Hegel said that the appearance is also a reality, that there is no distinction between the means and the end because all is part of one sole entity."[58] His campaign relied heavily on the professional packaging of the personality—the image—of Alan García.[59]

Like Haya de la Torre, García stretched various ideologies to fit his needs. Politically he professed to be a democratic socialist, based on the model of Spain's Felipe González. He began his campaign copying Haya's gestures and then cautiously moved toward his own style and message to "all Peruvians" and redefinition of aprismo in modern social-democratic terms: offering change without radicalism.[60] On the economic front he dismissed the debate over the difference between the state-capitalist and socialist stages of Peru's development that Haya had written about in 1931. He also dismissed an early claim of Haya that antiimperialism was anti-capitalism.[61] At least initially, García was aware of the costs of alienating the nation's entrepreneurial sectors and the large part of the middle class whose fortunes were tied in with those sectors, and he was trying to dispel their traditional fear of APRA. He insisted that the party was not "statist" and would not nationalize private banks or operations of foreign oil companies and that it would sell off any superfluous state industries. Finally, he spoke of a social pact with private industry.[62] "The history of Latin America is filled with the blood of those who tried to alter the system too energetically and too quickly."[63] His pragmatic approach, his dismissal of politically dangerous polemical debates, and his vocal commitment to change through electoral and legislative rather than radical means were of great appeal to the new aprista generation, tired of quarrels about "which of Haya's books was right" and much more interested in rebuilding their party's bases of support: "first let's win, then we'll talk."[64]

Although García's campaign made a point of building support outside the party, he also clearly benefited from being affiliated with APRA. His rapid rise to national renown was in part due to his heading Peru's longest-lasting and most famous political party. He also benefited from his legacy as right-hand man to Haya, and it was no accident that he began his campaign imitating Haya's style. Finally, despite his own distinct beliefs and the strategy of opening up the party, the crux of the campaign theme still rested on the traditional APRA ideology and legacy. "He struck a number of responsive themes in the presidential campaign—in-

tegration of the Indian population, an emphasis on agricultural development, decentralization of the size and scope of the national government,
and an offer of hope to the country's poor. The campaign promises were
part and parcel of APRA's program since the 1920's."[65]

The success of the APRA campaign is attributable to García's and the
"new" apristas' ability to perceive the changes that had occurred in
Peruvian society and to provide a coherent political response. The rise of
the electoral left in Peru since 1978, following a series of strikes led by
Communist unions, which were a major force in toppling the military
government, pointed to an increasing radicalization of the working class
in Peru. The traditional aprista union base alone clearly could not capture
this momentum. The radicalization was in part a function of the prevalence on a national level of reformist ideology, and then the subsequent
retrenchment of reforms. It was also a function of demographic changes.
While the working class of the 1950s and 1960s was composed to a large
extent of recent migrants, in the 1970s and 1980s it was increasingly
composed of the children of migrants, who had been exposed to higher
levels of education and to a stronger union movement and consequently
had greater expectations. The heightening of expectations in the face of
retrenchment of reforms in the late 1970s and the economic debacle of the
1980s, led to increased radicalization. These groups, particularly working-
class youths, by the 1980s began to play an increasingly important role in
society: their presence became more prevalent in unions, parties, and
neighborhood organizations,[66] and was reflected in the plethora of Marxist
parties that sprang up with the political opening.[67]

Alan García recognized the need to appeal to these radicalized sectors
without alienating his primary support base in the middle class. His
confrontational remarks on the debt issue, for example, were intended for
internal consumption. His rhetoric was deliberately vague. In retrospect
the government's actual policies were much more radical than its campaign speeches had forecast. On the debt issue, an uncertain 20–25 percent
limit was spoken of, and not until the inauguration did the more radical
10 percent figure emerge. García could afford to be vague because of his
favored status among the candidates in the race, because of his position
as the head of APRA, and because of a traditional focus in Peruvian
politics on personality and leadership rather than specific policy. It is
striking that APRA put forth no concrete policy proposals until after
García's April 1985 election. The party strategy of "first let's win, then
we'll talk," which focused on a pragmatic, nondogmatic approach, on the
extension of grassroots organization, and on García's charisma, was extraordinarily successful.

It was the left and not APRA that suffered from an image problem.
Izquierda Unida's (IU's) campaign platform was much more specific and,
unlike both the AP and APRA, it spelled out a detailed program with

specific policy proposals. The IU's proposals included the nationalization of Southern Peru Copper, the reversing of oil contracts with Occidental and Belco, a selective moratorium on debt, and nationalization of the nation's banks.[68] The IU's candidate, Alfonso Barrantes, a former aprista, represented the more moderate aspects of the coalition, and in the minority, opposed bank nationalization and condemned Sendero Luminoso. While he supported a policy of national consensus with whomever attained power, many IU members deemed this an electorally risky strategy. They felt that while business leaders might be responsive to such rhetoric coming from APRA, they never would accept it from the left. "If the left stops being the left, it risks losing its own base of support."[69] The IU continued to suffer from internal divisions due to the diversity of its coalition, which extends from Maoists and Trotskyites to non-Marxists, yet it was still able to appeal to substantial portions of the population, especially in Lima's pueblos jóvenes and the sierra. The party was able to hold a firm second place in almost every department. Given the front's newness—it formed only in 1981—and the traditional military and elite opposition to any form of Marxism, its electoral success was indeed remarkable.

It could not, however, overcome the challenge posed by a highly organized and pragmatically oriented APRA and the charismatic persona of Alan García. APRA's victory in 1985 indicated that the Peruvian political spectrum still leaned toward the center. APRA was very careful in its campaign rhetoric not to diverge too far from the center, a tactic that paid off handsomely. APRA, as a party of the center with an institutionalized commitment to social reform, was uniquely positioned to fulfill a popular mandate for change at a time when even traditionally conservative elites recognized its necessity. The results of the 1985 elections demonstrated the strength of this position.

The 1985 Elections

In the May 1985 elections APRA's García won more votes than all the other candidates together. He captured over 47 percent of the national vote, but for the first time the figure requiring a runoff election was raised from 35 to 50 percent. Therefore, despite the fact that Belaúnde had garnered only 28.4 percent of the electorate in 1980 versus García's 43.9 percent (including null and blank votes) in 1985, a runoff was required by the Constitution.[70] The runoff was avoided, as Barrantes, the second-place candidate with 22 percent of the votes, declined to run. He felt that the IU had no chance of winning, and he feared further violence between IU and APRA militants, as clashes had occurred prior to the election.[71] The left was to continue to play a vital role in the nation's politics, however.

There were no other significant challenges to García in the 1985 elections. The AP's Alva obtained only 6.4 percent of the vote, and the PPC's Bedoya only 12.2 percent (see Table 4.1). APRA won on a platform that emphasized party and national unity. In the last two weeks of the campaign the party reined in the campaigns of individual congressmen to add to the image of unity behind García. This contrasted sharply with the "cacophonic scores of names, symbols, and numbers from the other parties."[72]

APRA also made great headway in non-APRA regions: Lima's pueblos jóvenes, Cuzco and Puno, and the selva. This reflected García's decision to devote much of his campaigning time to these regions and to create a much more open image for the party. Also reflecting this is the unprecedented 91 percent of the electorate that voted in the elections: a stark contrast with 1980.[73] Of particular interest is the Ayacucho region, where null and blank voting was 50 percent in 1980, possibly to some extent because of Sendero's efforts to disrupt voting. In 1985 this rate fell drastically, and García took the region with 62 percent of the vote.[74] While APRA under Haya was a very regional party, primarily northern-based, "with Alan it has penetrated the mysterious heart of the Andes."[75]

The election results of 1983–1985 demonstrate the "step back" that the country took by reelecting Belaúnde and Acción Popular; and the lessons learned and implemented by the other parties during that time, resulting in the 1983 successes of APRA and the IU, and finally in the 1985 APRA victory. The results point to a substantial decline in the power of the right, and to the institutionalization of the left as a force to be reckoned with in Peruvian politics. However, they also point to a preference among voters for parties closer to the center rather than for the Marxist left. There was most likely a perception, as was expressed by Barrantes, that the Peruvian military and probably most business interests would not tolerate a Marxist government. There was also the traditional appeal of APRA: a united, organized, uniquely Peruvian party with a strong leader, which inspired voter confidence more than the IU's conglomerate of blocs with competing ideologies, united only by the persona of Barrantes.

The image of strength and activism was key to APRA's success. García's focus on the pragmatic and possible and his following through on words with rapid action were welcome changes from the grandiose visions and inactivity in the face of disaster of the second Belaúnde administration. This contrast was also a factor in García's success, both in the campaign and his first years in office. "In the Palace of Government we have passed from the versaillesque state of Fernando Belaúnde, to one very appropriate for Lima 1985. The doors of the Palace have been opened to the directors of the popular sectors; the president himself appears at the balcony or at the door; he speaks with the people, who have begun to wait for him on the streets."[76]

García's bold, direct contact with the people during the campaign continued through frequent *balconazos* after his inauguration; his initial avoidance of polemical debates, yet willingness to challenge politically dangerous issues—such as his calling organized labor privileged, his stance on the debt, and his cutting of the military budget—and finally his base in the legacy of the revolutionary image of APRA, were all fundamental to his initial success. García, through the balconazos, was also able to continue a practice of Haya de la Torre: that of using the tradition of street protests to organize mass demonstrations in his favor. This tradition in Peru was perhaps more prevalent and effective than that of organized labor, at least until the late 1970s, for instigating popular sentiment and involvement.[77] Most important, perhaps, was his ability to take on a seemingly desperate political and economic situation using new ideas that sprang from a young generation of both apristas and nonapristas, and to perceive the nation's desire for change and action. "In the end it was his self-assured enthusiasm, drumming in the message that Peru was not condemned to failure, that made the difference."[78]

FROM CAMPAIGN TO GOVERNMENT: THE OBSTACLES

While García's rapid rise to power can be explained with relative ease, there were some fundamental issues it did not resolve, which increasingly became obstacles in government, particularly after García's initial popularity was eroded. While the APRA machinery was well suited for running an effective political campaign, it was evident early on that it was not as suited for the tasks of democratic government. The relationship between García and the APRA leaders and party mechanism was a changing one and often the source of controversy. Eclectic campaign rhetoric, which appealed across diverse social sectors, became much more controversial when it was developed into actual policies directed at specific interest groups. These tensions were exacerbated by the incompetent manner in which policies were often implemented. Two traditional characteristics of Peruvian politics were still evident: APRA's lack of experience with democratic government, and its record of violence; and the dominance of a populist leader whose personal ambitions precluded the development of lasting, competitive political parties that work to integrate the population into a participatory system. APRA's lack of skill and experience and García's own behavior were to demonstrate that these traits predominated, and that the renovation that the APRA party had undergone was one of image rather than substance. Such a renovation proved much more effective for a political campaign than for the task of governing.

García aroused a great deal of animosity within the party by approaching the government with his own personal team of *técnicos* and intellectuals—which had been part and parcel of his campaign—and by not extending government posts to party militants. The approach is in part due to García's autocratic, exclusionary habit of decisionmaking and in part to the prevalent mediocrity within the ranks of APRA. Party militants had no practical experience with issues of national significance, and there was a shortage of talent within their ranks. As APRA minister of energy and mines, Wilfred Huaita, stated, "you do not find technocrats in APRA. Let us be honest with ourselves. We have not prepared ourselves to govern."[79] The party remained much more an electoral machine than a resource base for government. Thus García surrounded himself with his own team: Luis Gonzales Posada, who became justice minister; Javier Tantalean, who became chief of the National Planning Institute; and Héctor Delgado Parker.[80] Alva Castro, who had his own team of técnicos, was to play a key role as premier. The most important of the old guard were awarded attractive parliamentary posts. Meanwhile the rank-and-file *compañeros* became increasingly bitter as they waited for a convocation that never arrived.

More than anything else, the transition from campaign to government exposed the complex and heterogeneous nature of the "renovated" APRA. "One day I compared APRA with the procession of the God of the Miracles, where certainly there are all kinds: devout and shameless; liberals and totalitarians, 'búfalos' and doves. APRA is Peru . . . I know many democratic apristas and I presume there are many without much desire to be so."[81] The image of unity and capability that succeeded in the electoral contest did not hold up under the much more difficult test of being in government. García's own image was soon tarnished, as his tendency to grant image more importance than action proved disastrous when translated into policy. Meanwhile the diversity that characterizes the modern APRA, as well as an overall shortage of skilled personnel, also affected the party's performance. At the macro level, party influence was initially minimal, yet it increased precisely at the time when political and economic crisis was most acute. The absence of trained and capable leaders was dire. At the micro level—in the implementation of programs such as the Programa de Apoyo de Ingreso Temporal (PAIT) and the Rimanacúy—the party's authoritarian and sectarian nature were frighteningly evident. The party youths, meanwhile, frustrated with the pace of reforms, grew increasingly radicalized. In part as a response to these sentiments, and in part to inconsistencies of his own, García—after an initial period of remarkably successful consensus building—attempted to project two images: one of the confrontational revolutionary and the other of the pragmatic reformer, a strategy that cost him credibility in all political camps.

García's own ambitions and the nature of his leadership proved critical for the fate of APRA and for Peru. García's commitment to democratic reform was revealed as shallow. His tendency to attempt to govern singlehandedly and his lack of tolerance for dissent among his close circle of advisors were evident from the start. García was indeed a "populist" of sorts and made no attempts to improve administrative capacity, or to solidify APRA's political base. While APRA initially took advantage of García's popularity to build up its bases of support, this strategy was inherently limited. The prevalence of García's personal political ambitions exposed the extent to which the party's renovation had been one of image alone—effective for the political campaign, but not for the difficult tasks of government. Ultimately it was disastrous for both his nation and his party. "His youth and energy captured the country's imagination during his long months of campaigning. But he also exuded the paternalism of a natural populist and projected the strong leadership—some would even say the authoritarian streak—that many Peruvians are seeking. At times the candidate seemed more important than his party, his personality more important than his platform."[82]

The 1968 military revolution, the social forces that it stimulated, and the transition back to civilian government all had substantial impact on Peru's society and polity. Heightened expectations in the face of economic crisis and limited state capacity made the task of consolidating democracy, and indeed even governing, a difficult one. During this time APRA's role evolved from one of stunned spectator, while the military "stole" its revolution, to that of institutional basis for the transition to democracy. Its subsequent electoral debacle in 1980 and the five-year Belaúnde interlude instigated and provided the time for necessary changes and leadership transition within the party. By 1985 the consensus for reform in Peru was the strongest it had ever been, and APRA, a party with an institutional commitment to reform, a highly popular leader, and located in the "acceptable" center arena of the political spectrum, was uniquely positioned to take advantage of that consensus.

Yet consensus for reform was strong precisely because of the visible manifestations of years without progress on the reform front. When APRA took over in July 1985 Peru's economy, society, and polity were in deep crisis. The living standards of the population had deteriorated substantially since 1973. Capital flight was on the rise; criminal kidnapings and urban and rural terrorism had become daily occurrences; and finally Sendero Luminoso had become a genuine threat to national security and stability. Peru was on the brink of chaos. APRA, through good grassroots organization, pragmatic campaigning, and a focus on regions and groups neglected in the past, capitalized on both the sense of crisis and the desperate search for an alternative to the status quo.

APRA thus had both a historic opportunity and a daunting challenge. The party had a very strong political mandate and base of support and an extremely popular leader. Yet the APRA government still had to contend with the age-old characteristics of its own party, which were particularly prevalent among the rank and file and at the regional levels. The party's renovation and new progressive bent had by no means permeated all levels. With the absence of a genuine renovation of party leadership structure and doctrine, the party's—and the nation's—fate was to a large extent to be determined by the whims of the popular and inexperienced Alan García. Thus, despite the strong mandate for reform and APRA's unique position, many of the party's traits were in themselves obstacles to its ability to govern, to successful relations with society, and ultimately to the prospects for democratic consolidation.

2
APRA in Power

5

From Unprecedented
Consensus to Policy Collapse

*There is one road to the solution of the historic problem of our society.
There is one means through which to conquer poverty and injustice ... the
different future. ... It is the aprismo that is founded in the permanent truths
that in 1924 signaled the necessity of a great transformation.*
—Alan García Pérez, *El futuro diferente*

*Alan García started his presidential term at thirty-six years, without much
administrative experience. He had been a lucid and determined activist,
which taught him to manage masses, but neither offices nor workshops.*
—Luis Alberto Sánchez, *Testimonio personal*, vol. 6

Alan García and APRA took power in July 1985 amid high expectations
and a great deal of uncertainty. The nation's oldest political party—more
than any other political force the subject of intense animosities and
loyalties—had finally reached its goal, after sixty years in opposition. At
its helm was an eloquent and charismatic leader, the youngest president
in Peru's history, and supporting him was the largest electoral margin of
any elected president of Peru. For the past decade the nation had been
buffeted by acute economic crisis, and since the transition to democracy,
in 1980, by the brutal insurgent activities of Sendero Luminoso. Peru's
population was on average younger, less well-off, and more urban than it
had been a decade before. This population was the poorest in South
America, with the exception of Bolivia's and Paraguay's, and at the same
time one of the most politicized. Since 1980 the left in Peru had the
strongest electoral performance on the continent, and the Izquierda
Unida, a coalition of Marxist, Maoist, and Trotskyite parties, was to be
APRA's main opposition in Congress. The expectations facing the new
government were great; the challenges formidable.

Alan García's boldness and energy were evident from the day he took
office, declaring that he would transform Peru and challenge international
imperialism at the same time. He was, both within and outside Peru,
something of a phenomenon. How that phenomenon would govern and
what role his party would play in that government was not clear at the
outset. APRA was not a monolithic entity; rather it was a complex,

multi-generational, ideologically disparate, and culturally diverse movement. In the government's first stage, when García's popularity was at its height, the party had little influence on his decisionmaking. Yet from the start the party was able to infiltrate the state bureaucracy, staking claims on all positions that entailed authority. Posts were filled according to political rather than technical criteria—in part because the party was extremely short of trained personnel. Party members were well aware that while APRA's victory was made possible by Alan García's popularity, his election owed much to APRA's well-oiled electoral machinery. After so many years of persecution and being blocked from power, the desire to enjoy the fruits of government was quite strong among party members.

As García's popularity declined precipitously after mid-1987, so did his power in APRA, which increasingly asserted its control. As was noted in the first chapter, the predominance of nonmerit appointments undermines the ability to respond to already-underdeveloped and inefficient state sectors. With the challenge of governing the country, both García's relations with the party and the party's with society in general deteriorated. APRA had no coherent program for governing, and decisions were soon concentrated solely in García's hands, the outcome of both his own character and the party's tradition of not questioning the *jefe máximo*. This resulted in a great deal of party resentment, especially as policies became more controversial. García's interpretation of aprista doctrine was mercurial and reflected different currents within the party. One day he called for cooperation with the private sector, and the next for revolution and a war on the middle class.

The government's initial coherence in policymaking soon fell prey to the contradictory goals and ideologies of García and his close circle of advisors, and the party's inability to supersede personal and ideological rivalries made it impossible to govern efficaciously. APRA's perennial role as opposition had not emphasized the need for realistic proposals for governing, a tendency that Sartori attributes to parties that are less likely to get into power. The rifts that emerged after Haya's death—which were a function of conflicting interpretations of party doctrine stemming from generational and ideological differences—soon resurfaced. At the same time the sectarian nature and history of the party precluded any potential cooperation with the political opposition. The result was an extremely polarized atmosphere and an economic crisis on the one hand, and the age-old divide, now accentuated by the party's control of the state, between APRA and society on the other. This was reflected by both a resurgence of the right and by a dramatic increase in insurgent activity. "Alan García arrived in government without having previously organized the sectors that he wanted to reach, without trusting APRA as his partner as a party, without having technicians familiar with the details of his project, without having constructed a popular base of support to sustain it."[1]

Initially the APRA government projected a bold and coherent image and succeeded in an effective economic reactivation, in implementing several innovative policies concerning the poor, and in fostering a strong base in the private sector. By mid-1987, however, the economy began to falter as the government failed to respond to the exhaustion of short-term reactivation policies, and the president himself caused a political crisis with disastrous consequences. The latter part of APRA's tenure in power yielded record levels of political mudslinging, a dramatic increase in terrorist and paramilitary violence, hyperinflation, and a sharp drop in the living standards of all social sectors. The speed and the extent of the deterioration of policymaking coherence was dramatic; as the crisis deepened, the inability of APRA as a party to deal with it became increasingly evident. The nature of the party was a key determinant in the polarization that ensued.

STRATEGY AND ECONOMIC PROGRAM

Alan García and APRA were able to achieve victory by a large margin in April 1985 without publicizing any sort of detailed program or strategy. This was in part possible because of García's popularity and oratorical skills and in part due to his generation's success in renovating the party's image and opening it up to new social sectors and regions. It was also possible because of the discrediting of previous options on the right and the widely perceived opposition of the army to a Marxist government. In contrast to APRA, Izquierda Unida's program—much of which was later adopted by APRA once in power—was well publicized. APRA was deliberately vague in order to maintain its traditional middle-class support and to appeal to the emerging "technocratic" working class as well. Apristas were extremely cautious about confronting the entrepreneurial sector, and there was no talk of nationalization. The more radical aspects of the program were not presented until after García's inauguration.

No specific policy proposals or overall strategy were announced during the time between García's election in April and inauguration in July; there was an aura of suspense, and among the business community an attitude of cautious watching and waiting. García finally announced his strategy in his July 28 inaugural address. In a subsequent series of announcements, culminating in the October package of economic measures, the government's economic reactivation scheme—which was the pivotal part of what García had in his address labeled "productive social reactivation"[2]—was gradually released. The government's strategy was to address the deepening crisis in Peru's economy and society through an internally based economic reactivation scheme that would benefit, first and foremost, the marginalized sectors: the impoverished peasants of the

Andes and the burgeoning population of the pueblos jóvenes in the cities, primarily Lima. Reactivation depended to a large extent on the cooperation of domestic entrepreneurial sectors, as even before García's stance on the debt issue it was evident that no new foreign credit was heading in Peru's direction. The government had to appeal to two audiences and relay two messages: first to the poor, that the state was actively going to change the structure of the economy and society by "democratizing" it; and second to the entrepreneurial classes, that despite these proposed "revolutionary" changes their interests and assets would not be threatened.

García's strategy was reminiscent of the original APRA program of the 1930s; yet he also added his own themes: focus on ethical behavior among state employees; a crackdown on the drug traffic; and the idea of a social pyramid. In García's pyramid organized labor and state workers fit into the privileged category at the top—those who were protected by a "bureaucratic cushion."[3] Attention was to focus on the 70 percent of the population that was at the bottom: the unemployed; street vendors; and shantytown dwellers. The social pyramid, while revolutionary in some senses, did not focus the issues of reform on a labor (presumably backed by the state) versus capital confrontation, and in this sense was much more palatable to the entrepreneurial class than a more classical Marxist strategy. While García did call for a role for the "nationalist state," that role was to provide education and health services and to protect the economy from monopoly and excess profits. That was immediately followed by a clause that stated that private property and free initiative were linked to the common good and rejected dogmatic egalitarianism and sterile statism. García also devoted a section of his speech to the importance of security for investment by foreign and national capital. Nor did he forget to appeal to the traditional support base of his party. "I do not ignore the industrialists, or the laborers, or the employees, or the professionals. Faithful to the ideology of my party, I believe . . . the small and medium proprietor classes have a great responsibility."[4]

Many of the government's themes were also reminiscent of those of the Velasco era. This was in part due to the presence of several former velasquistas in García's circle of advisors, in particular Carlos Franco, who had been a close companion of Carlos Delgado's in SINAMOS. APRA was in a much better position than the military officers—who were trusted neither by the civilians nor the politically astute—to play the delicate game of offering prospects of radical change to the poor without alienating powerful entrepreneurial interests. The new APRA government, with an innovative approach and the benefit of the lessons of past APRA failures and Velasco's errors, was able to produce a strategy that did not lead to an immediate confrontation with the elites. The government was clearly bolstered by the business community's willingness to try a reformist strategy after the economic debacle of the Belaúnde years and the fears of more-radical alternatives raised by the growth of terrorist activity. "The 'new' elite is very aware that Peru could be on the brink of civil war, and like the military officers, they know that their economic interests would be devastated in such strife."[5] However, to the new APRA leaders' credit, it was able to do what heretofore had been impossible in Peru: to openly propose social change without automatically alienating powerful elites.

In contrast, García challenged the international financial community and the armed forces early on. He unilaterally declared a cap on interest payments of 10 percent of export earnings. In October, after the discovery of an army massacre of seventy-five civilian "suspects," he fired three top generals; and in a blow to traditional army budgetary autonomy, he halved an order for French Mirage jets.[6]

> The whole policy approach . . . comes out of the long and hard experience of Peru with orthodox approaches to inflation and balance of payments problems. By 1985 it was at last possible for many academics and policymakers to conclude that . . . recession-inducing policies were inappropriate as measures to deal with inflation, and exceedingly inefficient in dealing with balance of payments equilibrium. . . . By July 1985 it was abundantly clear that inflation did not come from excess demand. . . . The balance of payments disequilibrium had its roots in long run supply problems on the export side . . . and in the capital flight induced by the very recession itself and the resulting lack of confidence and "desmoralización."[7]

Support bases for a heterodox policy grew with the drastic failures of orthodox adjustment policies under Belaúnde. In May 1986 the former president of the Central Bank, Richard Webb, wrote that, "despite the limitation of the 10% rule, Peru will remit $500 million more in interest and debt payments than it will receive from lenders in 1986. On the other hand, Peru stands to gain a degree of self-reliance that would be healthy from both economic and political points of view."[8] Peru's recovery had to be internally generated, as past dependence on foreign capital and on the international markets had led to unstable, poor growth rates, a large debt burden, and a dualistic economic structure.

The García government inherited a depressed economy; growth was a negative 12 percent in 1983 and made only a partial recovery in 1984. With ample reserves and excess productive capacity, it was ripe for reactivation. The first stage was primarily antiinflationary, with an initial rise and then the freezing of key prices, coupled with a rise of the minimum wage and cutting of interest rates. Luxury imports were curtailed; employment and agriculture were stressed.[9] By 1986 inflation was substantially reduced and growth became the priority, with incentives introduced for

the manufacturing sector.[10] Employment creation was a major priority—
over 50 percent of the population of 18.7 million was under- or unemployed. Companies that operated extra shifts were allowed to take on staff
without guaranteed job security. One of the main policy programs for the
urban poor, the PAIT, was created to provide jobs and improve living
conditions in the pueblos jóvenes and poor rural regions. In urban areas
the program hired thousands of workers on a temporary basis. The
government also sponsored the Instituto para Desarrollo del Sector Informal (IDESI), an associated agency to provide credit to informal sector
entrepreneurs.

By the end of 1985 most business sectors were lending the government
and its plan their confidence. After almost a decade of "decisionmaking
paralysis" in which economic policy was caught in a web of intense
confrontation between business and labor into which the state sometimes
intervened, and in which the conditionality imposed by external creditors
had played an increasingly restrictive part, an active government role in
economic policymaking was welcomed.[11] In addition, IMF–sanctioned
austerity and stabilization measures had not only negatively affected
standards of living, but the business sectors and the internal market as well.
Business and labor leaders seemed willing to cooperate with the reactivation solution. In practice, however, the government's policy of
concertación, or cooperation with the private sector, consisted primarily
of García's meeting with the so-called twelve apostles—the most powerful
businessmen in the country.

> The government's decision to rely on the private sector . . . was perfectly
> consistent with the APRA's historical position and García's own earlier
> writings. . . . Many industrialists . . . had supported the APRA in the 1985
> election. The unexpected aspect was the particular form that
> concertación assumed—primarily negotiations with the largest business
> conglomerates in the country, popularly known as the "twelve apostles."
> CONFIEP, the umbrella business association formed in 1984, was by-
> passed in favor of . . . large businesses in the hopes that smaller entrepre-
> neurs would follow suit.[12]

Despite dire predictions and condemnations from international agencies and critics, Peru's economic performance for 1986 and 1987 was
remarkable. Real gross domestic product (GDP) growth was 8.5 and 7
percent, respectively, compared with 1.5 percent for 1985, and inflation
was 64 percent compared with the previous year's 163.4 percent. Manufacturing production rose, and real wage levels increased (see Table 2.2).
While a full-scale renovation of agriculture was hardly likely, given the
constraints and the backwardness of Andean agriculture, a growth rate of
3 percent was still attained. Reserves rose dramatically by mid-1986 as a
result of the restrictions on debt payments and profit remittances, al-

though the trend was reversed by capital flight at the end of the year. Inflation was clearly cost-induced, and thus the price-controls policy was on the mark, although inflation reduction was also achieved at the price of an overvalued exchange rate. Terms of trade turned toward agriculture, a trend for which the government quickly took credit.[13]

International agencies and creditors neither welcomed nor supported Peru's economic strategy and its stance on the debt. In October 1985 the World Bank reiterated its past prescription that inflation in Peru was demand-induced. The IMF, which had been unduly harsh during the Belaúnde years—calling for extremely restrictive adjustment measures in the face of El Niño disasters and severe deterioration in terms of trade, and pressing for import liberalization at a time of severe balance of payments crisis—rejected price controls as a support to an anti-inflation program, at least in Peru's case. The Fund may have feared that García's radical stance on debt would start a worldwide trend. Despite the few attempts at goodwill payments made by Peru in 1986,[14] the Fund declared Peru ineligible for credits.

One key aspect of the economic recovery was its concentration in the informal sector. Because the informal sector pays no taxes, this exacerbated the government budget deficit. Price controls favored the informal sector, as certain key prices, particularly for gasoline, fell significantly in real terms, while informal sector enterprises were not affected by controls. Some firms shifted their activities into the informal sector to restore profitability, and there were resulting shortages of inputs and labor in the formal sector.[15] The labor shortage could in part be explained by the seventy-five thousand jobs created by the PAIT, but overall was due to the unprecedented boom of activity in the informal sector.[16] The informal sector plays a critical role in generating desperately needed employment.

A growing disparity between the official and parallel exchange rates, a resurgence of inflation in early 1987, and a general strike in May of that year, signaled that the first, so-called honeymoon, stage of the government's reactivation policy had come to a close. There are a variety of reasons for this. The recovery was based to a large extent on existing idle capacity. Supply bottlenecks began to appear in some key inputs and raw materials, such as cement. State enterprises, after years of mismanagement, were unable to respond to necessary production increases. Reserves fell to dangerously low levels. Accompanying these trends was increasing skepticism in the business community about the government's credibility and economic management. This was exacerbated in April 1987 by the government's announcement—and then subsequent withdrawal—of compulsory bond purchases for certain industrial sectors.[17] While this does not signify that the overall reactivation approach was flawed, it does point to the difficulty of managing an unorthodox and interventionist set of policies,[18] and to the limitations to their profitable duration. The government's failure to adjust promptly (in fact it delayed implementing any policy at all until March 1988) created disastrous supply problems and inflation due to uncertainty and expectations.

Along with the end of the honeymoon phase came an end to the overall consensus over reactivation policy in general, and over the future course of the economy among García and his advisors. As early as July 1986 many of his advisors had a plan for the nationalization of certain key firms, including banks and financial houses. García at that point opted for a concertación strategy instead,[19] and included in his July 28 speech an explanation of why the government should not nationalize the nation's banks.

In the meantime rifts within the government, in part a function of the party's exclusion from it, became increasingly blatant and public. Luis Alva Castro, who had wanted to resign for several months, did so in June. Alva Castro, with an eye on APRA's 1990 presidential nomination, wanted to distance himself from the government before the honeymoon phase ended. There were also disagreements within the cabinet and economic team over the future course of economic policy. The most powerful group, known as *los audaces* (the bold ones), primarily made up of the velasquistas and Daniel Carbonetto, an Argentine economist who had the most influence on García's economic policy, supported the president's determination to maintain growth as a priority and favored increased state intervention in the economy. Only two of the audaces were apristas: the finance minister, Gustavo Saberbein; and Javier Tantalean, the head of the influential Instituto Nacional de Planificación (INP). The split was clear by April 1987, with the audaces wanting to implement another heterodox shock plan by July if inflation had not been curbed by then.[20]

Pressure for change from the audaces contributed to García's decision to announce the nationalization of all domestically owned banks and insurance companies and the closing of all private foreign exchange houses on July 28, 1987.[21] These measures were extremely unpopular among the business community and disrupted the entire strategy of concertación. García used highly confrontational tones when he presented the measures to the public, a tactic that hardly served to foster private sector cooperation.

The business community, which had accepted the transitional and stimulating role the APRA government assigned to the state, with these measures grew extremely suspicious of the government's motives and fearful that "APRA seems to be returning to its statist whims."[22] The traditional antagonism between the nation's powerful entrepreneurs and APRA quickly resurfaced when the threat of a genuine transition to a socialist economy was perceived. The expropriation of the banks also sparked a political polarization and a crisis that was clearly not foreseen by García.

The end of the honeymoon phase of unprecedented growth, low inflation, and almost unchallenged consensus would not have meant instant collapse for the heterodox strategy, however, had the government acted in a flexible and cooperative manner rather than a desperate and confrontational one. There was much more potential for a policy of concertación to work in Peru's small business community than in larger ones such as Brazil's, for example. Also, there was more consensus in the Peruvian community for rejecting the IMF route, as Peru had so little hope of receiving any new credit.[23] This does not imply that there were no limitations to heterodoxy in Peru's case. The economy and state sector were severely underdeveloped. Not only did bottlenecks exist, but the state's capacity to ameliorate them was limited. This underdevelopment was a serious drawback to the audaces' strategy of expanding the role of the state in the economy. The expropriations forfeited the sorely needed cooperation of the business community. Labor, meanwhile, already irked by García's calling them "privileged," became increasingly antiregime as inflation heated up. They resented the way concertación excluded labor unions and business organizations.[24]

A general strike, led by the Communist-run CGTP, proved relatively successful on May 19, 1987. Besides opposition to the concertación strategy, strikers sought to preserve the economic gains made in 1986 and to extend union coverage to workers in industries that received exceptional legal treatment; nontraditional export companies and industries eligible to hire Programa de Empleo (PROEM) workers were both exempted from the labor stability law. The erosion of wage gains was a legitimate concern, as average salaries reached their peak in October 1986 and then began a steady decline; by March 1987 the minimum wage was only 4 percent in real terms above the lowest level in its history—which was during the second Belaúnde term.[25] Finally, after several years of eroding power, the unions sought to reassert themselves as a political force. The number of strikers was only one-third what it was in 1977; yet given the extremely different context of the unpopular Morales regime, this number was indicative of a noticeable amount of support for organized labor. It is also significant that García met with the directorate of the CGTP after the strike.[26]

The labor relations scene continued to heat up into 1988 as inflation began to rise and the government postponed economic adjustment. The CGTP sponsored relatively successful general strikes, disrupting the economy if not totally paralyzing it, on January 28, June 19 and 20, October 14, and December 1 of that year. APRA was in a poor position to deal with organized labor for a variety of reasons. First, the government had provoked the ire of the unions even at the height of the growth boom by excluding them from its concertación efforts. Its strategy in the PAIT and PROEM showed disdain for organized labor, and García had launched several tirades attacking labor as privileged. Finally, APRA's affiliated union confederation, the CTP, was on the margin of labor disputes.

The CTP controlled only 15 percent of the labor movement; its influence was strong in a few sectors such as textiles and sugar, but even in these traditional strongholds it had diminished in favor of the CGTP.[27] The CTP's actions were limited in part by the conservative views of its leader, Julio Cruzado. Cruzado was strongly opposed by the APRA youth, which had demanded his resignation for several years. During the Belaúnde years Cruzado failed to support one of the major strikes, drawing severe criticism from many sectors of the party.[28] The CTP was also limited by its affiliation with the government and did not participate in any of the general strikes. When some CTP factions participated in a transport workers' general strike on July 4, 1988, the aprista minister of transportation accused them of being "infraternal."[29]

APRA was never able to regain the dominant position that it had held in the labor unions prior to 1968. Given its position as affiliated to a government that had expressed disdain for organized labor, and given the increased participation of the insurgent left in the movement, its influence was likely to deteriorate. Finally, because the CTP never had full independence from the party and its goals were always subordinate to the party's, its potential as a major force in labor was limited. "There always was an ongoing contradiction between the concept of pure nonparty syndicalism and political, partisan syndicalism."[30]

In the aftermath of the nationalization of the banks and the political crisis that it caused, there was a devastating policymaking paralysis. The government failed to implement any policies, with the exception of a 40 percent devaluation—not accompanied by any of the necessary adjustment measures—in December. In the meantime rumors abounded for months over what the upcoming measures would be. With price increases expected, there was hoarding by store owners on the one hand, and severe shortages of basic inputs—such as tires and cement—due to the balance of payments crisis on the other. The fiscal deficit reached 16 percent of GDP.[31] There was clearly a need to replace the short-term reactivation model with a long-term growth one, and there was no government consensus on how to do it. García called in a host of external advisors, several of them from the political opposition. He was apparently finally convinced of the need for adjustment, and in particular for raising the heavily subsidized price of gasoline—a politically sensitive issue.[32] The afternoon before he was to announce adjustment measures, in a characteristic display of concern for his image, he had opinion polls taken; upon finding public opinion negative, he canceled his speech and rewrote the entire package himself. The following evening he announced a watered-down adjustment package that was neither adequate to correct the economic imbalances nor able to assuage negative public opinion, which had already been prepared for the worst by abounding rumors. García announced a focus on basic goods and imposed what he called an economía de guerra, declaring immoral anyone who owned an electric blender or a car. Prices of most basic goods were raised 40 percent and then frozen; minimum wage was raised 60 percent. Gas prices were raised 50 percent rather than the originally proposed 100 percent. A necessary devaluation was not implemented.[33] Public opinion in general was negative, as the package pleased neither the left nor the right.[34] Inflation took off on a hyperinflationary path, going from an annual rate of 360 percent in the first quarter of 1988 to nearly 7,000 percent in the second,[35] a surge caused to a large extent by the uncertainty and sudden policy shifts. García may not have been aware of the severity of the ensuing crisis, but "at a less precise level he [was] totally aware that he [had] decided to go for broke with an inflationary program."[36] While firm in his refusal to turn to orthodoxy, neither he nor his advisors had a long-term strategy. "They . . . appear to have taken the gamble that their reserves, and perhaps some ingenuity, could get them by. Interview evidence suggests no serious long-term planning had been done when the decision to challenge the international system was taken."[37]

By forgoing gradual adjustment early on, García had left himself few options. Because he destroyed the fragile consensus with the private sector that was key to the heterodox growth strategy, and at the same time allowed inflation to spiral out of control, a heterodox adjustment strategy became increasingly less viable. Both radicals and the IMF agreed that the only way to break the hyperinflationary spiral was with a shock program such as the one Bolivia recently took, cutting both the deficit and inflation through sharply recessionary policy. The political capital required for such a program is enormous. Instead García opted to accept chaos, Allende style, with the hopes of being remembered as an *hombre del pueblo*.[38]

The shortsighted approach of the economic team, coupled with a lack of concern for orthodox financial constraints, is strikingly similar to the approach to economic policymaking that was the demise of the Allende government. Former Unidad Popular Minister and Vice-President Clodomiro Almeyda related how "in the first meeting of the economic team after the elections the CEPAL-oriented technocrats, expressly and convincingly it would seem, argued that monetary and financial management did not deserve too much attention."[39] There was the widely held belief among the team that fiscal deficits would not be harmful if channeled to the right groups and with controls. As in the case of APRA, reserve stocks were depleted very rapidly in the early stages of the government.[40]

Mid-1988 yielded several cabinet reshuffles that involved the reassertion of APRA leaders, particularly Villanueva, the prime minister, in an attempt to save the party from the political costs of economic collapse as hyperinflation set in. Most of García's key economic advisors—Carbonetto, Tantalean, and other audaces—were forced to resign or did so by choice. The first of two shock packages was announced in September, tripling the prices of basic goods and devaluing by 100 percent.[41] In keeping with the record of inconsistent policy, it was announced that all prices would be frozen in ten days' time; the freeze was subsequently canceled. Prices soared in anticipation of a freeze that did not occur, and inflation was over 100 percent for September.[42] Abel Salinas, the new economics minister, was sent to negotiate with the IMF, yet García continued to denounce such negotiations as impossible. This was not the first time that García had authorized and then undermined such efforts: preliminary agreements had been initiated and then canceled with both the Paris Club and the IMF.[43] According to Bourricaud, García's perception of the IMF as the "Great Satan," and his belief that *los malos capitalistas*—the industrialists—had betrayed him, stemmed from the importance he placed on image and of his lack of understanding of basic business behavior: that firms operate to maximize profits.[44] He shared these perceptions with many in APRA: a result of training rich in doctrine and short on practical skills.

Ironically, the end result was a default into an IMF-style policy of the worst kind—austerity-induced recession—without the IMF and the credit relief that it provides. By mid-1988 it was virtually impossible to run a functioning business in Peru. On top of input shortages and spiraling inflation, there was a morass of state interference in the daily conduct of business, with the rules changing constantly. While there were three exchange-rate categories in 1985, for example, by 1987 there were nine. While interference existed before the APRA government, the vast growth of regulations and permits required led to a pervasive increase in corruption. While the extent of such corruption is difficult to quantify, there were enough public episodes to make it obvious that corruption was widespread. Such episodes included the allegations of extensive misappropriation of funds that accompanied the resignation of the agriculture minister, Romigio Morales Bermúdez, in mid-1988; the resignation of the first head of the PAIT, Víctor López, amid corruption charges; and a highly publicized scandal at the aprista-directed Instituto Peruano de Seguridad Social.[45] While corruption is hardly a novelty in Peru, APRA was also blatant in its use of partisan criteria to infiltrate the public sector. "Aprista party militants without professional capacity or ethical service credentials invaded the bureaucratic structure from the bottom to the top, paralyzing whatever was already in motion."[46] The combination of sectarianism and shortage of skill, and the prevalence of nonmerit appointments, not surprisingly, had negative effects on an already inefficient public sector.

Policymaking coherence was severely limited by the inadequate and inefficient nature of the state machinery. The technical and administrative skills necessary to implement a heterodox policy were in short supply, limiting García's ability to implement a coherent strategy.[47] García's autocratic style further undermined the state by continually bypassing it. Nevertheless, his constant changing of strategies and priorities, more than anything else, led to the collapse of the consensus he had created into political and economic chaos.

Key to explaining the economic deterioration were the political events at the time: García's relationship with his advisors, his party, the left, and the private sector, as well as inconsistencies within his own ideology. The 1987 banks expropriation, which marked an end to the consensus that had been so crucial to the successes of the first years, was clearly a turning point for the APRA regime.

THE BANKS EXPROPRIATION: A TURNING POINT

No episode during the García government's tenure so demonstrates the importance of the manner in which the reformist debate is presented as well as the July 1987 banks expropriation. President García's expropriation of the nation's ten private banks, six finance and seventeen insurance companies, announced on the second anniversary of his inauguration, came as a major surprise not only to the public, but to many high-ranking members of his party as well. The announcement of the measure caused a widespread public reaction and a severe political crisis. The president was apparently surprised by the extent and intensity of political opposition. However, he must have been aware that the expropriation would signify for the public a definitive change of political and economic strategy: a change that would result in the alienation of the economic actors he had been cooperating closely with for two years. The measure caused a resurgence of the political center and right. For almost two months the topic was the sole focus of political and legislative activity; there was a plethora of demonstrations and protests, precluding all attention to the other pressing items on the national agenda—in particular an ensuing economic crisis and the marked increase in strength of insurgent movements. The controversy dragged on for well over a year because of the poor planning behind the measure and a host of legal flaws that bungled attempts to implement it.

The expropriation came as a total surprise for several reasons. First and foremost, it was a direct contradiction of all of García's previous campaign and inaugural addresses, in which he had explicitly rejected state expropriation of private industry and had emphasized the goals of reducing state bureaucracy and pursuing economic reactivation based on cooperation, or concertación, with the private sector. Second, the measure neither originated in the high-level ranks of APRA nor was strongly supported by them. At the time it was announced most high-ranking apristas refrained from substantive comment. Finally, while the expropriation affected only 20 percent of the nation's banks, as the rest were already state-owned, it omitted foreign banks—quite a paradox coming from the nationalistic García. García seemed willing to forfeit his entire economic strategy at high cost for very little benefit. In presenting the measure, he used confrontational rhetoric, pitting the rich against the poor, the "hardworking pueblo" against the "lazy and exploitative bankers"—a tactic he had in the past avoided—and claiming the move would "democratize" credit. Ironically, APRA's slogan in opposition to Velasco had been "estatizar no es socializar" (nationalizing is not socializing).

García and a few close advisors came up with the plan less than two weeks before its announcement; the lack of preparation was blatant. García first attempted to take over direction of the banks prior to the congressional approval of the law required by the Constitution. After a rash of protests and the intervention of a Lima civil court judge, Eduardo Raffo Otero, García backed down on August 10 and agreed to wait for the measure to pass in Congress and for court ruling on its constitutional validity.

The argument that nationalizing the banks would democratize credit lacked credibility. There is a definite need for the reform of the credit system in Peru, as credit is allotted primarily through personal guarantees and a *compadrazgo* system rather than by market or profitability criteria. With interest rates at an artificially low level—as is demonstrated by the much higher rates in the informal sector—resulting in a credit shortage, the system of personal ties and guarantees takes on increased importance. The losers are the new entrants to the system who, though they might propose profitable schemes, have no major personal assets to guarantee their loans.[48] Ironically, the compadrazgo system is even more prevalent in the state banks, with their extended bureaucracy, than in the private banks.[49] Since the Velasco years the state has controlled 80 percent of the nation's credit. The noncommercial state banks—the Banco de la Nación and the Bancos de Fomento—control two-thirds of Peru's credit and should in theory already have been serving to democratize it. Most programs extending credit to the informal sector relied on private rather than state bank support. Finally, the country's productive structure was oriented around large-scale enterprises, many of them state-owned, and the concentration of credit in state hands would only exacerbate this trend. While the case for credit reform was clear, nationalization hardly seemed the solution. "If one does not change the productive structure of the country...where an important part of the production occurs in very large firms, including state firms, then it is very difficult and perhaps does not make any sense to radically change the orientation of credit."[50]

The economic power of Peru's private banking groups was indeed extensive. A web of credit and ownership links between the five largest banks and several entrepreneurial groups controlled, by some estimates, over 50 percent of private industrial production and services.[51] Four of the five most powerful bankers, Romero, Raffo, Wiese, and Brescia, also belonged to the group of twelve apostles upon whom García had based his concertación strategy. There was no doubt that, by expropriating the banks, García destroyed this relationship as well as undermined overall business confidence in the government. From the industrialists' perspective, if García were willing to expropriate the holdings of those with whom he worked most closely, then he would probably have fewer qualms about doing so in the case of less powerful industries.[52]

García's logic was baffling. If he sincerely sought credit reform, there was a host of more effective and less controversial ways to pursue it. If he sought increased investment, the total destruction of business confidence was contradictory. He clearly sought to curb the power of the bankers, particularly Dionisio Romero, with whom it was rumored that he had a personal rivalry. This rivalry cannot be totally dismissed as a factor in the decisionmaking process, given Alan García's volatile temper and autocratic style. While he seemed determined to continue to pursue an economic model based on private investment, he also was making a definite move toward an increased state role in the economy and a confrontational government stance against big business. In Peru's business community, which is relatively small and has highly concentrated entrepreneurial interests, García's two positions were hardly compatible. Finally, and ironically in light of García's antiimperialist stance, foreign bank branches were exempted.[53]

The measure was not a product of the APRA ranks, and the exclusion of the party from such a major and controversial decision fueled existing resentment. Luis Alberto Sánchez, vice-president of the Republic and the highest-ranking aprista after García, was informed of the decision only one hour before its announcement; he was told by none other than ex-President Belaúnde! The cabinet ministers were informed only the day before. Both Premier Larco Cox and Foreign Minister Alan Wagner privately expressed reservations, while Economics Minister Saberbein— one of the bold ones—supported the measure. The minister of industry, Romero Caro, resigned in protest a week later. He was followed, in the next ten days, by twenty-two other high-level functionaries, vice-ministers, and agency directors.[54] The surprise and opposition, although expressed with restraint, of many apristas was obvious.

The expropriation measure was thus not a direct form of credit reform nor was it backed by the party, and it was extremely disruptive to the overall economic strategy. The move had primarily political objectives: to distract attention from a faltering economic strategy; to reassert García's leadership after several defeats within his own party; and to strengthen his relationship with the left. An important reason underlying García's change of strategy was the obvious exhaustion by early 1987 of the heterodox reactivation model. The logical next step was to increase productive investment, conceivably by the private sector, as the state had neither the resources nor the capacity to provide it.

Economic strategy was one of the key points of the García–Alva Castro rift, which stemmed from Alva's ambitions for APRA's nomination for the 1990 elections. Alva had let it be known for almost a year that he wanted to resign, a move that indicated his desire to disassociate himself from the government before economic performance declined. The rift culminated in a major political defeat for García: Alva was elected president of the Chamber of Deputies, an outcome that García had campaigned actively against. Sánchez, Priale, and León de Vivero all opposed García's tactics to prevent Alva's election. Priale was involved with Alva in a project to modernize the Parliament and strengthen its role—a move that would assert party control over García. Of the top old-guard apristas, only Villanueva stood by García.[55] The Alva-Alan rift was an old and bitter one, and the election of Alva Castro on top of the impending economic crisis marked the lowest point yet in García's presidency. The decision to expropriate the banks grew out of a need to revitalize the president politically.

García's key supporters and advisors were not apristas, the most important ones being Daniel Carbonetto and Carlos Franco. Franco, a sociologist, had been active in SINAMOS. He was particularly persuasive in convincing García that he had to curb the power of the economic elites, more specifically the bankers. "We are confronting a crisis of the economy, of society, of the State. But it is also a crisis of dependency and of internal domination. The different cycles of the historical dependence of Peru in some manner always allowed certain national groups to find . . . ways in which to exercise their domination."[56] Carbonetto, the most influential advisor in economic matters, later admitted that the banks measure was primarily politically motivated and stated that the goal was "to create the stable political environment necessary for development when you have kidnappings, an active Sendero Luminoso guerrilla problem and a government party representing not the business community but the middle and poor sectors of society."[57] These goals, although laudable, were hardly rendered achievable by the banks expropriation, which totally destabilized both economic and political climates.

The move was also a function of the drifting apart of García and the twelve apostles. García claimed that industrialists had not invested sufficiently and that they were putting their money into "narcodollars" that were leaving the country. While figures differ, there is no doubt that business investment was far greater in 1986 than in the previous year, and even Finance Minister Saberbein's figures indicated a 32 percent increase in the first semester 1987 over the same period for 1986.[58] Final official data estimated that private investment doubled between 1985 and 1987, although a big share of that increase was in construction and inventories rather than in equipment.[59] Meanwhile concertación had resulted in an unprecedented $400 million in letters of intent through the newly founded National Private Investment Board. A great many of these were canceled following the expropriations.[60] Finally, neither in Peru nor in any country does most capital flight occur through the banks.[61]

The debate should perhaps have centered on the nature of future investment, as it is not clear to what extent entrepreneurs were willing to continue to invest in the face of bottlenecks and the absence of a longer-term economic strategy. This uncertainty might have been a factor in García's decision to totally change his approach. Yet as the true figures for 1987 investment were not available at the time of the expropriation, and the numbers being quoted were subjective estimates, the concertación strategy was disrupted before it had the chance to fulfill its potential and be fairly evaluated. Meanwhile, if García planned, as he consistently stated after the expropriation announcement, to continue to rely on private investment, taking over the nation's banks was neither a wise nor a productive decision. His lack of understanding of how the private sector functions led to misconstrued accusations. At a certain level it seemed as though he believed his own rhetoric about *los malos capitalistas*.

Political factors were prevalent in the decisionmaking process. Besides upstaging Alva, García decided to retake the political initiative from his main political rival, Izquierda Unida, and at the same time to reforge the link with the left that he had lost with Barrantes's resignation from the leadership of the coalition. In order to generate popular support for the banks measure, he undertook a strenuous schedule of speechmaking in the pueblos jóvenes that was reminiscent of his campaigning days. There was talk of a new *populismo* that would merge the more radical wing of APRA and the moderate factions of Izquierda Unida. Carlos Roca, a radical aprista, referred to this potential merger as *el abrazo histórico* (the historic embrace).[62] Carlos Franco was also a major proponent of expropriation of the banks as a way of forging the link between APRA and the IU.[63] This new populismo, however, had two fundamental problems. The first was that, with the government's alienation of investors as a resource base, to distribute more the state would have to expropriate more, not necessarily a viable solution and one increasingly being rejected as inefficient in a wide range of nations on all sides of the political spectrum. The second was that most members of both groups were not willing to cooperate with their main political rivals.

The members of Izquierda Unida, mindful of maintaining the coalition's political identity, and many of whom had deeply resented

Barrantes's support of the APRA government, were quick to criticize the banks expropriation as insufficient to reform the credit structure and for its failure to affect foreign banks. Alfonso Barrantes, while praising the project for its breaking with the oligopolistic power of the bankers, warned that this power and wealth could as easily be concentrated in the state.[64] While the law passed in the APRA-dominated Chamber of Deputies, it was held up in the Senate where the government needed the IU's support for passage. The left demanded that the government pass an amnesty law for imprisoned terrorist suspects and backed their demands with a hunger strike in the Congress by six IU deputies and two senators. This placed the government in an awkward position, as Sendero's primary targets since 1985 had been APRA party and government officials. In August 1987, when the hunger strike was occurring in the halls of Congress, Rodrigo Franco, the thirty-year-old aprista head of Empresa Nacional de Comercializacion de Insumos (ENCI)—the government food-distribution agency—was brutally assassinated by Sendero in front of his wife and children. Not surprisingly, this incident precipitated the cancellation of the proposed amnesty deal. García clearly made no gains in his relations with the IU.

The banks proposal also disrupted APRA. García's autocratic style and frequent bypassing of the party apparatus was deeply resented by many apristas, particularly those high-ranking officials of the generation García had skipped over. Other key actors from García's own generation, such as a previously influential advisor, Héctor Delgado Parker, and chairman of the External Debt Committee, Hernán Garrido Lecca, also resigned at that time, if not publicly in protest. Those apristas who had been the proponents of an economic model hinged on cooperation with industry could hardly favor abandoning that model, nor were many apristas pleased with the increasing preeminence of nonaprista advisors to the president. A rift of sorts between the president and his party was apparent. One prominent aprista noted that the president's actions were resulting in a loss of contact with APRA's main support base, the middle classes.[65] Meanwhile the party youths, presumably those to whom García was trying to appeal, were becoming increasingly radical and violent, and their actions during the political rallies at the time served to confirm APRA's reputation for undemocratic tendencies. Their links with the old-guard apristas were virtually nonexistent.

Most notable, however, and also indicative of APRA's still-dominant hierarchical structure and messianic rather than rational political tradition, was the lack of public opposition to the measure by party members. Initially one aprista spoke out publicly against it: Alfredo Barnechea, a deputy from Lima and a supporter of García prior to the measure. As a result he was threatened with party disciplinary measures; he resigned before he was expelled. Jorge Torres Vallejo, one of García's main supporters during his rise to power, subsequently spoke out against the measure; he too was threatened with expulsion from the party. All other APRA senators and deputies voted for the project, despite their misgivings or disagreements. The lack of public criticism of the party leader stems from the history and hierarchical nature of the party, both of which were a function of forty years of unquestioned dominance by Haya de la Torre. As Barnechea stated, "There just is no dissent in the APRA. . . . This is what is difficult for an outsider to understand."[66]

The lack of public dissent from the party stems in part from a tradition of obeying without question the jefe máximo, Haya de la Torre. While García by no means had the godlike stature that Haya had in the party, an in-bred tradition of hierarchical order and behavior remained. This hierarchical structure and personal domination of the party is distinct from party discipline, which is strong in many parties, such as the AD in Venezuela. Such parties are usually more democratic internally, however, than is APRA.[67] At the same time non-APRA opposition to the measure was such that for several months there was little other debate or legislative activity. This was in part due to the IU's attempted "sabotage," but primarily to the extent of the opposition and the support the nation's beleaguered center and right were able to rally.[68]

A series of opposition rallies was organized by an independent front headed by Mario Vargas Llosa, the nation's best-known writer; Miguel Cruchaga, an architect and organizer of past political rallies; and Hernando de Soto, author of *El otro sendero,* a widely read study of the informal sector that attributes the marginalization of that sector to a discriminatory and inefficient state bureaucracy and regulatory system. Vargas Llosa launched a campaign based on the threat to liberty posed by the expropriation. His main concern, presumably a sincere one, was that the state monopoly of all credit and savings would result in authoritarian control, particularly in light of the indebted status of much of the press. He interpreted the lack of respect for constitutional guarantees as forewarning of a return to the Velasco-era style of dictatorship.

The movement was supported by many members of Belaúnde's Acción Popular, the Partido Popular Cristiano, and a variety of independents, including the Frente Nacional de Trabajadores y Campesinos (FRENATRACA). While the political right was involved in the movement, it was not alone, as many of the middle sectors who voted for APRA in 1985 latched onto the movement. The first of the movement's demonstrations attracted unprecedented numbers of people—approximately thirty thousand—to Lima's Plaza San Martín. The attendance was far greater than at similar rallies held by each of the particular political parties that same week. At the second demonstration, in Arequipa, the participants were violently attacked by IU and APRA militants, and national television coverage, run by the state-owned channel, was cut off because of reported "mechanical difficulties" a few seconds after Vargas Llosa began to speak. APRA launched a defamation campaign against Vargas Llosa in the newspapers and on television, accusing him of having been a strong supporter of the Velasco regime. While Vargas Llosa had supported some of Velasco's reforms, such as the land reform, he also had been a constant critic of the absence of civil liberties. The fact that the APRA government felt threatened enough to engage in such a campaign—and presumably even to censor the coverage of Vargas Llosa's speech—was indicative of a lack of confidence and a worrisome disintegration of the political climate. The movement behind Vargas Llosa actually developed into a political front, the Frente Democrático, which backed Vargas Llosa's candidacy for 1990 and was favored to win by a large margin until the last-minute appearance of political dark horse Alberto Fujimori. García and his advisors clearly had not foreseen this renovation of the right as a formidable opponent.

The haphazard way in which the expropriation was presented added fuel to the opposition's fire. There were two lawyers on the advisory team, but neither was particularly astute at constitutional law. A host of legal loopholes was left open for the opposition. At the same time no attempt was made to build prior support for the measure among the left, which resulted in García's failure to gain any political capital, while providing a rallying point for the right. An example of the incongruities in the measure's planning and presentation was García's calling for, in the very same speech, the privatization of the nation's social security system. These failures are a result of García's authoritarian style of leadership and decisionmaking strategy, and the reliance on a very small and select group of advisors. A comment by one was telling: "There aren't many of us in the team, and we overlooked the legal aspect."[69] It is surprising that García did not foresee the negative reaction to the measure, despite his previous relations with the private sector. (In light of the effects of the banks measure, it is interesting to note the example of Mexico's 1982, largely unsuccessful, banks nationalization, and to ponder what sort of conclusions García's advisors drew from this case, if they studied it at all.)[70]

Unfortunately, the political debate over the banks issue was turned into a crisis by proponents of both sides. Both García's calls to battle, pitting the exploited pueblo against the lazy bankers, and the right's threats of impending totalitarian doom were attempts to generate crisis and benefit politically from it.[71] The controversy dragged on, involving several extraordinary legislatures and the illegal and violent takeover of the banks by the government. While the situation was resolved in part by a solution proposed by the Banco de Crédito—the devolution of 51 percent of the bank's shares to its workers—it was not applicable to all the banks, and an entire year after the measure had been announced the status of some was still pending. The government's handling of the controversy was viewed negatively both at home and abroad.[72] Ultimately the government created a plethora of new and unnecessary problems for itself at a time when it already faced a faltering economy and a growing insurgent threat.

The banks issue reveals a great deal about García's government and party. It is evident that it was García and whichever advisors he fancied at the time who made policy, not individual ministers or the party. His underestimation of the opposition was in part due to his intolerance of dissent among his advisors. The lack of tolerance for discussion and dissent within APRA reveals the pervasiveness of undemocratic traits within the organization. With the banks move, García—nicknamed Caballo Loco (Crazy Horse) by the opposition—shot himself and his party in the foot, and APRA barely whimpered, despite the fact that many high-level party members disagreed fundamentally with the measure. Despite the renovated image that APRA was able to project for the 1985 elections, the old strains of hierarchical order and intolerance were frighteningly evident.

Another old strain was also evident: the party's self-perception as martyr—victim of oppression from all sides. Within this interpretation there was no room for analysis of the party's own errors. At the time of the expropriation and Sendero's murder of Rodrigo Franco, APRA could once again play this role: its efforts at reform were being sabotaged by the resurgent oligarchic forces that it had once again challenged, and at the same time it was a victim of the terrorists. "We apristas were faced with blind and destructive terrorism on the one side, and on the other by the rancorous and also cowardly attack of diverse enemies who tried to take general political advantage of a particular situation: the banks. I believe that the tragedy of Rodrigo and the perverse comedy of the sudden love for liberty by those who traditionally repressed it, has been the best 'recall to order' for the Peruvian people and especially APRA."[73]

The nature of decisionmaking underlying the banks expropriation brings to the fore the issue of García's leadership style and personal ambitions. His typical style was to launch a harsh attack and then retreat, as he did in taking over the banks and then supporting modifications of the law, or ordering the police into the banks with tanks and then agreeing to wait for the courts' ruling. This was a function of his ambitious and bold approach coupled with a volatile character. García aimed for center stage. He seemed indispensable for APRA in 1983 and for Peru in 1985, and presumably wanted to maintain that image.[74] In the event of a military coup, García would have been thrown out for attacking the oligarchy and would remain an *hombre del pueblo*. In the same vein was his rumored threat to resign, in protest of the September 1988 economic shock program that his own mismanagement had necessitated. The political and legal controversy after the banks measure was extremely damaging to both the president and his party. García's popularity fell from an almost 70 percent approval rating in June to as low as 30 percent after the violent takeover of the banks in October.[75]

The controversy over the banks expropriation exposed the fundamental weaknesses of Peru's political institutions. The political and legal debates reached almost ludicrous heights, and the government's lack of respect for the judicial system was painfully obvious. The extent to which proponents on all sides were willing to generate a crisis over the issue threatened the viability of democratic government and suggested that the desires of the diverse political forces in Peru to destroy each other were stronger than their concern for democratic government.

Finally, the banks controversy demonstrated the importance of how the reformist debate is framed. García was able to create a sense of unity for the first two years he was in office largely because he provided a reformist platform while avoiding the politically divisive property-relations issue. While the reformist debate had for the past two decades, particularly during the Velasco years, focused on the structure of property relations, causing much controversy and at the expense of an approach that directly addressed the needs of the poor, the APRA government had avoided the long-prevalent belief of the Peruvian left that state takeover of the economy would solve the nation's problems. It is surprising indeed that García chose to forsake this unity by once again framing the reformist debate in controversial terms. At a time when the solution of state control was increasingly being challenged by leftist movements throughout Latin America, it is astonishing that García and his advisors chose this path. It is even more surprising given the weak and inefficient nature of the Peruvian state machinery, and thus the obvious barriers to extending its control. The choice may have been a function of the prevalence of velasquistas among García's advisors, who, instead of learning from the failures of the military revolution, may still have clung to their faith in reform from above and their disdain for political parties and autonomous popular participation. This might explain the lack of concern for building support for the measure prior to its implementation, an oversight prevalent in the Velasco years as well.

Unfortunately, the reform-from-above approach was incompatible with democratic government, as the banks issue demonstrated, and instead pitted the various actors against each other at the expense of much needed political consensus. A well-known Peruvian scholar, initially enthusiastic about the APRA government, noted that "the problem is that nationalization will neither signify the solution for Peru nor bring us to totalitarianism.... Property reforms in and of themselves have no way to ensure a change in social relations.... If one wants to have democracy, one has to think in terms of agreement between the parts.... A democracy does not signify one part's destroying the other."[76]

The desire to reform from above and to take a confrontational rather than consensus-building approach was also a function of the nature of the APRA party. Reforms always entail confrontation, and APRA alone could implement them correctly: "solo el APRA salvara al Peru." This sort of sectarianism tends to lead to polarized politics. Again a comparison with Allende's Chile, and the animosity between the Christian Democrats and the Socialists is useful. "The two major parties in Chile had strong utopian elements, had programmes that offered a complete transformation of Chilean society, that saw the key to change in changing property relations, that saw compromise as betrayal, and that saw politics as polarization."[77] The utopian vision, the calls for a total transformation, and the focus on changing property relations all fit in with APRA's original doctrine, as well as with Alan García's personal vision, although they contradicted all the claims made in his inaugural address. In his book *El futuro diferente* he wrote at length about the *circuitos financieros de poder* as the current form of imperialist domination that had to be overthrown. The nationalization of key lands and industries was a fundamental part of aprista doctrine, but had been toned down by Haya in his later, more conservative years. The debate within APRA was not over whether the banks expropriation was right in the context of present-day Peru, but over whether or not the measure was sanctioned by Haya's writing. This exposed the lack of doctrinal clarity in the party, as well as a tendency to value dogma and utopian vision before reality, leading to the polarization that was comparable to Allende's Chile prior to the coup. Unfortunately, the polarization that resulted after the banks expropriation squandered the opportunity that APRA had, at least for the near future, to implement democratic reform in Peru.

POLITICAL "SOLUTIONS" TO ECONOMIC CRISIS

The total loss of consensus and the extent of political infighting that occurred after the banks expropriation, both within and outside APRA, diverted attention from all other issues, regardless of their importance. Policymaking in most arenas from that time forward was a victim of power struggles within the party and government. Insurgent activity in particular increased dramatically. Economic policy became a series of shock packages, or *paquetazos:* inadequate and poorly implemented sets of austerity measures designed to curb the hyperinflation and economic collapse that the government's loss of coherence had generated.

Faced with a rapidly deteriorating international reserves situation, the INP proposed a plan for "selective growth" in late 1987. The underlying assumption was that the problem was not the enormous number of subsidies, the multitiered and overvalued exchange rate, or the dramatic loss of private sector confidence caused by the banks expropriation, but rather that subsidies had been applied too generously and generally and should be targeted at a few priority sectors. In addition, there purportedly was an attempt—the Programa Trienal—by Daniel Carbonetto to reverse the precarious financial situation by simplifying the exchange-rate structure, increasing the tax burden ratio, and divesting several public enterprises. Such a course was never taken, however.[78] There were three paquetazos announced in 1988: the March announcement of an economía de guerra; the September shock program during which García remained in seclusion in the palace and threatened to resign; and one more in November. Like the March package, the other two were austerity packages, drafted by a technical team, that subsequently went through "a substantial political filter."[79] All three packages included decreed adjustments to public prices, exchange rates, interest rates, and wages. *Nominal* wage hikes were granted at higher rates than those decreed for regulated prices and the exchange rate, but nominal wage hikes could hardly keep up with the erosion of purchasing power that resulted from hyperinflation. Inflation was generated by fiscal imbalances, inadequate price adjustment and major distortions throughout the complex regulated price system, and the lack of confidence and inflationary expectations generated by the government's incoherent policy measures, particularly the stop-go cycles of raising and then freezing prices.

> By late 1988, the economy had taken off on a hyperinflationary path with inflation accelerating from an annual rate of 360% in the first quarter to nearly 7000% in the second and real money plummeting to one third of the level one year earlier. Economic agents had rationally interpreted the Government's corrective attempts as destabilizing, prompting a massive rush on the dollar, unprecedented black market premia (up to 400%) and a free fall of both GDP and real wages that had been initiated in early 1988. Hyper-recession walked hand-by-hand with hyperinflation.[80]

The social costs of the economic collapse were tremendous. GDP per capita fell by an accumulated 20 percent for the 1988–1989 period. Labor unrest increased dramatically, amid widespread protests by unions over imperfect indexation of wages to inflation and widespread shortages of basic foods. Hours lost in strikes increased tenfold; in particular a two-month strike in the mining sector crippled Peru's main foreign exchange-earning sector, thus aggravating the reserves crisis and inflationary expectations.[81] Unemployment soared. While in 1985 approximately 50 percent of the economically active population were under- or unemployed, by 1990 this figure had increased to 75 percent.[82]

The crisis had particularly negative effects on the informal sector. The sharp reversal and rapid deterioration of positive trends put new pressure on an already precarious situation. The urban poor, who spend up to 70 percent of their income on food and are not protected by wage indexation, suffer the worst from hyperinflation. The results were stark and immediately visible. By early 1990 studies in poor urban areas were reporting worsening trends in basic nutritional status, height-weight measures, and infant mortality indicators. There were reports of a reappearance of incidences of types of malnutrition that had not been seen in urban Lima for over a decade. Horror stories included mothers not taking their sick children to get free medical attention because they could not afford the bus fare to the clinic.[83]

There was clearly no agreement within the APRA administration over how to handle the crisis. There were some voices calling for technically coherent economic policies designed to replenish the depleted reserves stock, reduce the fiscal deficit, and curb inflation. Yet there were also strong pressures, from President García in particular, to avoid implementing policies that would be perceived as "antipopular." The result was a high turnover of finance ministers and other officials and half-hearted or watered-down austerity measures that lacked the coherence and credibility to halt the inflationary spiral. Ábel Salinas, for example, resigned from his position as finance minister in November 1988 when his original proposal for an economic package was turned down. Pedro Coronado, as president of the Central Bank, had an ongoing struggle with the executive branch from September 1988 until July 1989, as he remained stubborn in his commitment to a tight monetary supply and to building up the sorely depleted reserve base. He even went as far as refusing to provide the funds for the government agency ENCI to pay the freight charges for a ship carrying wheat and corn donations from the US Agency for International Development, which thus sat in Callao harbor for several weeks! While foreign exchange losses in 1988 alone had reached over 2 percent of GDP, when Coronado left office in mid-1989 net international reserves had increased by $700 million, or 3.5 percent of GDP over the September 1988 level. The month that Coronado resigned, money printed for government financing—nicknamed a *maquinazo* or "huge machine"—totaled 21 percent of the entire money supply, compared to zero for the first semester. For example, in one day—July 20, 1989—the government issued 500 million intis of new money.[84]

There was clearly pressure from the executive to continue deficit spending, regardless of the inflationary effects. In May 1989 García appointed César Vásquez Bazán, a young economist from the left wing of APRA, finance minister. Vásquez Bazán was little known with the exception of a book he published titled *La propuesta olvidada* (The forgotten proposal), which criticized the García government as a populist one that had abandoned APRA's original agenda of structural reform. The appointment of the little-known and inexperienced Vásquez did not signal any major changes in economic strategy; rather it indicated that García wanted to assert more control over economic policy for the last year of his term.[85] There were no significant policy innovations during Vásquez's tenure, with the exception of the new flood of credit from the Central Bank, which from the departure of Coronado until the end of the APRA government had only an acting head. President García clearly wanted to use the reserves that had been accumulated in 1988–1989 to reactivate the economy prior to the November 1989 municipal and April 1990 presidential elections, regardless of the inflationary effects and of the reserve situation that he turned over to his successor.

As if the current Byzantine economic situation were not enough, the APRA government left several economic time bombs for the next government. The Central Bank had virtually no international reserves—a very different situation from the one that the APRA government inherited—and the fiscal deficit was equivalent to almost 10 percent of gross national product (GNP). In addition García decreed various labor laws in his final months that promised to make the future labor relations scene explosive. The laws, which appear to have been accepted if not initiated by García in order to buy future support in the labor movement, eliminated limits on indemnization payments, extended compensation to state sector workers after a certain period of service, and expanded the scope of collective bargaining legislation.[86] While these laws may have been progressive in some sense, they were hardly viable in the Peruvian context: a state treasury totally devoid of resources and 75 percent under- and unemployment. In addition, the timing of the measures indicates that García did not want to have to accept the consequences once they were passed.

García's manipulation of economic management for political reasons—and APRA's willingness to provide institutional support for this manipulation—worsened an already critical situation. He apparently wanted his last months in power to consist of economic reactivation and the passage of "progressive" legislation in order to depart on a positive note. He could thus be remembered as a "man of the people" when he reappeared on the political scene in 1990. The last few months of the APRA administration, however chaotic, would probably contrast favorably with the initial months of any sort of stabilization plan the new government might attempt. In any event, at that point García and APRA would be in the opposition and could point to the "better" times at the end of the APRA government. This was neither responsible leadership nor was it guaranteed to play favorably into García's or APRA's hands, particularly as the government's legacy was prolonged and unprecedented crisis. But given the volatility of public opinion in Peru, the extent to which fear of *el shock* was behind Fujimori's victory over Vargas Llosa, the odds against any government's inheriting the 1990 situtation, and García's remaining a gifted orator with the ability to capture crowds—and APRA the only party in the country with a strong institutional base—from a political standpoint, it may have been a good strategy. Nothing more needs to be said about the effects of that strategy on the Peruvian nation, particularly its poor.

It seems plausible to conclude that the APRA government's economic management was disasterous and severely exacerbated a crisis of economy and society that was becoming increasingly chaotic and violent. It is also plausible to conclude that the nature of the APRA party was a principal cause of *why* economic management was so disasterous. This conclusion is a component of the central question posed in this book: why was the tenure in power of the nation's only truly institutionalized party, a party with a commitment to socioeconomic reform, such a dramatic failure, and what are the consequences of this failure for democratic consolidation in Peru? I posit that the nature of the APRA party was a determining factor in that failure. Yet I also place that assertion in the context of the formidable social and economic challenges that Peru faced in the 1980s, and the difficulties that any party or leader would have faced. The issue of García's own personal ambitions, above and beyond those of APRA, cannot be ignored. Yet the nature of APRA's relations with García were critical in determining the freedom that he had to act and provided him with an unwavering institutionalized core of support. The party's relations with the opposition and with society in general, meanwhile, were key determinants of the polarization that set in.

In the next chapter I focus on party-government relations and on the effects on the APRA party of being in government. I turn in Chapter 7 to the party's relations with the opposition, parliamentary and insurrectionary, and with the military, as well as the results of the 1990 elections. Finally, in Chapter 8 I examine party relations with society, particularly the poor, at the microlevel.

6

Partido de Gobierno o
Partido del Gobierno?

*But, there having evolved in Peru an important process of modernization
and industrialization . . . locating the very IU on the right margin of the
young Haya, we stand today for the evident inapplicability of the Hayista
principles of 1928. This helps us to understand, to some extent, the existing
doctrinal vacuum in the governing party.*
— Pedro Planes, "La alanización del estado,"
Debate 8, no. 42 (December 1986)

*We have always lived persecuted. From that comes our habit of receiving
orders and blindly obeying principles, because circumstances truly justified it. Now that we have this democratic spring, we are not prepared for
it. Those of us who have wanted to act have been perceived as undisciplined
or disloyal.*
— Jorge Torres Vallejo, interviewed in *Caretas* (Lima),
November 16, 1987

APRA was the quintessential opposition party: power had consistently
eluded it, both because of persecution or proscription and at times its own
mistakes. The years of opposition and secrecy had resulted in a disciplined
and hierarchical party machine, but not in the development of a strategy
or a leadership ranks for governing. To repeat our maxim: the less likely
a party is to get into power, the less likely it is to have realistic programs
for governing. APRA came to power in part riding on the wave of
popularity of its young presidential candidate and in part on its long-es-
tablished party apparatus, and the complex baggage of party loyalties,
intense personal experiences, and diverse interpretations of ideology that
it carried with it. APRA was not the homogeneous and unified organization that most outsiders saw it as. The party came to power with a shortage
of skilled personnel and a plethora of internal discrepancies, coupled with
a tradition of unquestioned loyalty to the party leader. There was a lack
of consensus over party doctrine, which the reprinting of *El antimperialismo
y el APRA* in the 1970s had not solved, nor had debate focused on many of
the questions that the party would face once in power.

These discrepancies became evident early on. The shortage of talent within the ranks of the party was one reason that García surrounded himself primarily with nonaprista advisors, which led to a great deal of resentment in the party. It also led, at the bureaucratic and municipal levels, to mismanagement and poor execution of policy. The tradition of unquestioned loyalty to the jefe máximo, coupled with García's own autocratic tendencies, led to the concentration of all decisionmaking at the executive level, with the president personally making all decisions. Although Alan was not "el Jefe," as Haya was referred to, and many of the party resented such dominance by someone so young, the party, because of its dearth of experience, lacked the ability to deal with dissent either with García or within its own ranks. Meanwhile the differences in interpretation of aprista doctrine led to major discrepancies in reaction to actual policies. There were elements within the party that could be labeled center-right politically, and based their view of "aprismo" on Haya's later works. At the same time there were also those who felt that Haya's early works should be implemented to the letter, which clearly placed them to the left of the moderates in the IU coalition. These elements in the party leadership were supported by the bulk of the party youths.

García's own ideology did not seem to be clear, as one day he would speak in confrontational revolutionary terms to placate the radicals and youths, and the next of the need to cooperate with other political parties and the private sector (the effects of this inconsistency on both economic and counterinsurgency policy are discussed in other chapters; it also had an effect on the party as an institution). These contradictions, coupled with the lack of attention to party matters that inevitably came with the responsibilities of being in government, resulted in a disintegration of the unity and loyalty that had in the past held APRA together. This was exacerbated by new tendencies in the party—the opportunists who had joined the party at the last minute to reap the benefits of being in power, and old, antiquated strains such as the existence of paramilitary squads (búfalos)—that confirmed the view of many outsiders that APRA had not lost its violent and sectarian tendencies. The lack of consensus, coupled with the shortage of skilled people at the rank-and-file level and the party's tradition of sectarianism, led to APRA's inability to integrate effectively with existing social organizations, unions, and the private sector. Initially the APRA government was virtually García's government, and García's government had all the characteristics of a classic populist regime. Yet the party was able to penetrate the state bureaucracy through patronage appointments, with substantial effects on its ability to operate. Meanwhile, as García's popularity plummeted after the nationalization of the banks and the onset of economic crisis, the party's power in the executive branch increased, and the discrepancies and contradictions within its ranks had substantial impact on the course the government took. The experience of governing, meanwhile, also had negative effects on the party's internal cohesiveness. As Randall notes, when the boundary between party and bureaucracy is blurred, in the long run the party's legitimacy and integrity are damaged. In addition, when the party leader is also the national leader, with power independent of the party, then the party's adaptibility is likely to suffer.[1] This clearly occurred in the case of APRA, which was prepared neither to govern nor to respond to the crisis that the behavior of its autocratic leader precipitated.

At the same time there continued to exist a different APRA phenomenon: the cultural APRA. There was another aprismo, at the popular rather than leadership level, which to a large extent had more to do with family ties, a shared history of persecution, and an almost religious faith based on Haya de la Torre than with the issues and conflicts facing the García government. The APRA mística continued to exist, but like the party and the government, it existed as a piece of an incomplete puzzle, rather than as a cog in an efficiently operating machine. APRA was a complex and constantly changing entity, and its changes were in large part a result of the challenges that it faced and was ill equipped to handle as a party of government.

THE GARCÍA PHENOMENON AND APRA

Alan García's personality was without a doubt the most important dynamic affecting the APRA party during its tenure in government. At first this was due to APRA's winning the 1985 elections thanks to García's opening up of the party during the political campaign and to the appeal he had as a presidential candidate. There were several results. During the honeymoon phase of the government, party members felt completely indebted to García, and he at the same time took them for granted. He acted unilaterally and expected that they would follow. Despite the claims of the opposition, the party, while it did fill many posts with those of the APRA ranks, was not able to *apristizar* the government.[2] What did occur was an *alanización* of the government. Policies such as the PAIT and the Rimanacuy were not presented as gifts from APRA, although all positions within the programs were given to apristas; rather they were gifts from Alan. Slogans such as "Alan—Peru" and "Alan contigo" followed the campaign slogan of "mi compromiso es con todos los peruanos."

Along with this was the dominance of nonapristas, or younger rather than old-guard high-ranking apristas, among García's advisors or close confidants. His closest colleagues were either nonapristas (and often former advisors to the Velasco government such as Carlos Franco and Guillermo Thorndike) or apristas of his own generation (Luis Gonzales Posada, Romúlo León Alegría, Carlos Blancas, Hugo Otero, and Jorge del Castillo).[3] The old-guard apristas such as Sánchez, Priale, Villanueva, and Negreiros had posts in the Senate or in the party but were not included in the close circle that advised García. There are several reasons for this. First, it was well known that the most talented economists and sociologists were not within APRA's ranks. Second, García was not Haya, the founder and *compañero jefe* of APRA, and thus was probably much more comfortable with advisors of his own age rather than those who were two generations older.[4] With the younger generation García could build up a circle of advisors who were dependent on him rather than established in their own right, something that someone with his autocratic tendencies would clearly prefer. García trusted no one and was intolerant of dissent. He purportedly once stated, "Yo quiero ministros enmudecidos" (I want silenced ministers).[5]

This older generation was tolerant of García, as they were indebted to him for achieving power, and as in most cases their aspirations for the presidency had already come and gone. It was the middle generation of leaders, the generation that García skipped, that was most piqued. Resentment of García's exclusion of the party grew substantially as the honeymoon period came to a close, and APRA, rather than reaping benefits from García's presidency, was getting the blame for failed policies. They were unable, however, to express this resentment in the form of effective opposition to García's controversial measures.

This became particularly evident at the time of the banks expropriation. The party's lack of tolerance for publicly expressed dissent gave García even freer rein and fueled latent ill-will. The absence of open party debate of a measure that so negatively affected the overall political and economic situation and broached the touchy issue of state versus private sector ownership of industry—a measure that a large number of apristas were fundamentally opposed to—demonstrated the party's dependence on its jefe máximo for any sort of substantive initiative. At the same time the sharp divisions over the measure exposed ideological discrepencies within the party.

The extent of the ire of many members of the party not only to the banks measure but also to García's overall style and to his perceived disregard for fundamental aprista values, as was demonstrated by his shelving many of APRA's traditional symbols during the campaign, became evident at this time, albeit in subtle ways. As García's popularity deteriorated, and it was perceived that he needed the party, dissent became more open, rifts became more evident, and the old APRA symbols, such as the five-pointed star instead of the dove of peace and the APRA Marseillaise, began to reappear. The conservative sectors within the party blamed the *socialistas* who were advising the president for the mismanaged banks measure. "Once the aprista government began to operate, I was surprised that in the beginning decisions were taken without always consulting the relevant party organization. The advisors who intervened in the beginning were alien to the party. Perhaps it was they who proposed the changing of the five-pointed star, for that dove. . . . The forgetting of the beligerant aprista Marseillaise? Perhaps it was they who wanted to use 'socialist' instead of 'aprista' vocabulary?"[6]

At the same time the more radical sectors of the party, in particular the youth, who also felt excluded from the government, felt that the government was not revolutionary enough. They felt that García should never have backed down on the banks issue and accepted judicial intervention, and that Haya's true doctrine, *El antimperialsimo y el APRA*, was not being implemented. Their reading of APRA doctrine was Marxist and revolutionary, and the García government clearly was not. For these sectors, "aprismo in the form of doctrine, program, and direction does not govern. On the contrary, they posit that political power in the country is held by a sterile variation of Latin American populism."[7] These ideologically opposed criticisms from the conservatives on one hand and the youth on the other stemmed from the same causes: the lack of doctrinal clarity in APRA and García's exclusion of the party from matters of government.

The critique of the García regime as populist, coming from within his own party, was a forceful one. The basic characteristics of a populist regime are nationalism, a vertical decisionmaking structure, a reliance on political mobilization and recurrent rhetoric and symbols, and emphasis on a dominant personality.[8] In addition there was García's penchant for grand gestures. Besides being presented as the giver of programs such as the PAIT, he had a habit of personally "fixing" things. After a land invasion at Garagay in June 1986 was repressed by orders of the Interior Ministry, García rushed to the area and declared in a grandiose manner that he would expropriate the land for the settlers.[9] After the prison massacres, for which his executive order was ultimately responsible, García rushed to the prisons in the middle of the night to see what had actually happened. It was clear to the public that the government was García's and not APRA's, and he was clearly in control. This had the effect of undermining the party, which was already in a weak position. The ability of the government, through its party, to incorporate the participation of the marginalized sectors was extremely limited.[10] APRA's connections with the marginalized were shallow, and they were further eroded by García's populist methods. The way in which programs such as the PAIT and the Rimanacuy were implemented—always from above and with no respect for existing organizations—limited their potential. Because they failed to incorporate the poor in the process of reform, the programs were ill suited to stimulating the popular initiative necessary for meaningful and lasting reform.

Populist style and methods were key to APRA's victory in the 1986 municipal elections, when APRA was able to make substantial headway in Lima and in the sierra, where it had traditionally been weak. The party made the most of the mechanisms available: the PAIT and the Rimanacuy. In the 1986 elections eight IU mayors were defeated by APRA candidates. APRA made great strides in Cusco and Puno. In Cusco APRA's margin rose from 27 percent in 1983 to 57 percent in 1986. The party also made headway in Lima's pueblos jóvenes, and even narrowed the left's margin in its stronghold Villa El Salvador from 55 percent to 10 percent.[11] Yet the reformist impetus proved to be short-lived; the Rimanacuy faded out after 1986 and the PAIT was scaled down significantly after 1988.

APRA's approach was vertical and manipulative rather than genuinely reformist. The party did not attempt to adopt the logic of the horizontal and democratic style that characterized the spontaneous social movements of the 1970s, as the left had in its municipal administration, such as in the highly successful Vaso de Leche program. APRA instead maintained its vertical style, which was partially responsible, along with its sectarianism, for its failure to give continuity to its viable experience in democratic municipal government from 1983 to 1986.[12]

García had questionable respect for the democratic system as well. His autocratic style and his impatience often led him to step well beyond constitutional norms, as when he sent army tanks to break down bank doors. His impatience with a Congress that could spend months disputing dogmatic points while the nation disintegrated into chaos may have been warranted, yet his own practice of unilaterally decreeing surprise measures often left the opposition in Congress with no choice but to use legal and technical criteria to stall major legislation after the fact. García's statement to APRA youth, in which he apologized for the slow pace of revolutionary transformation, is telling. "It is because we drag along the democratic, parliamentary, bourgois results of doing things the easiest way possible. . . . From 1956 we have cohabitated with democracy, taking advantage of its benefits. We have gotten accustomed not to the battle, but instead to journalism; not to confrontation, but instead to parliamentary debate."[13] These are hardly the words of a leader fully committed to democratic government, and they reflect the unresolved dilemma in García's own mind: whether or not revolutionary change is possible in democratic context. García's increasingly confrontational behavior after 1987 and his framing the debate in terms of class conflict demonstrate his impatience and perhaps his loss of faith in such a possibility. The name of the semiofficial biography of García, written in 1988 by one of his advisors, Guillermo Thorndike—*La revolución imposible*—is also demonstrative of this frustration.

García's behavior could be ascribed to his frustration with an institutional system that was heavily bureaucratized but had absolutely no procedural structure. Indeed, García had very few people he could rely on within the system to actually get things done.[14] His shift to confrontational rhetoric and his statements to APRA youth, meanwhile, could be ascribed to the need to respond to radical sectors within and outside his party. The emotional baggage surrounding Alan García was by no means simple, however, and while rationale did play a role in explaining his erratic and autocratic behavior, the fact that he had not made a clear choice between a commitment to the democratic process and the alternative—a revolution either from above or from below—undermined the viability of the democratic system. This dilemma existed within the party ranks as well. A concrete example of this dilemma in process was the debate over changing the Constitution to allow García to run for reelection.

Early on in the García government's administration, the proposal to alter the Constitution to permit him to run again began to circulate among the APRA ranks. The proposal was debated in Congress, and its sole supporters were the *Alanistas* in Congress—the apristas who were strong supporters of Alan García, led by Alfonso Ramos Alva. The opposition and those apristas whose concern for the future of the constitutional system in Peru was greater than for the short-term political goals were strongly opposed. Altering the Constitution to suit the political fancies of the leader in power would obviously undermine its legitimacy. García was evidently interested in seeing how much potential the proposal had and let the debate continue without taking a stance on the issue. His own political ambitions were paramount to the fate of the constitutional system. Only when the political and economic situation was in severe deterioration, and his political future would clearly benefit from an absence from power, did he, in an open letter to APRA in July 1988, denounce the reelection proposal as offensive to him. García had enough control and influence over the behavior of the apristas in Congress to have put a halt to the reelection speculations immediately, had he so desired.

Interestingly enough, at the same time, he renounced the post that had been created for him of president of the party. His explanation was the conflicting responsibilities of government and party. Clearly the responsibilities of being president had preempted attention to the party since García took office, but his renouncing of this post two months prior to the party congress scheduled for October 1988—the first to be held since August 1985—definitely had political connotations. "The exercise of government and its relation with the party inevitably mixes the charge of president with the daily conflicts and problems of the party. What's more, I am conscious that I am now the object of the worst of the reactionary attacks.... It is my obligation to avoid allowing those attacks to affect the party."[15]

It is not clear why García chose to distance himself from the party at the time, nor was his resignation accepted at that point. He may have wanted to distance himself from APRA at a time when the most likely candidate for secretary-general was his main rival in the party, Luis Alva Castro—and Alva Castro did indeed get that post when the congress was finally held in December. The results of the December congress were a sound rejection of García's wishes, as the party reasserted itself in the face of the president's increasingly erratic behavior and plummeting popularity. After Alva's election the president again submitted his resignation as party president, and this time it was accepted. The Alva-Alan rivalry was a deep-seated one. Alva clearly had his own support base within APRA, a base he had built up by taking the time to listen to the concerns of regional party leaders and directors, something that García, both because of his style and because of time constraints, could not do. García also probably felt that he would be better off disassociated from an Alva-led party in 1990, as Alva had very little appeal as a candidate outside APRA. As an external observer, García would have much less to lose were APRA defeated, and then would be free to lead the party in 1995. Perhaps most important, if García could not be the unquestioned jefe máximo of the party, which he would not be if Alva had a high post, then he would rather be nothing at all. Alan García did not play second fiddle to anyone.

García's concern for his political image became even more evident at the time of the September 1988 economic shock plan. He did not appear in public for thirty days,[16] in an attempt to distance himself from the economic crisis of his own making. There were also highly credible rumors that he threatened to resign at the time. García seemed more concerned with his political image than with commitments to the party[17] or even, when crisis set in, to the presidency.

It is interesting to note that García called for the October congress, which was finally held in December 1988, to be the congress of unity, and for a revamping of party doctrine and mística.[18] After three years in government García was publicly recognizing that the party had no real program, and that being in power had had negative effects on it. His chances of uniting APRA, however, were not very good, as his own position was to be substantially weakened by the election of Alva to the secretary-generalship, and the fundamental disagreements within the party over doctrine and ideology would not be easily resolved.

THE DOCTRINAL DEBATE

> The responsibility that we all have now that the party is compromised in the task of government is very great. And we cannot evade that responsibility simply by saying that we need more apristas in positions in the bureaucracy. Aprismo should be the promoter and the ideological and programmatic gauge for the government and not the instrument of the satisfaction of bureaucratic ambitions. . . . In the administration and management of the affairs of the state all Peruvians should participate

with the larger ideological orientations and social commitment of aprismo. The essential mission of the party is to point out and defend those orientations.[19]

In this message to APRA, the same letter in which he resigned as president of the party, García was publicly recognizing that APRA as a unified party had virtually ceased to function, and that there was no agreement among the party leaders on doctrine or government program. On one side of the party leaders of several generations, such as José Barba, Alfredo Barnechea, Jorge Torres Vallejo, Guillermo Larco Cox, and Luis Alberto Sánchez, were opposed to increased state control of industry on principle, favored a tougher stance on terrorism, and held constitutional principles in high esteem. They were pragmatists of the political center. Barba even suggested reforming APRA doctrine, as he asserted that Haya's 1928 writings were ill equipped to deal with Peruvian realities. There was then a center-left group that corresponded to the García supporters and to such personalities as Javier Valle Riestra, who had been in the MIR and was an active proponent of the human rights of suspected terrorists. This group supported the nationalizations in particular and García in general, and behaved according to the president's wishes in Congress. There was also a more radical wing of the leadership ranks, led by Carlos Roca—one of Haya's favorites in the Buro de Conjunciones. Roca espoused the most radical of Haya's writings and felt that not enough was being done to put Peru on a revolutionary path of a decidedly Marxist bent. He had little concern for constitutional government. Most of the party youth favored the Roca route, if not a more radical one, and had a great deal of sympathy for those groups involved in armed struggle. At the same time the director of the party's Commission for Ideology, Alfonso Ramos Alva, asserted that aprismo was not socialism, and that the radical publications that emanated from the party youths must be receiving funds from an outside source.[20] APRA doctrine does not even have a definition of private property or a clear stance regarding it.[21]

There was a plethora of movements within APRA. One, called Generación en Marcha, was the last generation of the party, the one that followed García's, to know Haya. Most of its seven leaders had government or municipal posts. This group felt that Haya's and APRA's platform was anachronistic and incomplete, and that the party needed a political platform. The party was more of a front, with diverse views such as those of Barba and Barnechea at one extreme and those of the ex-aprista head of the MRTA at the other. APRA, they felt, needed to define its position on issues such as private property and to distance its doctrine from the IU's. At the same time the group wanted to revive the mística and dedication of the Haya-led APRA and was attempting to stress the importance of the traditional APRA symbols. They felt that the trappings of power and the domination by Alan García harmed the traditional unity of the party.[22] They wanted to democratize the party by expanding the links of the leaders to party youth—the Juventud Aprista Peruana (JAP), the students, the Comando Universitario Aprista (CUA)—and to the adult militants.[23]

The number of currents and personalities was clearly more complicated than this brief analysis permits; the point is that there was a diversity of views within the party that stretched from a constitutional reformist view to a radical Marxist vision. Haya de la Torre's writings were so extensive, so varied, and so elusive that all of these groups could justify their views using his works. His theory of *espacio-tiempo-histórico* (space-time-history) is so all-encompassing that it justifies both calling for immediate insurrection in the name of revolution and postponing revolutionary change for decades. Without the jefe máximo to determine what the party's ideology would be at the moment—whether it be the convivencia with conservative elites or the participation in revolts such as the 1948 uprising against Bustamante—there was an absence of doctrinal clarity that led to a great deal of confusion. While Alan García was president of the nation, he was not Haya, the jefe máximo, and he himself also did not seem to have a set view of the party's doctrine. Thus there was a genuine lack of consensus in the party, not just over how to govern, but over what the party's official doctrine really was. Since Haya's death, the rifts between the conservative Treinta Años de Aprismo wing led by Townsend and the Antimperialismo wing led by Villanueva were never resolved; rather they were set aside in order to win the 1985 election. As disagreement over key decisions followed, however, the rifts once again became clear.

It can easily be argued that Peruvian politics would be greatly enhanced by much less attention to doctrine and more to the nation's realities. Yet because there is no consensus in Peru over basic political tenets, such as respect for constitutional guarantees, a market versus a state-run economy, and the type of society that Peru should aspire to have, dogma and doctrine take on an increased importance. There is an absence of consensus on basic societal values[24]—an equilibrium that is missing in revolutionary societies. In absence of agreement over basic values, debates over daily policy measures carry an additional and often overblown ideological charge.

Another problem that surfaced from the party's lack of clarity on certain critical principles was a tacitly condoned reemergence of APRA paramilitary squads, the infamous búfalos named after the 1932 insurrectionary Búfalo Barreto. APRA's attitude toward armed insurrection has always been ambiguous, as was demonstrated by Haya's tacit support for uprisings in the past and the appeal that the MRTA had among the party's youth ranks. The specific armed groups with links to the party will be detailed in the section on armed opposition in the next chapter; suffice it to say here that political violence emanating from within the ranks of the governing party clearly demonstrated the lack of agreement on commitment to democratic practices and principles within the party, undermined the legitimacy of the state, and severely exacerbated the political polarization process.

The problems that plagued the party at the leadership level also were evident at the rank-and-file level. There were many cases of party youths clashing with conservative regional directors; most extreme perhaps was the case of an avidly anti-Communist director in Cusco, Julio Lara, who was involved in violent attacks against radical youth.[25] The discrepancies at the leadership level were far greater at the rank-and-file level. Particularly since the party had taken power, party activities were relegated to secondary priority, and most party leaders opted for government-related posts. The party mechanism as such virtually ceased to function. "In APRA, the principal leaders understand that their personal political future does not lie in the party but rather in the government. ... No one wants to dedicate many hours to party work. ... The APRA party, as such, is no longer the organization of cadres and masses that aroused so much love and hate. ... It is now only an organization of masses articulated by that charismatic leader ... Alan García."[26] Party activity at the rank-and-file level was greatly reduced, and there were even cases of aprista ranks who had not seen a director in forty years.[27] Disillusion at the rank-and-file level showed up in the widespread failure to pay party dues. The party's funding depended much more on the 5 percent of salaries that was required from aprista public functionaries.[28] The existence of a Federation of Forgotten Apristas was telling.[29]

There remained two strong and relatively independent currents in the party that were not part of the government, but had more of a sense of loyalty to the party in many ways than did its leaders: the JAP and the many apristas for whom APRA signified family ties and national identity, and almost substituted for religion—APRA culture.

THE PARTY YOUTH

"It is the party that has a title to its legitimacy and the true and sublime expression of its moral power, a glorious martyrdom ... that signifies the voluntary offering by a people, ready to give their blood because aprista ideas maintain justice and liberty as their eminent aspiration."[30] More than any other sector of APRA, the party's youth looked for inspiration to its history of martyrdom and insurrection. For the first time in APRA's history, however, it was the holder of power, and thus the force that other insurrectionist movements were rebelling against. This created a fundamental dilemma for young apristas, and they became disillusioned to a large extent with both party leadership and government. Their support was clearly a concern of party leaders, as is evidenced by García's speeches designed to placate their more radical sentiments and the attempts to elicit that support through measures such as the banks nationalization. Party leaders were well aware that the loss of that support often translated directly into support for the Marxist left or for guerrilla movements such as the MRTA. APRA had lost the best and brightest of its young leaders in the 1960s, an experience that was not easily forgotten.

APRA began almost as a youth movement, with the activities of the 1920s generation. Until the convivencia era APRA dominated the youth movement in the universities. After that time its dominance was substantially eroded by groups to the left, which had more appeal to young sectors than the aging and increasingly conservative APRA leaders. The defections of the youths were primarily a function of their ideological disillusion: at the time when the events of the Cuban revolution were inciting revolutionary activity in the left throughout Latin America, APRA was making alliances with the conservative forces that had been its persecutors. APRA maintained the organizational bases of its youthful sectors, however, throughout this period, and among other things the organization of the party's youths is what gives it the distinct characteristics of a mass party.[31]

The JAP was made up of youths aged fourteen to twenty-four whose goal was to enroll in the party. The JAP had a national directorate and within it were the CUA and the Comando Escolar Aprista. There were different currents within this national youth movement, as was demonstrated by the existence of the Izquierda Democrática Estudiantil (IDE) and the more radical ARE in the 1970s, and by groups such as Vanguardia Aprista, Nueva Izquierda, and the ARE in the 1980s. The youths were the focus of Haya's attention during the military years, and that generation are the leaders who were in power in the APRA government. The generations that followed, however, had a very different training experience. Rather than knowing APRA as a binding family led by the paternal guiding hand of Haya, these young people never met Haya and instead experienced the divided party of the early 1980s and then the governing party. Thus there was among them a strong current searching for the "lost" values that they had been told about but had not seen, for the mística experienced by the older generations who had been persecuted. The youths of the 1980s wanted to return to the doctrine of the early 1920s, and also to the experience of belonging to a party that was actually fighting for its revolution. Thus their political views were much more radical than those of the government, and the appeal for them of the MRTA was greater than that of seemingly ineffective parliamentary debate.

The majority of APRA youth on average wanted a much more radical,

Marxist-oriented approach on the part of the government. They consistently revolted against corrupt regional officials, who were in many cases of the conservative strain, as well as being corrupt, which fueled rebellion. On several occasions high-ranking party leaders were sent to JAP congresses to attempt to quell rebellious APRA youth. Luis Negreiros, the general-secretary of the party, for example, had to travel to the North in October 1987 to deal with a rebellion in the youth movement that stretched across four traditional APRA strongholds: Chimbote; Trujillo; Chiclayo; and Lambayeque. The youths were accusing their regional directorates of having split up their charges irregularly. They accused one official, the head of Cooperación Popular in Lambayeque, of robbing the PAIT of 200,000 intis, and called for his resignation.[32] In February of that same year Carlos Roca was sent to temper the rhetoric of a national convention of APRA university leaders. Roca, the leader of APRA's most radical wing, disassociated the radical rhetoric of the youth congress from the party. Roca's stance was denounced by the majority of the young, and the event went on, with only a minority allying with the party's CEN.[33]

The party youths wanted an APRA that was "a doctrine and a complete response."[34] Their respect was greatest for those who were willing to die for their ideals, as was demonstrated by their naming their 1983 CUA Congress "Edith Lagos"[35] after a well-known *senderista* who was killed by the military; and by the movement to name the 1988 JAP Congress "Luis de la Puente Uceda" (the name "Martyrs of Aprismo" was finally chosen.)[36] This had an effect at all levels of the party, as was demonstrated by García's controversial address at the 1988 congress in which he said that he too admired the dedication of senderistas. This cult of the martyr, which pervaded not just the party youths but also the party rank and file, is analogous to that of the Peronist party in Argentina, and was a powerful sentiment behind the formation of the Montonero guerrilla movement that grew out of the Peronist party; not unlike the many APRA youths who joined the MRTA. In both cases the utopian elements of party culture translated into tangible challenges to coherent government. A government cannot be constitutionally elected on the one hand and sanction armed struggle on the other.

The party youths also deplored the fact that prior to the 1985 closing of new inscriptions into the party many nonidealistic technicians, such as INP head Javier Tantalean, joined the party. The young people saw these new apristas who were not products of the JAP ranks as "opportunists."[37] Party leaders, not surprisingly, had a difficult time responding to the increasing isolation and radicalization of the youth movement.[38]

The increasing divergence between the bulk of the party youths and the party line was demonstrated by a 1988 APRA youth meeting where the speakers included Agustín Haya and Javier Díez Canseco of the Partido Unido Mariáteguista (PUM), and a representative of the Nicaraguan embassy, but not one APRA leader.[39] The lack of communication between the youth and the top levels of the party was accentuated by the fact that most of the recently "graduated" JAP leaders, the twenty-four-to-twenty-seven-year-old generation that was organized and trained by García and Carlos Roca in the late 1970s and early 1980s, which might have served as the natural link between the JAP and the older party leaders, took positions in the government rather than dedicating their time to party activity.[40] As the party took on the responsibilities of government the youths' traditionally strong influence in party decisionmaking diminished.[41]

The main divergence of the youth wing was its clear definition of society along the lines of class struggle. The young saw APRA as "a Marxist movement, which believes in a revolution conducted and executed principally by the workers and peasants."[42] This sector apparently was supported by the more radical elements of the labor movement, those elements of the CTP that broke with Cruzado and participated in the 1988 national strike.[43]

The leftward shift of the student movement had its origins as early as the mid-1970s, with the division of APRA youth into the IDE and the more radical ARE. Haya initially disavowed the ARE but eventually he granted it recognition, such as his tacit approval of its participation in the events of February 5, 1975. Haya formed the CUA to avoid such splits and problems, but it was unable to solve the factional disputes over ideology. In 1980 one of the key party issues was the student movement's harsh criticism of Julio Cruzado and the failure of the CTP to support the national strikes of the late 1970s. In the split between Townsend and Villanueva, the IDE supported Townsend and Cruzado, while the ARE went with Villanueva.[44] The ARE remains one of APRA's main representatives in the universities today, along with Vanguardia Aprista and Nueva Izquierda. The ARE's support in universities does not compare to that for the more extreme left, however. In the 1988 elections at San Marcos, the ARE came in a poor fourth place after a Sendero-and-MRTA–aligned group, the Frente Democratica Revolucionaria (FDR); the Frente Amplio San Marquino, aligned with the IU; and the Partido Comunista del Perú (PCP)–Bandera Roja.[45] The radicalization of APRA youth must be seen in the context of the overall radicalization of the young in Peru and the challenges that it poses for democratic government.

Coexisting with the leftist elements of APRA youth was a small group—primarily from longtime APRA families—that had unquestioning loyalty to the party and retained the age-old animosity for the Marxist left. This group very much resented APRA's being labeled as similar to the IU or other elements of the left, and was, on several occasions, involved in violent clashes with IU militants. The most notable was the October 1987 assault by Jaime Bedón, then national secretary of the JAP, on an IU congressman.[46] This sort of violence, which also contributed to the speculations about a resurgence of the búfalos, or paramilitary squads, was justified by one staunchly loyal APRA militant. "It is when they tell 'compañeros' that it is the left that is sabotaging the government and when one believes that the APRA really could and should implement a great transformation . . . many of them are willing and will resort to anything that they are told to do so that the great historical project is not jeopardized."[47]

This group of young people was a product of the aprismo that continued to exist apart from and independent of the government. The blind loyalty to APRA as an ideal is *aprismo popular*, and it maintains what the radical and disillusioned sectors of the youths were seeking: mística. The changes that occurred as the party sought power and then met the challenges of government caused APRA to behave more as an electoral front than as an organized mass party. The APRA mística was clearly less prevalent and of a different nature in the 1980s than it was during Haya's time. It had by no means, however, disappeared.

MÍSTICA: APRISMO AS A CULTURE

The same way in which aprismo tends to confuse the people with itself, so does the left. . . . Regardless, it is precisely in defining the popular, we should say then that the popular is that part of reality that is accumulated, inorganic, and spontaneous, but active, creative and dynamic, which the popular masses live, express, and communicate. The popular is the ancestral experience, life, social customs and symbols, that translates into a vision of the world and of history.[48]

There was clearly in existence an aprismo popular that was relatively independent of the García phenomenon. For this group of people, APRA is the equivalent of a religious faith, and Haya de la Torre their god. While this faith in Haya and his ideas also exists at the leadership level, it involves ideological conviction, while at the popular level it is more of a spiritual one. At the popular level, aprismo is part of a family tradition and is handed down from generation to generation. It is not unlike Peronism in Argentina and entails a similar cult of the hero or martyr. Aprista families often have members who either died or were imprisoned during the persecution years. Persecution was felt by families as a whole, as wives were often left alone for years to support households. In one family interviewed, seven of the eight male members of one generation were imprisoned at the same time. Faith in APRA—in Haya in particular—was the guiding principle throughout such experiences. When references were made to Haya, even in the present context, it was to a man with superhuman qualities, a leader, a savior.[49]

The shared faith throughout these painful experiences became an integral part of aprismo. Alan García's father was imprisoned for the first five years of García's life, and this aprismo popular was a part of García's formative years and is one of the qualities that made him acceptable as a successor to Haya. García and Haya are not referred to in the same way, however, and past times, particularly the era of persecution, are spoken about with an aura of mystery and awe. Aprismo popular seems to be based much more on the "then" than the "now." In the same way that faith in Haya got these families through persecution, it would in the future get them through whatever other problems they might face, and resulted in unquestioning support for the party that was blind to any criticism from outside.

It is necessary to distinguish APRA at the leadership level from aprismo popular. From its initiation in 1924, APRA had an institutional-ized leadership ranks that formed the crux of the political and intellectual bases of the party. But beginning with the 1930 electoral campaign and with a basis in the popular movements of the times, there arose a popular movement that was also APRA. Yet the two currents were distinct from each other intellectually and sociologically, with the leaders being primar-ily coastal, white, wealthier, and better educated, and the popular move-ment adherents more likely to be of provincial origin, mestizo, and less educated. Haya's genius allowed these two movements to form a political alliance, but they were not necessarily united on other levels.[50]

Although Haya was a *costeño* with European tastes, it was no coinci-dence that he chose symbols of Andean origin for his graphic representa-tions, such as the famous *chavin*—the Andean bird that is one of the party's best-known symbols. Thus he cultivated a political faith in the popular APRA movement that was not grounded in politics but in mística: a complex combination of shared historical experiences, symbolism, and spiritual faith in the personality of Haya himself. This movement is, to a large extent, cultivated independently rather than by the party leaders.[51]

Aprismo popular thus functions in a cross between autonomy and submission, and its role in the reactivation of the party is significant but not totally clear. There were sectors of APRA that had not seen a *dirigente* in forty years at the time of the 1981 split between Townsend and Villanueva. The conflict was viewed as distant by such sectors, as a "squabble of older brothers (whites)," although these sectors did go along with the ruling of the secretariat of discipline's expelling Townsend. APRA's vertical and authoritarian structure was thus able to maintain loyalty and obedience on matters of national political importance, but for the most part functioned as a separate entity from APRA as a culture. Once the party attained power, the control of the party mechanism over these sectors took on a clientelistic nature, in keeping with the approach of the García government.[52]

Aprismo popular was both independent of and linked to the party mechanism and the government. It clearly will always deliver its votes to APRA in the way that the youth sectors will not. In 1983, for example, many of the youths purportedly voted for Barrantes over the more conservative aprista candidate Alfredo Barnechea.[53] This is clearly part of the reason that despite its disasterous record in power APRA was still able to garner almost 20 percent of the national vote in 1990. The popular movement that is aprismo fundamentally is an expression, however, of the world vision, the religion, the *razón de ser* (reason for being) that is aprismo. It is, more than anything else, an expression of the need for cultural integration in Peru, of the need for agreement on fundamental values, and of the brilliance of Víctor Raúl Haya de la Torre in perceiving that need. He may not have succeeded in founding the most capable group of leaders or the most socially integrated group of followers—indeed APRA's sectarianism has always been one of its downfalls—but he did succeed in giving Peru, through APRA, a unique form of cultural and political identity.

Yet by combining cultural identity with political utopia, Haya also created precisely the kind of party that was least suited to the consensus building that is so critical to democratic reform and ultimately consolidation. Like the Peronist party in Argentina, the combination of cultural identity, hierarchical structure, sectarianism, utopian philosophy, and cult of the martyr and hero that was aprismo created artificial cleavages in polity and society; cleavages that made it impossible to attain the political and cultural integration that the party's utopia envisioned.

7

APRA's Relations
with the Opposition

In order to evaluate APRA's performance, it is important to understand the forces of opposition, both parliamentary and insurrectionary, that it faced. APRA, as the oldest revolutionary party and the starting point for many of the leaders of other movements, was in a unique, and often difficult, position to deal with opposition from the left. Alfonso Barrantes, leader of the Izquierda Unida, and Víctor Polay Campos, leader of the MRTA, both began their political careers as apristas. The defections to the left during the convivencia and Velasco era left a permanent scar. The criticism from much of the left—that APRA was not genuinely revolutionary—was difficult for the party to deflect, particularly since it often came from former members of APRA's own ranks. The party's sectarian nature, meanwhile, made cooperation with the left impossible, except at the highest level. Alan García relied a great deal on advisors affiliated with the left, which was deeply resented by the members of his own party.

On the other end of the spectrum the moribund right was revitalized after the banks nationalization. The Frente Democrático (FREDEMO), led by Mario Vargas Llosa, not only incorporated the support of the Peruvian oligarchy, but much of the political center and middle class, as well as the private sector, which had supported García and APRA until that time. While FREDEMO had little success in appealing to the nation's poor, it was able to erode APRA's traditional support base in the middle class and was the primary contender for the 1990 elections until the unexpected surge of support for Fujimori one month prior to the first round. In addition, the resurgence of the new right in the midst of the banks controversy led to a rise in antiaprismo, which had been dormant during the first part of the García government.

Finally, and posing the greatest challenge, the existence of revolutionary groups actively opting for the insurrectionary route placed both APRA and the left, as supporters of revolution, in difficult positions ideologically, particularly as members of APRA youth and the largest faction of the IU supported armed struggle. APRA's past as an insurrectionary movement was also a factor. This issue was made more difficult by the brutal and fanatical nature of the Sendero Luminoso, and the fact that its main targets were APRA government officials. By the middle of the García government's term, both Sendero and the MRTA had made substantial headway, violence had become a daily event, the judicial system became subordinate to terrorist sabotage; armed APRA paramilitary groups, or búfalos, had reappeared; and there was overt support for a violent path among young apristas and half of the parliamentary left. APRA's relations with its opposition were complex at best, and had substantial impact on the party's ability to govern.

IZQUIERDA UNIDA

> Any convincing explanation of the weakness and even more so of the sectarianism of the Peruvian left would have to enter into a detailed examination of that country's political history and of its complex and fragmented social structure. Historically, one would have to examine the influence of APRA which monopolized the resistance to dictatorial government. . . . The way that the Communist party supported the military government after 1968 helps to explain why many opponents of the government looked to more radical groups. . . . Whatever the reasons for these deep and sectarian differences, the fact that they exist and that so much time is spent on sterile debate about what Mao or Trotsky really meant . . . isolates would-be leaders from the mass of the people.[1]

The Izquierda Unida is an electoral front formed after the 1980 elections, comprising the majority of the nation's socialist and Communist parties until its formal split in 1989. The parties varied from Maoists and Trotskyites to Moscow-aligned Communists to independent socialists, and were originally united by the personality of Alfonso Barrantes. The moderate and likable Barrantes, a former aprista, was palatable to many outside the left as well. He was mayor of Lima from 1983 to 1986 and consistently remained one of the most popular leaders in Peru, according to most opinion polls. In the 1985 elections the left was the only political force other than APRA with any substantial backing.

After 1986 the IU grew increasingly divided between the moderate Barrantes-led faction, which was composed primarily of independents and socialists, and the more radical factions, led by the largest party within the IU, the PUM. In 1989 the IU formally split, with the moderate socialists led by Barrantes forming the Acuerdo Socialista Izquierdista (ASI), and the majority remaining in the IU. The PUM–led faction was openly sympathetic to groups engaged in or supporting armed struggle and had formal links with three of them: Union Democratica y Popular (UDP); Pueblo en Marcha; and the MIR. The Barrantes faction, on the other hand, strongly condemned Sendero Luminoso and terrorism in general. Barrantes himself, in response to an accusation that he was "to the right" of García, stated that his primary goal was to preserve democracy.[2] Barrantes took this stance for several reasons. First, he genuinely was a pragmatist in his ideological convictions. Second, he was one of the top targets of Sendero, which condemns him as a revisionist. Finally, he was aware that the left in general would not fare well were there a military coup inspired by guerrilla violence.

The more radical factions of the IU, on the other hand, are extremely dogmatic and have little concern for democratic government. The militants and leaders of the PUM are sympathetic and have ties to the MRTA guerrillas. Before the MRTA launched its armed struggle, it was affiliated with the UDP, Pueblo en Marcha, and the MIR, all of which have ties to the PUM. When the MRTA began its violent route, part of the MIR joined it. The other groups remained proponents of armed struggle, while not actively engaged. The PUM's stance is that of using democracy as a stage of preparing the "consciousness" of the masses before going to war. This approach is unacceptable to Barrantes, who maintains that there is an explicit choice between reform in a democratic context and armed struggle. This fundamental difference created an unbridgeable rift between the two factions. The other large party in the coalition, the Moscow-linked Partido Comunista (PC) remained affiliated with the IU after the formal split, although it clearly is not as radical as its counterparts in the coalition. The PC has a history of negotiating[3] and it also controls the powerful CGTP; its position in the split was a critical one.

The PUM, meanwhile, would rather engage in armed struggle than accept the Barrantes approach. It is ironic that the PUM was led by Javier Díez Canseco—a member of one of Peru's oldest aristocratic families and educated at the elitist Universidad Católica—and also by Agustín Haya de la Torre, a nephew of Haya. The PUM was clearly a force to be reckoned with, as it has substantial party mechanisms at the grassroots level. Díez Canseco received more votes than any other IU senator in the 1985 elections, and again in the April 1990 elections, when only six IU senators were reelected.[4] While until its split the IU coalition had managed to retain its unity at election time, at the grassroots level the different parties functioned independently and had—and continue to have—different strongholds.[5] This may result in good grassroots organization, but also in a less coherent core of support at the macrolevel.

The radical wing of the IU accused Barrantes of being a pseudoaprista because of his close relationship with García and his stance of "critical support" for the APRA government. His desire to cooperate with the APRA government probably stemmed from concern for Peruvian democracy and for reform within that context, rather than from ideological affinity with APRA. Like most APRA dissidents, his distancing from the party, which occurred in 1958, entailed an ideological breach. He refers to his time in APRA as his *edad de piedra* (Stone Age) and maintains that the main benefit of the experience was getting to know the bases of the party. Haya's incoherent ideology in the face of Mariátegui's pure vision was what spurred him to leave the party.[6] "For example I was anti-imperialist when I worked with APRA, and as a socialist, I still am. But it is unquestionable that the aprista vision differs from a Marxist or a Mariáteguista vision. The analytical tools are different, and therefore so is the analysis of Peruvian reality."[7]

Despite the fact that Barrantes was probably the most capable and popular leader in the IU coalition, he admitted prior to the split that he was in a tenuous position: as an independent, he had no formal leadership position in any of the parties in the front.[8] Without such organized support, he was unable to draw the majority of the left with him when he broke off from the IU. To some extent the break was a tactical decision to distance himself from the extremist elements in the coalition. It proved disastrous for the left in electoral terms, however, as the IU obtained only 7.12 percent of the vote in the first round of the 1990 elections, and the ASI only 4.16 percent.[9] (See Table 4.1). Both factions backed Fujimori in the second round.

The future of the nation's left remains as uncertain as Peru's. Barrantes maintained that the instability of the political situation was a function of the deteriorating condition of the governing party; however, he also admitted that the left was not united enough to fill its place. While the animosity between the Mariáteguista left and the hayista APRA was reduced substantially after Haya's death, an intense rivalry remained as the two forces competed for the same social sectors: unions; universities; and pueblos jóvenes.[10] This competition took various forms. In Puno, for example, there were constant violent clashes between PUM-controlled campesino organizations and APRA authorities.[11] In Lima, where Barrantes ran what most observers agree was an efficient and nonpartisan municipality, APRA control of the municipality has signified the creation of many parallel and competing organizations, such as mothers' clubs and Vaso de Leche program committees. Meanwhile, in a 1988 attempt to build up the non-party-affiliated left, Barrantes chose Trujillo, the traditional APRA stronghold, as a base of operations.[12]

In general, while competition for social sectors was intense on the part of both parties, APRA's approach, resulting from both its sectarian nature and the advantage of controlling the central government, was far more exclusionary in nature than the IU's. The IU's advantage seemed to lie in its superior competence at the directorate level, as many IU functionaries are either from upper-middle-class "bourgeois" families and have the advantage of an education at "La Católica" or were able to take advantage of the increase in funding for left-affiliated think tanks during the Velasco years. This competence difference was such that García purportedly offered a host of government posts to several high-level IU functionaries at a series of dinners early on in his administration; the IU functionaries declined.[13] There was definitely a presence of IU functionaries in the government, however. "It is the capacity and the level of some technocrats in the left that makes them indispensable."[14]

Despite the competition, there was also ideological convergence between the younger, García-led wing of APRA and the moderate Barrantes-led faction of the IU, which was strengthened by the friendship of Barrantes and García. This was resented by both the old guard of APRA and the radical wing of the IU. There were similarities between the youths of the Izquierda Unida and those of APRA, who constitute the most radicalized sector of the party. In the long run a convergence of these forces could be an important core of support for Peruvian democracy, acting as a counterforce to the more radical and violent groups further to the left, which provide increasing competition for social support bases in unions and popular organizations, for example. Yet APRA's sectarianism, particularly at the rank-and-file level, and the extent of support for armed struggle among the radical left, to a large extent precludes such cooperation; and this plays into the hands of the more radical faction of the IU, which spurned all cooperation with APRA. The PUM's Augustín Haya noted with satisfaction that "the 'socialismo y participación' group's intent to act as a bridge between APRA and the IU existed from the years prior to the 1985 elections. But with time those intending to initiate a historical alliance have been disillusioned because of the behavior of APRA."[15]

Democracy in Peru might indeed have been enhanced by an abrazo histórico between these two forces, but the possibility of such an alliance was jeopardized by APRA's inability to rid itself of its sectarianism and dogmatism, and by the weakened electoral position of the more moderate elements of the left once they disassociated themselves from their colleagues who consider democracy a transient stage en route to revolution. The friendship between García and Barrantes could have been a positive political force, and is interesting historically in light of the relationship between Haya and Mariátegui. The potential of this relationship was limited, unfortunately, by the ideological differences of the parties and García's autocratic nature. Indeed the failure of these forces to form an alliance that could have offered a viable alternative to the radical left or the discredited APRA left a vacuum in an important sector of Peru's political spectrum, providing the political space for widespread support first for the conservative FREDEMO coalition and subsequently for Alberto Fujimori and his Cambio 90 front.

FREDEMO

The resurgence of the right in Peru indeed had consequences for APRA. In the same way that the left was competing with the party for support in unions and pueblos jóvenes, the new right provided APRA with a major competitor among the middle class. By moving to a confrontational approach to politics, and framing the political debate in antagonistic class terms, something that he had previously avoided, García's rhetoric at the time of the banks expropriation opened the door for a resurgence of latent antiaprismo among the conservative elites. Not necessarily to Vargas Llosa's benefit, these groups also lent him their active support. Once again APRA was embroiled in an "us versus them" controversy, and the "them"—the conservative elites—had been given an excuse to participate by the APRA government.

While the banks controversy gave the new right impetus to organize, the idea of providing a political alternative had been discussed several times previously by Vargas Llosa and his campaign organizer Miguel Cruchaga.[16] The banks crisis opened a new political space that had until then been filled by APRA after the demise of Acción Popular. First, it gave Vargas Llosa impetus to act in name of a cause that he felt deeply about. While critics contended that the "Libertad" slogan was indeed a sham, Vargas Llosa truly seemed to believe that state control of the country's credit was a threat to freedom of the press, both because of the government's lack of respect for constitutional norms and because of the heavy financial dependence of the press on the banks. Second, the banks measure alienated not just large-scale financial interests, but entrepreneurs of all sizes and a large segment of the middle class that had supported APRA. The measure also alienated several members of the more conservative ranks within APRA. Besides the highly publicized defections in Congress of Jorge Torres Vallejo and Alfredo Barnechea, there were also a few defections at the rank-and-file level, some of whom purportedly translated their support to the Vargas Llosa movement.[17]

The anti–banks expropriation movement grew from an informal alliance of protestors into a formal political front—the Frente Democrático—between Vargas Llosa, Fernando Belaúnde, and Luis Bedoya, and their respective party mechanisms. Vargas Llosa formalized this alliance out of a perceived need for organization, particularly in remote areas.[18] However, the alliance with the AP and PPC narrowed the movement's political space by placing it squarely in the right, rather than remaining as a new political alternative. Hernando de Soto, one of the Libertad movement's original proponents, purportedly disassociated himself from the movement because of his opposition to the alliance.[19]

The Libertad movement formalized its organization in March 1988 by establishing a party headquarters and political platform. Its general theme was to seek technical rather than political solutions to Peru's problems, with five main points: to transform the state from a large and weak one into a small and strong one; to reinsert Peru into the international financial system; to integrate the country's two coexisting—or more accurately, warring—cultures; to stimulate the private sector so as to create wealth;

and to ensure a civilian presence in antiterrorism strategy. Poverty and terrorism were the most pressing issues.[20]

The Libertad movement was able to generate a great deal of support because of "the extent to which the leftist alternative in general" was discredited by economic crisis.[21] FREDEMO's links with the discredited political parties of the right, and the fact that all of the members of its nine-member directorate were of the elite, limited its appeal to the poor, as did Vargas Llosa's lack of ties to the poor and less-educated population. Yet the Frente's underlying theme—a rejection of dogma and the search for technical solutions—attracted some of the nation's most talented economists and sociologists, José Matos Mar and Felipe Ortiz de Zevallos, among others.

Until one month prior to the April 8, 1990, first round of elections, FREDEMO was favored to win easily, with opinion polls predicting Vargas Llosa would obtain 40–50 percent of the national vote. This support was due largely to the general discrediting of APRA. The widespread perception of a FREDEMO victory resulted in its running a heavy-handed and extremely ideological campaign. Vargas Llosa's lack of political experience and the fervor with which he espoused free-market principles frightened a great many voters, particularly the poor, as did his promises of a shock austerity program and the laying off of thousands of state sector workers. In addition, he was unable to control the diverse elements within his coalition, many of them members of AP and PPC, the parties that had been soundly rejected in the 1985 elections. Campaign propaganda was often in poor taste, and a barrage of television commercials led to the widespread perception that an inordinate amount of money was being spent on the FREDEMO campaign. Initial misgivings on the part of the moderate left and the poor—that FREDEMO was a spruced-up version of the old right and big business—were confirmed by the campaign tactics of many of the members of the front, as well as by Vargas Llosa's lack of sensitivity to the political concerns of the poor.[22] This, coupled with the split of Izquierda Unida, opened the door for the sudden and surprising growth of support for Alberto Fujimori in March 1990 and his eventual victory in the second round. The FREDEMO coalition dissolved shortly after the election, meanwhile, as the separate parties attempted to reassert their individual identities.

THE FUJIMORI TSUNAMI

There are countless theories as to why Alberto Fujimori was able to surface from virtual unknown to the national presidency in the course of three months. More than anything else, the Fujimori tsunami, as it was called, was a rejection of all established political parties: the right, despite its refurbished FREDEMO image; the squabbling and hopelessly divided left; and APRA because of its disastrous performance in government. Fujimori was able to capture APRA's traditional support base: small entrepreneurial groups and those sectors of the middle class for whom APRA was no longer an alternative, and the conservative FREDEMO equally unacceptable. In addition, Fujimori's success was due largely to a great deal of support at the grassroots level. As is mentioned in the opening chapter (and will be discussed further below), the importance of local, autonomous grassroots organizations grows in conjunction with the relative size of the informal sector. These groups play a critical role not only in the day-to-day survival strategy of the poor, but also in political participation. The relationship that such groups have with political parties is by no means clear-cut, although evidence suggests that they are reluctant to support political parties that threaten their autonomy. As we will see in the next chapter, APRA's attempts to politicize and subordinate autonomous local groups created substantial resentment, and it is thus no surprise, particularly given the severity of the economic crisis of 1988–1990, that there was a movement at the grassroots level to participate politically outside the realm of traditional parties.

Fujimori had been rector of the National Agrarian University from 1984 to 1989 and host of a popular television program called "Concertado," and had entered politics only in 1989. The son of Japanese immigrants, Fujimori ran on a simple, and vague, platform of "Work, Honesty, and Technology." Fujimori's appeal had several dimensions. First, his experience as an engineer rather than as a politician, and his lack of ties to any of the established parties, clearly was in his favor. APRA's incoherent conduct of government had led to an economic crisis of unprecedented proportions; at the same time the polarized political debate and the derogatory mudslinging that characterized the electoral campaign did not seem to offer any positive solutions. The right preached free-market ideology with fervor and made little attempt to appeal to the poor. The left was hopelessly divided and unable to provide a credible alternative to the failure of heterodox economic policy. Thus not only APRA was discredited, but so were all established politicians. In addition, and key to his popular appeal, were Fujimori's non-elite origins. His Japanese ties also aroused some hopes, whether realistic or not, that in the event of his victory the Japanese would extend substantial aid to Peru. He capitalized on Vargas Llosa's lack of appeal to the poor by promising not to implement a painful shock economic adjustment program to end inflation, and with such slogans as "Un Presidente como tú" (a president just like you). The claims of this first-generation Japanese-Peruvian—that he was "just like" the majority in a predominantly mestizo-Indian nation—seem less than credible, and his vague promises of "gradually" ending hyperinflation glibly unrealistic. Yet his message was much more palatable to an already severely impoverished population than Vargas Llosa's perhaps more responsible but bluntly phrased calls for a shock austerity program to end inflation. "El shock" had become a common term in the electoral campaign and among all sectors of society.

Fujimori's success was also enhanced by his rather eclectic political team, Cambio 90 (Change 90). Cambio's two main bases of support were small businessmen—including the National Association of Small and Medium Industrialists of Peru—and the evangelical movement. While approximately 4 percent of Peru's population is Protestant, the evangelical movement has increased its activity and scope of operations in recent years, and was extremely active in campaigning for Fujimori at the grassroots level. While Fujimori became a known phenomenon at the national level only in April 1990, his team was actively campaigning at least as early as January of that year and made a major effort in the pueblos jóvenes and in the sierra regions, both of which received relatively little attention from FREDEMO. By the April elections Cambio had 200,000 registered members in its ranks, as well as substantial popular following.[23] The Catholic church felt sufficiently threatened by the surge in support for a movement backed by evangelicals to make it clear in no uncertain terms that it backed Vargas Llosa. This included the staging of a mass procession in Lima a week before the election, purportedly for El Señor de los Milagros. Ironically this placed the church in the camp of Vargas Llosa, an agnostic, against Fujimori, a Catholic.

In the first round of elections Vargas Llosa attained 28.19 percent of the vote, Fujimori 24.32 percent, APRA 19.57 percent, the IU 7.12 percent, and the ASI 4.16 percent. Null and blank votes were 14.38 percent of the total[24] (See Table 4.1). It was clear from that point on that the left and APRA would back Fujimori if for no other reason than to defeat Vargas Llosa in the second round. Vargas Llosa was seen as the representative of the traditional conservative elite and was thus unacceptable for ideological reasons if not for pragmatic ones. In Luis Alva Castro's words to APRA, "compañeros, our support for Fujimori is a given, but there is no need to make an institutional commitment."[25] A similar stance was taken by the left.

The support of the left and APRA virtually guaranteed Fujimori's victory in the second round, but it by no means signified an organized or institutionalized support base, either inside or outside Congress, adding another formidable challenge to an already uncertain future for the Fujimori government. The electoral campaign, meanwhile, was waged in extremely negative and personalistic terms and took on both racial and class confrontation tones. It became a struggle between the "rich whites" and the "poor Indians,"[26] which exacerbated the existing polarization in the system. The political mudslinging and personal attacks, first by FREDEMO against APRA and President García, and then between the

Fujimori and Vargas Llosa teams, offended the average voter and undermined general faith in the political system.

> This is the worst political campaign that I have seen and heard until
> now. . . . I think that 90 percent of Peruvians share this sentiment with
> me. . . . If it continues this way, then it will not be anything extraordinary
> that the next president of Peru will be Mr. Fujimori. Why? There are
> many reasons . . . People are tired of traditional politics."I offer, I ask,
> you give me, tomorrow I forget you." . . . FREDEMO is using a language
> that by no means is fitting for a writer like Vargas Llosa. . . . Perhaps
> the most grave error was all the attacks directed at Alan García. Perhaps
> he is not the best president we have had, perhaps this chaotic situation
> is his fault . . . but he is and continues to be the president, who represents
> us and, above all, whom the majority of people elected not because he
> offered paradise, but because he won the hearts and affection of the
> "pueblo."[27]

The disillusion of the people, more than anything else, played into the hands
of Alberto Fujimori and was responsible for his victory. He attained 56.53
percent of the vote, against 33.92 percent for Vargas Llosa, on June 10, 1990.

The prospects for the Fujimori government, which came to power
with neither a program nor a governing team, were most unclear. Only a
few weeks before his inauguration, there was no coherent team of advisors, no key appointments had yet been made, and Fujimori's own political
tendencies were not clear. His advisors were from diverse sides of the
political spectrum, and he had made no clear choice between them, as they
themselves admitted.[28] At the same time he made it clear that he would
reestablish relations with the international financial community, and that
he was not interested in a radical economic program. How he would
reconcile those goals—in a context of hyperinflation—with his promise
not to implement a shock stabilization plan was obscure at best.[29]

Recent comparative work on successful stabilization efforts and on
macroeconomic stability more generally points to a variety of political
factors that are critical. The role of the institutional arrangements, and in
particular the party systems, is singled out. "Macroeconomic stability is
most precarious, and stabilization most likely to be delayed, where the
party system is fragmented or polarized."30 In 1990 Peru's political spectrum and party system were fragmented and polarized to an unprecedented
degree. Peru was in a critical situation, in which there was little margin left
for error, for flawed economic policymaking, for bad government. Economist Jeffrey Sachs, during a visit to Lima following the June elections,
described the country as "slipping away from the rest of the world."31

The 1990 electoral results reflect the populace's total dissatisfaction
and lack of faith in traditional politicians and parties. Clearly
FREDEMO's dogmatic and heavy-handed political conduct were partially to blame for undermining that faith, as were a succession of weak or

inept governments for the past several decades. Yet in the short term the disastrous failure of APRA, Peru's only well-institutionalized political party, was most directly to blame. It was not only the crisis that mattered, but also the underlying reasons for its severity. The way in which García and APRA governed and interacted with society resulted in the total alienation of society from polity. The rejection of traditional parties clearly does not necessarily represent a rejection of the democratic system. Instead it reflects an ongoing evolution of participation occurring outside the realm of traditional political institutions,[32] and the increased importance in society of autonomous local groups and the informal economy. That electoral results reflect this phenomenon should be no surprise, as it has been the subject of academic analysis in the social and economic fields for at least a decade. One could conclude that the results of the 1990 elections merely demonstrate the exacerbation, from 1985 to 1990, of a preexisting breach between state and society.

Yet the results also show a crisis of representation. Political parties play a fundamental representative role in virtually all consolidated democracies; their utility in formulating and channeling demands in both directions—from society to state and from state to society—is irreplaceable. In Peru, as in many developing countries, demands upon the state have undeniably far outpaced its ability to respond. Thus the role of parties in channeling those demands—and, through the party platform or doctrine, indicating their relative importance—is critical.

Parties also play a role in providing a guarantee of institutional stability for important nondemocratic actors such as the military. The Peruvian military itself noted the importance of a strong institutionalized party during the transition to democracy in 1978–1980, and turned to APRA. It is likely that at the height of the crisis of confidence in the García government, the military was to some extent deterred from intervening by the assurance that, regardless of what García did, the APRA party would retain some semblance of control over the government—which is exactly what happened. But a similar scenario in the Fujimori government would result in the disintegration of a governing coalition that has no underlying institutional base to guarantee the continued functioning of the state. Such a scenario would provide increased incentive for the military to step in to fill that role as a last resort, the direction that events took (see the postscript on page 218).

In Peru dogmatic politics, on all sides of the political spectrum— whether the right's intransigent adherence to liberal or neoliberal economics, or APRA's belief that it was the only solution, or the left's endless debates and splits over Mao versus Trotsky, or García's implementing his "very own" revolution by nationalizing the banks—has resulted in a polity that is hopelessly out of touch with the needs of its society, and thus in parties that are unable to fulfil their representative function. The 1990 elections signified a rejection of dogmatic ideology, of traditional politicians, and of established parties, considerably weakening their position in the near future. APRA in particular was unable to play its role as a reformist party: providing the link between state and society, and an organized base of support for progressive macroeconomic policy. Democratic consolidation is, at least in the short term, an elusive goal, at any rate insofar as it is broadly defined as the establishment of stable political institutions and progress toward socioeconomic equality.

On the other hand, the rejection of not just APRA but of all political parties by the Peruvian electorate is bound to create an impetus for reform within political parties themselves. APRA, for the many reasons detailed here, may not be the party that is most adept at adapting to the changing needs of Peruvian society. Yet it remains the country's oldest and only truly institutionalized party: APRA received more votes—almost 20 percent—than any other single political party, as opposed to front, in the 1990 elections. It clearly has a role to play in the democratic consolidation in the future, despite its dramatic failure during its tenure in power.

The prospects for democratic consolidation remain tenuous at best, in part because of the severity of the economic crisis facing Peru, but even more so because of the extent of the challenge that armed insurrection poses to the democratic system and indeed to social order. The most dogmatic force in Peruvian politics is Sendero Luminoso, whose utmost goal is to destroy all established civil institutions. The death and destruction that Sendero has wreaked on Peru has not only retarded the development process, but has changed the entire nature of society to one where violence is an accepted norm. Yet Sendero's existence in a perverse way acts as a force in favor of democratic government, as almost all political rivals, most of the left and the military included, can unite, at least in principle, against the threat to democracy and civil society posed by the group.

THE CHALLENGE FROM THE ARMED LEFT

"Aprismo is Marxist because it fully utilizes historical materialism; because it accepts class struggle in principle . . . because it recognizes the possibility of the revolutionary use of violence."[33] The existence of violent revolutionary movements in Peru poses a challenge to any government in terms of confrontation, but a more complex ideological challenge to a government, like APRA's, that itself claims to be revolutionary. APRA could not both be a revolutionary party and pursue the same counterterrorism strategy as a right-wing government. This put the party in a difficult position when faced with the threat from a movement as vengeful and extreme as Sendero Luminoso, whose primary targets were APRA government officials and functionaries. In addition, another insurrectionary movement, the MRTA, led by a former aprista, launched armed struggle in the jungle region of the country in November 1987. This movement, a more conventional and less ruthless one than Sendero, found a great deal of support among the youth of APRA and the IU, as well as in the IU's more radical wing. This created a dilemma for the APRA government, which needed a support base among these radical groups. To further complicate matters, a paramilitary squad with links to the armed forces and the aprista minister of the interior, the Comando Rodrigo Franco, surfaced in July 1988. The group's main targets were strong critics of the government or of military human rights abuses. Like the Peronist party in Argentina in the mid-1970s, APRA found itself challenged by political violence of the right and the left, some of it from within its own ranks. The government's, and the party's, response was both incoherent and insufficient.

Sendero Luminoso is the most brutal and fanatical guerrilla group in Latin America and has succeeded in waging virtual civil war in the nation's southern sierra region. When Alan García took over in 1985, Sendero Luminoso's attacks coupled with the military's reprisals had taken over 5,000 lives. By June 1990 that toll had reached 17,119. Between 1980 and 1985 political violence took more lives in Peru than in any other Latin American nation save El Salvador, with official estimates at over 6,000 but others as high as 10,000. According to some sources, Peru in 1989 had the worst record in the world in terms of "disappearances."[34] In the meantime the other guerrilla group, the MRTA, which at the start of the García government was responsible only for a few sporadic urban bombings, grew so in size and strength that by the fall of 1987 it had military control of an entire province in Peru's jungle region. Most government and external observers agreed that terrorism was the nation's most pressing problem.

The García government came to power promising to take a different approach than the Belaúnde government's "letting loose" of the military. García both issued warnings to the military by firing three top generals after the massacre of seventy-five citizens[35] and launched several policies to improve living standards in the sierra—the stronghold of Sendero. For the first time in Peru's history, the terms of trade were turned in favor of Andean agriculture, and the Agrarian Bank instituted a policy of providing favorable credit to Andean farmers; loans to campesinos in the Ayacucho region rose by 380 percent from 1985 to 1986.[36] The García government also launched a series of unprecedented public dialogs, called Rimanacuy, between campesino leaders and government officials. Because of the uncompromising nature of Sendero, and the lack of follow-up on the part of the government, these initiatives had little impact on the spread of terrorism and soon ran out of steam.

The military's frustration with the advance of the guerrillas, meanwhile, was demonstrated by the massacre of over 250 imprisoned terrorists during a June 1986 uprising in Lima's prisons. While García's image suffered at the time, it suffered more as Sendero made continued advances and its victims included Rodrigo Franco, one of the brightest young apristas, slated to be the head of the Central Bank, and almost a dozen APRA mayors. By 1988 the cycle of violence was clearly out of hand. The judicial system was also victim, as lawyers and judges who ruled against terrorists became common assassination targets. García was forced to instal a retired Navy admiral, known as a hawk, as interior minister. In his July 1988 innaugural address, the main measures announced by García—in contrast to the banks nationalization of the previous year—were a toughening of antiterrorist laws, making it illegal to be associated with or to apologize for terrorist groups, and making holding unlicensed weapons or explosives a major offense.[37] Indicative of the inconsistency of approach was that only a month before, in what was supposed to be an off-the-record speech to APRA youth but soon made the front pages of the national press, García had lauded the revolutionary devotion of Sendero militants. "Mistaken or not, the senderista has what we do not have: mystique and dedication. . . . Those people have what merits our respect and my own personal admiration because they are, whether you like it or not, militants. Fanatics they call them. I believe that they have mystique and it is part of our self-criticism, compañeros, to know how to recognize that whoever, subordinated or not, gives himself to death, gives his life, has mystique."[38] The speech was, as could be expected, extremely controversial, and exposed the dilemma that APRA faced in trying to maintain its image as a revolutionary party while actively involved in a war against leftist revolutionaries. Despite initial hopes that the APRA government would introduce the nonmilitary component that was necessary to combat the growth of insurrectionary activity, the efforts were short-lived, much in the same way that innovation and initiative faded on the economic front. The strength and scope of the insurrectionary groups, on the other hand, particularly of Sendero, grew to a debilitating level.

Sendero Luminoso

"'It all began like a game,' say the lyrics of a popular song, which were more . . . appropriate to describe the armed movement . . . Sendero Luminoso. . . . A few electric towers over there, a few bombs over here—they did not predict or perceive the exponential dimensions that the actions would achieve, which began in a few Ayacucho provinces . . . reaching in reality a disquieting presence at the national level. Today the name of Sendero Luminoso is known around the world."[39]

Sendero Luminoso, or Shining Path, derives its name from a state-

ment made by Peru's first Communist ideologue and initially a collaborator of Haya de la Torre, Jose Carlos Mariátegui: "Marxism-Leninism will
open the shining path to revolution."[40] Sendero's ideology takes both from
Mariátegui's interpretation of Peruvian realities and the need to incorporate Indians as equal citizens in all spheres, and from Mao's focus on the
rural peasant as a basis for Communist revolution and future society. The
group professes to be the legitimate revolutionary representative of the
Peruvian people. While the origins of Sendero Luminoso are beyond the
scope of this study, and are well documented elsewhere,[41] it is relevant
here that the group's ruthlessness, its willingness to commit atrocities
against members of its own ethnic group and economic class, and its
distortions of indigenous culture and ritual, coupled with its unique blend
of Maoist and Mariáteguista ideology and its looking back to a mythical
Inca golden age, make it impossible to find a counterpart for the group in
Latin America. The comparison most often made is with Cambodia's
Khmer Rouge, which, while perhaps not totally accurate, points to the
formidable challenge for any government and society facing a group of
such an extreme nature.

By the mid-1980s, Sendero was a force to be reckoned with, not only
on its original rural turf, but on that of the political parties and the labor
and popular organizations that they traditionally competed for. The
movement had approximately five thousand members, and at least half of
them were women. Sendero had grown from a local, scarcely known
guerrilla movement in the early 1980s to an internationally renowned
revolutionary force, with an affiliated newspaper, El Diario, and logistical
support group—Socorro Popular, numbering as many as five hundred—in
Lima. The number of deaths from terrorist-related violence grew ever
greater after Sendero's decision to expand into urban arenas, with the toll
for 1988 at approximately two thousand and for 1989 at over three
thousand. The amount of territory controlled by the group increased to
alarming levels. At least one-third of the country was in a state of emergency throughout the course of the APRA regime. In such areas civil
authority is totally subordinate to the power struggles between Sendero
and the armed forces. In May 1989 the group displayed its strength with
the first of a series of armed strikes that paralyzed all the departments
surrounding Lima for over twenty-four hours, and in July with an attack
that paralyzed the center of the capital.[42] It subsequently staged sporadic
raids in Lima, with varying degrees of success.

A fundamental part of Sendero's strategy for 1989–1990 was to sabotage the municipal and presidential elections. In a ruthless campaign,
Sendero made all local elected officials or candidates for electoral office
its targets. From 1985 to 1989 the group assassinated forty-five mayors,
and in a campaign of violence prior to the 1989 municipal elections over
120 elected officials or municipal candidates were killed, resulting in the

withdrawal of approximately five hundred potential runners.[43] In both the municipal and presidential elections the group threatened to chop the index fingers off all those who voted. Yet despite Sendero's brutal challenge, elections were successfully held, although null and blank voting and absenteeism were quite high in the emergency zones where Sendero's presence was the strongest, Ayacucho in particular.[44] Indeed, it was rumored after the 1990 elections that there were rifts within the group, with one faction considering abandoning armed struggle because of the failure to successfully sabotage the electoral process.[45] It is difficult to assess the accuracy of these rumors; suffice it to say that despite the possibility of a split, by the end of APRA's tenure in power Sendero Luminoso remained a formidable threat with a significant capacity to disrupt civil society.

While Sendero's armed activities coincided with the 1980 transition to democracy, the group had made substantial inroads during the Belaúnde years, in part because of the ruthless nature of the counterinsurgency campaign.[46] Yet the initially popular García government was much more resistant to the group. In 1985 García took Ayacucho, Sendero's stronghold, with 62 percent of the vote, and null and blank voting fell dramatically. His victory was a reflection of APRA's grassroots campaigning and quite likely of the peasantry's rejection of Sendero for a perceived better option. Sendero responded by stepping up its activities, particularly in Lima. The group was threatened more by a democratic government, particularly by a popular one, than by dictatorship; no revolutionary guerrilla group has ever overthrown a genuinely elected democracy. Belaúnde's neoconservatism created far less of a challenge for Sendero than did the populist García and his "false revolution." Sendero seeks to precipitate a military coup, so as to polarize society further, a strategy that is frustrated by the success of democracy. Sendero labeled APRA corporatist and co-optative, and programs such as the PAIT as a means of popular control.[47]

Sendero is most threatened by any organization capable of attaining popular appeal, and thus APRA and IU functionaries, particularly in programs such as the PAIT, as well as popular organization leaders in mothers' clubs, communal kitchens, and the like were key targets in Sendero's urban strategy. Other targets were members of the Catholic clergy; the first clergy member was killed in Ayacucho in 1987, while saying mass on Guzmán's birthday.[48] Clergy members working in Lima's pueblos jóvenes have also been killed.[49] The attack on the few organizations esteemed highly by the poor most likely frustrates the group's goal of expanding its urban popular support base.

Nonetheless, as part of its urban strategy, Sendero has made substantial headway in Lima's universities and developed an affiliated labor group, the Movimiento de Trabajadores Clasistas (MOTC). In elections at San Marcos in May 1988, for example, the student group that sympathized with Sendero attained the most votes, and the APRA organization, ARE, the least.[50] Walls at most universities are covered with pro-Sendero slogans, and a February 1987 raid on several Lima universities uncovered caches of homemade bombs and other weapons.[51] Sendero's inroads in the union movement have also been notable. The MOTC virtually controls a whole region of Lima workers, those of the Carretera Central, and in April 1988, when the MOTC convened the first plenary meeting of the Carretera's Classist Workers, support for the *guerra popular* was guaranteed.[52] During the January 1988 general strike senderistas clashed with members of the CGTP in Lima's Plaza Dos de Mayo.[53] The pro-Senderista newspaper, *El Diario*, meanwhile, sold approximately five thousand copies daily until mid-1988, when it could no longer find a publisher.[54]

The number of actors in the battle has grown steadily year by year, as has the territory Sendero controls. This expansion created an even greater administrative problem for the government. Sendero effectively sabotaged all development efforts in the Ayacucho region.[55] It terrorized the judicial system by assassinating judges who ruled against its members in trials to such an extent that at the trial of Osman Morote, the supposed number-two man of the movement, whose participation in several assassinations was well documented, the judge found insufficient evidence to convict him. The lawyer who represented Morote, meanwhile, was assassinated shortly after by the Comando Rodrigo Franco. The situation is increasingly one of unrestrained violence.[56]

While the APRA government could clearly be blamed for inconsistency and lack of initiative in combating the movement, its failures also stemmed from Sendero's brutal and uncompromising nature and its commitment to destroying existing society. No party or government, particularly one that claimed to be revolutionary in its origins, would have an easy task of coping with the group. It seems capable not only of killing its targets, but also of preempting any legal or administrative programs to combat it. Whatever the outcome of the civil war scenario that Peruvian society has become, it will involve substantial bloodshed. There is only the hope that, as one IU member posited, "the more Sendero succeeds, the more society will be opposed to it."[57]

Movimiento Revolucionario Tupac Amaru

Sendero does not have the monopoly on insurrectionary activity. A major challenge to the government was posed by the launching of full-scale activities by the MRTA in late 1987. The MRTA, a more conventional guerrilla movement, had quite a bit of popular appeal to segments of the left and in particular to the youths of APRA and the IU. The leader of the movement was an ex-aprista who had held a coveted place in Haya's Buro de Conjunciones, with García. For young apristas who were convinced that the government was by no means revolutionary enough, the movement had a certain attraction and adventurous quality. No longer did APRA youth have to look to the mid-1960s guerrillas for genuine revolutionaries who had emerged from their party; they now had the option of participating directly, and indeed several members deserted to join the MRTA.[58] As the movement is young, middle class, and urban-based, its members were the contemporaries of the IU and APRA youths. In the case of the MRTA the contradictions raised by APRA's history of insurrection and revolutionary doctrine were felt more strongly than in that of Sendero. Alan García's statement in a 1988 speech to APRA youth is telling. "With Polay I had an alliance. He did not have the strength to remain in the party because he succumbed to impatience. . . . If he had remained within the party, he would be a leader."[59]

The MRTA initiated action in June 1984 with an assault on a bank, and its official slogan is "the war against the antipopular government and yankee imperialism."[60] From the beginning the MRTA projected an image different from Sendero's. Its actions were primarily to attract attention, and it avoided spilling blood, on principle. When an MRTA bomb killed a policeman in front of the Uruguayan Embassy it sent an apology. The MRTA held clandestine press conferences, took over radio stations to transmit messages, and focused on activities such as dynamite explosions and car bombs to attract attention. The ideology that the MRTA espouses is closer to the traditional Latin American guerrilla *foco* theory: the idea that a small group of guerrillas can act as the spark for revolution. Its heroes include Luis de la Puente Uceda, an ex-aprista who joined the APRA Rebelde and fought with the guerrillas in the sierra in the mid-1960s. The movement's strategy and organization is comparable to that of the *sandinistas* and the Frente Marxista de Libertad Nacional (FMLN), and it purports to have affinity with the M-19 in Colombia and Alfaro Vive in Ecuador.[61] The MRTA's ideology has links with that of the APRA Rebelde of the 1960s: Marxism-Leninism with analysis based on Peru's realities. It claimed that García was the most demagogic and dishonest president in the nation's history.[62] APRA's most vociferous enemies, like the dissident Carlos Delgado, are often the products of its own ranks.

The current leader of the MRTA, Víctor Polay Campos, fits into a Peruvian phenomenon of leftist politicians turned guerrilla, like de la Puente Uceda, or of guerrilla leaders turned politician, such as Hugo Blanco or Carlos Malpica of the IU, both of whom were guerrillas in the mid-1960s. Polay Campos comes from an aprista family; his father was an APRA congressional deputy in the 1960s, and Polay himself was secretary for external relations for the CUA, as well as being in the Buro de Conjunciones. His CUA group apparently was extremely militant. In 1973 Polay, along with seventeen others, was arrested for possessing explosives;

he was then sent by the party to Spain and France to study sociology—a path remarkably similar to Alan García's own. The two were rumored to have encountered each other in Europe at one point. Polay returned to Peru in 1985, convinced that Marxism-Leninism and not APRA was the solution.[63]

Polay Campos launched the operation that put the MRTA into the public eye in October 1987. The MRTA was able to quickly take control of the city of Juanjui and some of its environs in the San Martín department. President García, who had dismissed initial reports of the campaign as unimportant, was forced to send in the army and declare the entire department in a state of emergency. Government attempts to negotiate were thwarted by poor planning, and eventually the guerrillas were dispersed although not defeated by the military.[64] The group was bold and oriented toward the public eye, inviting members of the press to visit its operations when it took control of Juanjui.[65]

The aprista youth movement has a great deal of sympathy for the MRTA if not direct ties. "Aprista youth are very radical. If discipline is disrupted, be it through a military coup or through disillusion, they could easily change over to terrorism and guerrilla activity. . . . APRA is the *sierra maestra* of the contemporary Peruvian guerrilla."[66] Javier Díez Canseco's PUM movement has direct links to the group and supports it formally in parliament. This wing of the IU and the MRTA leaders both started as radicalized velasquistas[67] with links to the part of the APRA Rebelde that became the MIR in 1961. Offshoots of this group formed both the PUM and the MIR of the early 1980s, which is a substantial part of the MRTA. Among the APRA Rebelde/MIR group were two senators in Congress: Carlos Malpica of the IU; and Javier Valle Riestra, an aprista.[68] The sympathy for the MRTA's cause demonstrates the radicalized and complex political context within which the APRA government had to operate. The dilemma that APRA was in was not unlike that of the Peronists in Argentina in the 1970s, when they were faced with left- and right-wing violence, some of it from within their own ranks. Indeed, Perón tacitly encouraged the Montoneros from his exile in Madrid and then ordered his government to repress them when their activities were no longer useful to him. This is analogous to García's telling APRA youth that he admired the dedication that senderistas had and that he had had an alliance with Polay Campos, and then announcing to the nation that terrorism was Peru's number-one problem.

The MRTA's popular appeal contrasts with the racially oriented, rigid solution proposed by Sendero, which is unlikely to ever be acceptable on a broad scale in a society as complex culturally, racially, and ideologically as Peru's. Sendero's vision is alien even to former guerrillas, such as Héctor Bejar. "I never imagined, sincerely, that this kind of terrorism would be applied . . . in Peru."[69] Yet Sendero posed a much greater challenge militarily, and as the challenge increased on the one hand and public opinion in general favored increased repression of insurrectionary groups on the other, the government gave the armed forces an even freer rein (see the postscript on page 218).

Comando Rodrigo Franco

A significant indication that the situation had deteriorated into unrestrained violence was the emergence of a paramilitary squad, the Comando Rodrigo Franco, with links to APRA, to the armed forces, and even directly to the interior minister, Agustín Mantilla. About the same time that García gave his July 1988 speech declaring terrorism the country's primary problem, there was a visible resurgence of APRA-linked paramilitary squads, the búfalos. APRA's attitude to armed insurrection has historically been ambiguous, as was demonstrated by Haya de la Torre's tacit support for the student uprisings in February 1975 and apristas' participation in the 1948 military revolts. The influence of this heritage was demonstrated by the appeal that the MRTA had among APRA youth. There were several cases of isolated violence involving squadrons prior to 1988. Most publicized were a supposedly aprista bombing of the headquarters of the pro-Sendero paper, *El Diario;* the discovery of large caches of weapons and the assault on a *Caretas* journalist trying to investigate the Instituto Peruano de Seguridad Social;[70] and the discovery of large quantities of unregistered weapons being imported from North Korea, where APRA had links, by the then vice-minister of the interior, Mantilla,[71] who was known for his entourage of búfalos. Javier Valle Riestra, a high-ranking senator with a strong interest in human rights issues, admitted that "of course everyone knew that the party had *búfalos,*"[72] but maintained that a party had a right to protect itself. As Sendero-led violence grew more rampant in 1988, there was purportedly an intraparty campaign, led by Haya's former secretary, Jorge Idiaquez, to train more paramilitary types.[73]

The Comando Rodrigo Franco surfaced in July 1988. The command took its name "in honor" of the bright young aprista functionary killed by Sendero and was widely believed to have links to Mantilla—who became minister of the interior in May 1989—and to elements of the armed forces and the police. The group vowed to avenge all aprista victims of Sendero and was allegedly responsible for the murders of Manuel Febres, the defense lawyer of Sendero's Osman Morote; Saul Cantoral, the head of the powerful miners' union; and Arroyo Mio, a left-wing congressman, among others. The command also issued death threats to a special attorney investigating a military massacre at Cayara as well as to journalists of all political stripes critical of the government.[74]

The surge of government- and armed forces-linked violence and the dangerous deterioration of the social situation, in which the legitimacy of judicial and political institutions was increasingly called into question, was perpetrated to a large extent by the APRA's ambiguous stance on insurrectionary violence. As is noted in the first chapter, parties that are formed outside the parliamentary system—as most mass parties are—tend to be more hierarchically structured and centralized, in general place lower value on the constitutional system per se, and thus are more likely themselves to resort to violence, particularly if they have totalitarian or utopian ideologies. Exacerbating this tendency are the artificial cleavages that such parties often introduce into public opinion. Again this description fits not only APRA, but also the Peronists in the 1973–1976 era. As in the case of Agustín Mantilla in Peru, paramilitary squads had direct links to none other than the Peronist minister of the interior, López Rega, in Argentina. A major difference was, however, that in the Peruvian case, for a variety of reasons, the military was reluctant to take direct control of the government. There is no doubt, however, that in the chaos of the latter half of the APRA regime the de facto power of the armed forces increased.

THE APRA GOVERNMENT AND THE MILITARY

At least brief mention must be made of the APRA government's relationship with the armed forces. As has been discussed previously, at the beginning of his term García challenged the military over human rights abuses, firing three top generals, and on the issue of the military's budgetary autonomy, halving an order for French Mirages.[75] García further challenged the armed forces' autonomy with the creation of a Defense Ministry, placing all three wings of the military under the command of a single state agency. Yet the armed forces were gradually to reassert their autonomy. The military refrained, at least up to the end of APRA's term, from direct intervention, partly because of its bitter experience in power at the end of the 1970s and partly because of its perception of popular opposition to a military government. However, its de facto power increased as the government lost authority and control in the face of severe economic crisis and the escalation of insurgent violence.

The highly controversial proposal to create a Defense Ministry, which would maintain control over the three branches of the armed forces, was signed into law in April 1987 after a lengthy debate in Congress. It was strongly opposed by most high-level officers, as it promised to curtail significantly the autonomy of the three branches and their rights to separate budgets, and promised to give the government more direct control over counterinsurgency policy.[76] The opposition of the air force was made clear in early April, when its jets "buzzed" the government palace amid rumors of a possible coup. Although the leader of the air force rebellion was fired,[77] the government's control over the military through the Defense Ministry remained questionable, as a retired general rather than a civilian was appointed as minister.[78]

As political incoherence increased and economic crisis set in by 1988, the military attained de facto control over most regions of the country where there was an insurgent threat, even those that were not officially emergency zones. In the face of widespread assassination of APRA regional officials by Sendero in the Andean region, and the resignations in December 1988 of dozens of Andean mayors[79] who complained of lack of police protection from insurgents, the exercise of local government was increasingly left to the armed forces. Incidents such as the dismissal in late 1988 of Carlos Enrique Escobar, a government attorney who demonstrated that the armed forces were responsible for a massacre of over a dozen civilians in Cayara,[80] is a case in point. Also telling is that in July 1988, a retired naval admiral, Juan Soría—known as a hawk—was named interior minister.

The same contradictions that prevented APRA from implementing a coherent counterinsurgency strategy also jeopardized its relations with the armed forces. Antiaprismo had ceased to be a significant factor in civilian-military relations, as was shown by the aforementioned close collaboration of military officers with APRA's Plan de Gobierno team in the early 1980s. However, the APRA government's contradictory stances on armed insurrection fueled the armed forces' resentment of civilian direction of the counterinsurgency war. An example of APRA's contradictory behavior occurred at the time of the capture of Víctor Polay Campos in early 1989. Within hours of his arrival at the Dirección Contra Terrorismo (DIRCOTE) offices in Lima, Polay received a personal visit from Prime Minister Villanueva to ensure that he was not being mistreated. Although Villanueva was acting in response to a request from Polay's father, a former aprista deputy and personal friend,[81] his visit, and the public scandal it created, hardly improved the government's relations with the armed forces.

By late 1988 and early 1989 rumors of a coup were rampant. In January 1989 there was a mass resignation of over two thousand officers in protest of declining salary levels, a supposed movement in favor of a coup had been discovered, and the US ambassador had issued a public warning in which he stated that the United States was strongly opposed to any form of military intervention. Despite the rumors, there was no obvious leader of a coup movement within the upper ranks of the military,[82] in part a product of the military's bitter experience with power in the late 1970s, and also because there was little appetite to take power in a Peru so beset by economic and political problems. Perhaps most important was the widespread perception, both among the armed forces and among the civilian polity, that the population was adamantly opposed to a military government. According to a recent study of civilian and military attitudes by Cynthia McClintock, "by virtually all indications, every Peruvian social group now favors democratic political regime for Peru."[83] While 11 percent of those polled in 1982 favored a military government, only 6 percent did in April 1987.[84] While opinions may have altered slightly with the onset of severe economic crisis in 1988, it seems that the military option, unlike the "revolutionary" one, remained discredited among most Peruvians. This is in part a result of recent experience with the military's performance in power, the persistence of civilian government for almost a decade, and trends toward democratization in the region as a whole. Finally, there is the widespread perception that Sendero aims to provoke a coup with the aim of further polarizing society into civil war. It is widely believed that not only Sendero and the MRTA, but also significant sectors of the IU and APRA leadership and youth, would join armed struggle against a military regime.[85] Yet, while there are significant factors weighing against direct military intervention, the incoherence of the government in the face of a growing insurgent threat and economic chaos led to the military's extending its de facto control.

APRA's successor, Alberto Fujimori, also had to contend with the specter of military intervention. The social and economic situation at the end of APRA's tenure in power was the gravest in Peru's history, something that the armed forces are well aware of. There is also an important difference between the APRA government and its successor: the Fujimori government has no institutional base. While there were times when the García government lost all direction and coherence, with García himself in seclusion, there was always the institutional base of the party for the government to fall back on. The military itself pointed to the need for such a base at the time of transition in 1978–1980 and turned to APRA to play that role. The absence of such a base in the case of the new government signifies that in the case of a loss of leadership coherence or the collapse of a governing coalition, there will be more impetus for the military to step in and fill that institutional role (see the postscript on page 218).

The position of APRA, a reformist party challenged by a variety of insurgent revolutionary groups, was indeed a difficult one. Yet certain traits of the party made that position virtually untenable: its sectarian and hierarchical structure and the obstacles to dealing with society posed by that structure; its revolutionary legacy and ambiguous attitude to the use of violence; and the presence of radical sectors within its ranks. The need to cope with radical sentiments—both within and outside APRA—in part explains García's rationale in opting for a move such as the banks nationalization. Yet the urgent need for social reform made it even more important that the government not waste its precious few political cards, as APRA did, with lack of preparation, poor timing, and incoherent policy. APRA's political behavior, coupled with its sectarian nature, clearly forfeited any chance at cooperation with the opposition, and the system grew increasingly polarized. In the meantime the ideological challenge posed by APRA's revolutionary doctrine, particularly as interpreted by its more radical sectors, resulted in an inconsistent approach and an absence of policy in the face of insurrection. On the one hand García praised Sendero's dedication and willingness to die, and on the other increasingly gave the armed forces free rein. Violence from within the party's own ranks both undermined the legitimacy of state institutions and also exacerbated the rifts between the party—and the state mechanisms that it controlled—and civil society. The extent to which those rifts had grown was demonstrated by the results of the 1990 elections, in which not just APRA but all political parties with any ties to the established state were rejected.

A true revolution in Peru would substantially improve the fate of the poor, something that none of the "revolutionary" alternatives seems capable of doing. The APRA government's attempts, and the manner in which those attempts reflect traits inherent to the party, are the subject of the next chapter.

8

APRA and the Marginalized

URBAN POVERTY AND THE INFORMAL SECTOR

A central aspect of APRA's role in democratic reform was its addressing of the needs of Peru's large and continuously growing poor and marginalized population. Marginalization implies the exclusion of certain sectors of the population from participation in the socioeconomic change that occurs as a developing country industrializes its economy. This marginalized part of the population—often called the informal sector because of its peripheral relation to the modern economy—spans both rural and urban spheres. The "informal sector" is by origin an economic term, yet it describes both social and political realities as well. In rural regions the informal sector primarily refers to the peasants or campesinos who own little or no land, continue to use traditional agricultural methods, and exist at the bare subsistence level. In urban regions the term is a more comprehensive one and tends to encompass the ever-growing mass of urban poor, in large part migrants from rural areas, who primarily inhabit the pueblos jóvenes (shantytowns) and often survive on a day-to-day subsistence income derived from self-generated sales or service activities. Some of the self-employed, meanwhile, are able to earn incomes that are often quite a bit higher than the minimum wage. The terms *marginalized, urban poor,* and *informal sector* are often used interchangeably; all attempt, although none adequately, to describe the complex, heterogeneous, and interacting phenomena that have resulted in Peru's having the largest informal economy in Latin America, and a correspondingly high percentage of the population living in deplorable conditions in the pueblos jóvenes. As is noted in the first chapter, such a large percentage of the people living in a precarious legal as well as economic situation has substantial impact on societies and polities. The marginalized population has attracted the attention of academics and politicians alike, and has been looked upon both as the potential force for social transformation and as a target for clientelistic manipulation. The relationship that political parties have with this sector of society is by no means a simple or clear-cut one.

APRA, in its campaign, avoided using terms that implied class confrontation and adopted the term *marginalized* for this vast and heteroge-

Map 8.1 Lima

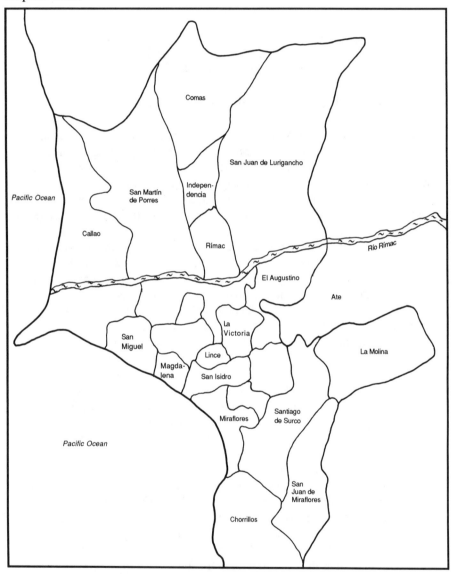

neous group—a tactic previously used by the Christian Democrats in Chile. García, upon coming to office, repeatedly declared that the nation's marginalized (70 percent of the total population according to his social pyramid) were to be the priority of his administration.

The García government implemented its policies for the marginalized in its first few months in power. In the rural arena it attempted to shift the terms of trade in favor of traditional agrarian products. The government embarked on an active credit extension program and conducted a series of government-sponsored dialogs with campesino leaders around the country. To its credit, the García government was the first in the nation's history to concentrate on and improve the terms of trade for the farmers of the Andean region. The actual shift, however, was mainly the result of its overall economic policy of freezing prices for many manufactured and basic goods, while floating those of Andean agricultural products;[1] thus the improvements were eroded with an end to the price freeze and the onset of hyperinflation. On the urban side the government implemented a variety of programs directed at the marginalized, the most important of which were the Programa de Apoyo de Ingreso Temporal (PAIT), an emergency employment program; the Programa de Apoyo Directo (PAD), which attempted to provide organizational support to pueblos jóvenes; and the Instituto para Desarrollo del Sector Informal (IDESI), a semiautonomous institute that was set up to provide credit to informal sector entrepreneurs.[2]

For two reasons the focus here will be on APRA's policies concerning the urban poor. The first is a practical one that stems from the existence of numerous programs—both of the APRA government and of its predecessors—and the enhanced feasibility of research in urban areas. The second stems from the dynamic characteristic of urban poverty in Peru. Concurrent with a dramatic increase in the numbers of urban poor in the past few decades is the emergence of an interest on the part of political leaders and parties, originating with APRA in the 1940s, in building a support base in this group. The current APRA's focus on the urban informal sector as a part of its overall economic strategy and as the central aspect of its policy toward the urban poor differed, in conception at least, from that of its predecessors, who primarily attempted political co-optation and did not make the poor a central point of economic strategy. A key underlying issue throughout the entire analysis is whether APRA made a genuine attempt to incorporate the marginalized population into the polity and economy; or whether APRA's was, like previous attempts, populist and co-optative. The analysis of how that conception translated into policy reveals a great deal about APRA's relations with the marginalized, a critical aspect of party-society relations in countries where a significant percentage of the population earns its living in the informal sector. Prior to examining APRA government's policies, it is necessary to describe briefly Peru's urban informal sector and its relation to the pueblos jóvenes, as well as the political behavior of those pueblos.

While poverty is an ambiguous term, a working definition is necessary. Absolute poverty is the condition of earning insufficient income to permit the consumption of adequate food and nonfood items.[3] A 1971/72 household survey of Peru stated that an estimated 31 percent of the total population lived in conditions of absolute poverty, with 14 percent of them in Lima and 52 percent in the southern sierra. Adverse economic trends from 1975 to 1990 suggest a worsening of these conditions, with estimates ranging from one-half to two-thirds of all households. The bulk of the deterioration has been in urban areas and the coastal region around Lima.[4] While rural poverty in many ways implies worse conditions, it is a relatively stable phenomenon in terms of numbers and standards of living. Urban poverty, on the other hand, because of constant migration, is a rapidly growing phenomenon that is more directly affected by economic trends, as well as by its dynamic nature: an already inadequate urban infrastructure is unable to meet the increasing demands for basic services and employment.

The population of Peru has nearly doubled since 1960, reaching over 21 million in 1989. Population growth was largely concentrated in the urban sector, which grew from 4.5 to over 14 million in that period.[5] Almost half of Lima's population and 25 percent of the country's population lived in pueblos jóvenes in 1982, as opposed to 18 percent in 1972. Half of these people were without running water, two-fifths without access to water supply, and one-third without electricity.[6] In 1985, 33 percent of Lima's population had a per capita income of less than one-third of the minimum wage of 540 intis, or $36 dollars per month. Of these, approximately 50 percent were in the pueblos jóvenes. These standards have deteriorated markedly since then with the steep economic decline of the last few years of APRA government, and the dramatic adjustments that they necessitated. In 1991, for example, it was estimated that less than 10 percent of Lima's economically active population was adequately employed.[7]

A large part of the population of the pueblos jóvenes makes its living in the so-called informal sector, which employs up to 60 percent of Peru's work force.[8] Most informal enterprises are characterized by a very low capital-labor ratio, low productivity, and small scale.[9] The existence of this sector poses the dual challenges of a massive reserve labor force and barriers to its incorporation into the informal economy: insufficient demand and limited access to productive factors.[10] A basic tenet of APRA's reactivation strategy was to overcome these barriers by providing employment on a mass scale and raising consumption capacity. The main program through which this was to occur was the PAIT, and the population targeted was that of the pueblos jóvenes.

Urban poverty and the informal sector are interrelated. They are not, however, synonymous. Not all informal sector workers are poor, and not all inhabitants of the pueblos jóvenes work in the informal sector. The most direct correlation between the pueblos jóvenes and the informal sector—besides the number of workers who live in these new *barrios*—is the concurrent and analogous nature of the context in which they developed and the strategies that both continue to use to survive. Like informal sector enterprises, pueblos jóvenes begin as spontaneous and extralegal responses to a need to survive in the absence of existing alternatives.

What sets the pueblos jóvenes apart from the informal sector in general, however, is their high level of cohesiveness and community organization. The settlements are often the result of coordinated action to invade a piece of land. While there are pueblos jóvenes that are settled in an ad hoc fashion, as well as constant additional settlers who build on to existing settlements, the sense of cohesiveness seems to prevail in a great many. The very nature of their survival strategy—the occasional need to defend their invasion from dislocation efforts by the state; the need to provide protection from crime in the absence of municipal enforcement; the need to work collectively to obtain legal recognition and public services such as electricity and water service—all serve to reinforce communal organizational capacity.[11]

The reliance on communal organization—in the form of neighborhood directorates, communal kitchens, and mothers' clubs, for example— is both a type of survival strategy and a response to an economic and legal system with which their relationship is "un poco afuera, un poco adentro" (a little outside, a little inside).[12] Community organization has had many and diverse effects, from an increased awareness and independence of women, who are the most active participants, to increased politicization in general. The importance of such organizations increased as a response to the heightened awareness that resulted from the Velasco "revolution" and to the steady deterioration in living standards since 1975. Attitudes toward community organization vary, as in some cases the resort to a strategy of joint survival is viewed as an acceptance of a degradation of economic level and loss of independence. The impulse to organize as a community often coexists with the desire of the settlers for their individual, or at least their childrens', progression to a more prosperous neighborhood: a desire that exists at many socioeconomic levels. The desire for independent progress is in part reflected in the lesser number of men who participate in such organizations; a recent study conducted in shantytowns in Chile found that two-thirds of the participants in communal organizations were women.[13] Lipset asserts that when there is faith in the prospect of social mobility, there may be a corresponding reduction in collective efforts at social change.[14]

This sense of community and capacity to organize can be used to distinguish between the visible manifestation of urban poverty, pueblos jóvenes, and the economically based concept of the informal sector. The organizational and communal practices of the *pobladores* are autonomous and democratic ones, and therefore any government that purports to be reformist and participatory should respect the existing communal organizations. In this sense, the record of various political forces and parties, including APRA's, is checkered.

Political parties and leaders have been quick to note the organizational capacity of the pobladores and, since the existence of the first settlements, then called *barriadas,* have sought to tap the communal structure as a support base, or to convert and co-opt it entirely for political ends. The pobladores, on the other hand, have shown a remarkable capacity to use this political attention for their own pragmatic ends, as is demonstrated by their mercurial capacity to shift support to whatever political alternative offers them tangible benefits at the time. They do not in general tend to be either revolutionary or pessimistic in their outlook and behavior; rather they are primarily rural migrants who have left behind them even worse conditions and have minimal expectations for employment for themselves or education and better opportunities for their children.[15]

In the past decade the urban poor of Lima have become an increasingly important force in Peruvian politics because of the vast growth in their number and their increased politicization. The emergence of the left as a viable political force was vital to this politicization and was reflected in the 1983 election of Alfonso Barrantes as mayor of Lima. "There is no causal relationship [in Peru] between poverty and radical voting, as is the experience of many countries. . . . [Other elements] in the Peruvian case were the urban social movement and the political parties of the left."[16]

In economic terms, the urban poor of Peru grew substantially poorer from 1978 to 1985. This deterioration concurrent with increased politicization resulted in increased awareness and skepticism among the poor voting population. The voting record during that period demonstrates pragmatism, adaptability, and opportunism in response to their deteriorating conditions rather than allegiance to party or personality. Studies of the urban poor in Venezuela have shown that leadership juntas eventually fall apart unless they can deliver services, and patronage is key to party recruitment among the urban poor.[17] The use of votes to obtain desperately needed services merely reflects rational behavior on the part of the poor.

While in the 1978 municipal and 1983 Constituent Assembly elections the urban poor leaned significantly more to the left than Lima as a whole, in 1980 the majority voted for Belaúnde and in 1985 for García (see Table 8.1). This indicates that the tendency to vote for the left is easily swayed by perceived opportunities. In 1983 and 1985 the results were a rejection of the Belaúnde government's policies. The growth of support for APRA

Table 8.1 Voting Behavior: The Urban Poor

Voting for Parties in the Twelve Poorest Lima Districts: 1978–1990

Party	1978	1980	1980	1983	1985	1986	1989	1990
APRA	28.7	20.9	16.1	26.5	53.6	41.8	12.4	13.5
AP	—	50.2	33.3	8.7	4.3	—	—	—
PPC	22.5	8.0	11.6	11.5	8.8	13.3	—	—
IU	55.2	18.2	38.9	49.9	31.3	43.9	15.1	7.1
ASI	—	—	—	—	—	—	3.0	5.6
Obras	—	—	—	—	—	—	49.2	—
FREDEMO	—	—	—	—	—	—	16.4	22.7
Cambio 90	—	—	—	—	—	—	—	39.6

Victory, by District

District	1978	1980	1980	1983	1985	1986	1989
Ate	IU	AP	IU	IU	APRA	IU	FREDEMO
Carabayallo	IU	AP	IU	IU	APRA	APRA	IU
Comas	IU	AP	IU	IU	APRA	IU	IU
Chorillos	PPC	AP	AP	IU	APRA	APRA	IND
El Augustino	IU	AP	IU	IU	APRA	IU	IND
Independencia	IU	AP	IU	IU	APRA	IU	IU
Lurigancho	IU	AP	AP	IU	APRA	APRA	FREDEMO
San Juan de Lurigancho	IU	AP	IU	IU	APRA	APRA	IU
San Juan/Miraflores	IU	AP	IU	IU	APRA	IU	FREDEMO
San Martín de Porres	IU	AP	IU	IU	APRA	IU	IND
Villa Maria del Triunfo	IU	AP	IU	IU	APRA	APRA	IU
Villa El Salvador	—	—	—	IU	APRA	IU	IU

Voting in San Juan de Lurigancho, 1990

Party	First Round	Second Round
Cambio 90	40.72	62.74
FREDEMO	22.16	30.70
APRA	12.20	
IU	7.60	
ASI	4.78	
Others	1.92	
Null/blank	10.62	

Sources: Fernando Tuesta Soldevilla, "Pobreza urbana y participación política: classes populares y cambios electorales en Lima" (unpublished manuscript, DESCO, Lima, 1988); *Qué Hacer* 62 (December 1989–January 1990); "El voto de los pobres," *Caretas* (Lima), May 14, 1990; and the Instituto de Investigación Nutricional (unpublished document, July 12, 1990).

at the municipal level in 1986 was a response both to García's popularity and to the opportunities perceived in supporting the central government's programs in the pueblos jóvenes, particularly the highly publicized PAIT, although Barrantes and the IU remained very popular. "Those sectors of the population that today support Alan García and Alfonso Barrantes do not do so in the unconditional and exclusive manner that characterized aprista populism fifty years ago. The support today . . . is much more critical."[18]

In the November 1989 municipal elections, Ricardo Belmont, a charismatic television entertainer running on a free-enterprise platform, took the municipality, although the conservative FREDEMO coalition fared quite well in poor urban areas. FREDEMO's margin was eroded in the 1990 presidential elections by Alberto Fujimori and his vague platform rather than by the left.[19] In 1989 and 1990 the poor's votes for Belmont and Fujimori reflected a rejection not only of the APRA party, but of all political parties associated with the established political system. The extent to which Marxist and socialist alternatives were associated with the hyperinflation of 1988–1990 played into the hands of Belmont, Vargas Llosa, and Fujimori, all of whom were centrists or right of center. In addition, the formal division of the Izquierda Unida and its fielding of separate candidates hardly promised a united governing coalition and proved disastrous at the polls.

The pragmatism of the urban poor is demonstrated by their response to attempts to use their support as a political stepping-stone or to utilize their organizational structure as a means of political control. The urban poor have shown themselves to be willing to lend their support only when it yields tangible benefit, and to be quick to drop that support if it is perceived to do no good. In this light it is important to note that most approaches to the problem of urban poverty were co-optative in nature, with no genuine attempt to eliminate the barriers to entry into the formal economy or access to housing and services. The failure of decades of government policy to address the needs of this rapidly growing population[20] was an incentive for the APRA team to focus on the urban marginalized as a major aspect of its policy. What differentiated the APRA government's approach, at least in theory, was its focus on programs for informal sector workers as a critical part of an economic reactivation strategy and not simply as instruments for political manipulation.

APRA POLICIES AND THE POOR

The APRA team's theoreticians concentrated on a policy designed to improve capacity and employment in the informal sector, rather than on any specific policy toward the "pueblos jóvenes." The approach, formulated by Daniel Carbonetto, who was to become García's main economics advisor during the first half of the regime, had two basic themes. The first was to narrow the gap between formal sector demand for labor and the size of the economically active population. The second was to reduce the plethora of restrictions—on access to capital and credit, for example—that handicapped the informal sector's strategy of *autogeneración,* or self-employment. The reactivation of the modern sector by increasing demand through wage increases and price freezes would also boost informal sector sales and absorb excess informal labor. Complementing this would be programs directed at structural informality: employment programs that in the long run would enable their workers to enter the modern sector; and policies to improve informal sector workers' access to financing.[21]

The first two years of the APRA government's heterodox reactivation strategy did achieve these goals, as demand for labor increased in the formal sector, as did demand for informal sector goods. In addition, APRA implemented four programs designed to complement this strategy, the most prominent among them being the PAIT employment program. The other programs—PROEM, IDESI, and PAD—are worthy of brief mention, as is APRA municipality's record in providing services to Lima's poor.

PROEM

PROEM, established in July 1986, allowed companies to hire employees for up to two years without adhering to normal job security or stability regulations. At its inception 2,290 workers were hired as PROEM labor in Lima. At its height, in August 1987, PROEM labor accounted for 42,160 posts in Lima and over fifty thousand nationwide. PROEM was primarily responsible for the 9 percent increase in textile industry employment.[22] The program's effects were eroded by severe recession after 1988, but its initial success points to the extent to which the labor stability laws implemented during the Velasco years, because of their excessive nature, have acted as an impediment to employment and restricted privileges to those lucky enough to have formal sector jobs. It is virtually impossible for a Peruvian industry to fire a worker for any reason after he has been with the firm for three months. Few, if any, advanced industrial economies have such labor provisions. Not surprisingly, PROEM aroused substantial opposition from organized labor and some sectors of the left.

IDESI

The government also established IDESI with the end of bettering working conditions for the informal sector by providing small-scale credit to informal sector workers. The mayor of Villa El Salvador, Miguel Azcueta, estimated that less than 3 percent of small producers in pueblos jóvenes had access to credit, and that they were asked to pay interest rates as high as 800 percent.[23] The design of IDESI was based in part on the experience of Acción Comunitaria in providing credit to informal sector workers based on group guarantees of repayment.[24] IDESI was a semiautonomous institution, working with credit lines from the Peruvian Central Bank, the Banco de Crédito, and international corporations. The program was perceived as highly successful, with over thirty thousand beneficiaries by August 1987 and with the extension of several hundred thousand dollars in new credits in early 1988. IDESI's strategy of group guarantees and gradual upscaling of loans resulted in a repayment record of 98 percent. The program's overall credit base was expanded in mid-1988 by the Central Bank's extension of approximately $150,000 in extra credits, and the Economic Ministry's promise that state banks would designate $300,000 to small entrepreneurs. In April 1988 a presidential decree obligated all banks to lend at least 10 percent of their credit to small businessmen, artisans, or groups of artisans. IDESI also obtained substantial international support, including a $1 million program from the United Nations Development Programme, at a time when Peru was receiving virtually no external credit.[25] Its status as an independent institution, meanwhile, meant that there was less potential for loans to be politicized and presented as a "favor" from APRA. Like PROEM's, IDESI's potential was severely curtailed by the onset of economic crisis, although the agency continued to function and maintain its high repayment ratio even after the onset of hyperinflation.

PAD

The government set up the PAD to deal with the pueblos jóvenes. The PAD had a checkered record early on. The program was designed to help equip communal kitchens, implement initial education programs for those not in school, provide primary health care, build child care centers and sports complexes, and organize local craft industries. With an initial budget of $45,000,[26] the PAD was run from the government palace, as it was a pet project of the president's wife. Her interest may have been modeled on the active role that Belaúnde's wife took in promoting communal kitchens, a role that made her extremely popular in many pueblos jóvenes. As it was run from the palace, the program often failed to coordinate efforts with municipalities and existing neighborhood organizations. A prime example is the government's spending, in conjunction with the PAD, 350 million intis (over $3 million)[27] on building two Olympic-sized pools in two pueblos jóvenes, one each north and south of the city. There is a need for recreation facilities in low-income areas; however, building swimming pools, which require expensive imported machinery and can be used only half the year, seemed a poor and ad hoc use of desperately needed funds, especially in areas that lack water and sewage facilities.

One of the dangers of any government's establishing new programs to "help" the pueblos jóvenes or the informal sector is the tendency to disregard or override existing organizations' programs. The PAD was primarily an attempt to centralize these organizations and quickly entered into conflict with them. There were several preexisting forms of organization and programs functioning in the pueblos jóvenes; some autonomous and some related to the IU municipal government. Over one thousand communal kitchens and seventy-five hundred committees of the Vaso de Leche program already existed.[28] Barrantes's highly successful "Vaso de Leche" program, instituted in 1983, distributed powdered milk, donated by international organizations, throughout the pueblos jóvenes. What proved to be one of the program's main assets was that it relied on existing and autonomous mothers' clubs to distribute the milk. Thus not only was the program able to distribute 1 million glasses of milk per day, with relatively few IU functionaries,[29] but it played the important role of strengthening rather than disrupting existing organizations. After the APRA takeover of the municipal government, there was an outbreak of conflicts in the administration of the Vaso de Leche program, both between IU and APRA functionaries and between the mothers' clubs and the new administration—hardly to APRA's credit. Jorge del Castillo, the new mayor, initially tried to end the program, as it was associated with the IU, but met with substantial opposition.[30]

The mothers' clubs, in a variety of pueblos jóvenes, often also are involved in sponsoring communal kitchens, of two types: autonomous and administered. While both are dependent on external sources for food, the latter are controlled or restricted in terms of their organization by external forces through a nondemocratic structure. The kitchens are not only an effective survival strategy for their communities but also promote the independence of women as organizers and community leaders. For the latter purpose, the record of autonomous kitchens is much better.[31] With the severe economic crisis after mid-1988, these kitchens took on increasing importance as a survival strategy.

Different political organizations have often tried to promote communal kitchens for political benefit. During the 1985 political campaign APRA and the AP competed with each other in sponsoring the kitchens; the poor's wizened response is well summed up by the slogan "APRA–AP kitchens: they appear quickly, they disappear quickly."[32] Izquierda Unida seems to have focused more on promoting autonomous kitchens.[33] The mothers involved complemented the IU's effort. "They provide the food and then leave us alone. The Municipality doesn't tell us what to do. This is important."[34]

The PAD established fifty-three centers in Lima's pueblos jóvenes that were to function through a general assembly with community representatives from each ministry; the assembly's task was to establish how and to what extent services and living conditions could be improved.[35] The PAD claimed to be supervising the "normal, institutional development of the Mother's Clubs."[36] Its aim in terms of communal kitchens was to turn the autonomous kitchens into administered ones and to dissolve the smaller ones. This attitude, coupled with certain new restrictions it imposed to make clubs eligible for its support, made the PAD an affront to the autonomy of existing mothers' clubs and the kitchens that they had organized. Comments of various mothers' clubs members about the PAD ranged from "the PAD is marginalizing some communal kitchens and mothers' clubs, because they were mistakenly identified with Izquierda Unida" to "we also know that they do not support organized women like the communal kitchens, the Vaso de Leche committees, and the independent mothers' clubs."[37] The insertion of the PAD where autonomous organizations already existed had little positive effect, resulting in a lack of coordination of the program's activities with those of the municipalities of the districts, as even members of APRA-run municipalities admit.[38] The concept of imposing external control on autonomous organizational capacity with the aim of channeling demand making was strikingly similar to the approach taken by the military government in the 1970s, and ran into similar barriers in terms of popular resistance.

THE PAIT PROGRAM[39]

The APRA government's most visible and expensive effort to address the needs of the marginalized was the PAIT employment program. This chapter is an analysis of the PAIT program: its design and implementation at the macrolevel, and then its implementation in one Lima municipality, and in one pueblo jóvene within it in greater detail. I detail how that program fit into the party's overall reactivation strategy and how political factors undermined its potential. A brief analysis of the manner in which AD operated at the "barrio"-level in Venezuela provides a comparative context. The study of the PAIT sheds light on how the APRA party operated at the municipal level, highlighting the sectarian and undemocratic traits of the party that proved barriers to its capacity to govern both at the municipal and central government levels, which were in part responsible for the political polarization that occurred during the course of its regime.

The PAIT was a crucial part of the government's strategy of raising domestic consumption capacity and was initiated with a great deal of propaganda and fanfare. It began with a budget of over $7 million for

Table 8.2 PAIT Enrollments

Nationwide		
Campaigns	Number of Workers	Investment (in Intis)
October–December 1985	35,114	99,400,000
January–March 1986	33,931	53,976,156
April–July 1986	41,949	107,925,806
September–December 1986	150,824	630,444,000
January–March 1987	12,273	66,219,932
April–June 1987	100,000	584,000,000
Total	374,091	1,541,965,894

San Juan de Lurigancho		
	Total Employed	Amount Invested (in thousands of Intis)
September–December 1986	4,526	17,706.46
April–June 1987	2,450	11,588.33
November–December 1987	584	5,350.00

Huascar		
September–December 1986	423	2,067.76
April–June 1987	554	2,638.48
November–December 1987	122	1,090.00

Sources: For nationwide figures see Nicholas Houghton, in *Empleos de emergencia* (Santiago: PREALC, 1988). Figures for San Juan de Lurigancho and Huscar were provided by the PAIT District Office, San Juan de Lurigancho.

September–December 1985. The budget for 1986 alone was $22 million, or 300 million intis in a total public investment budget for that year of 20,000 million intis.[40] By mid-1988, the program had employed approximately 500,000 people countrywide on a three-month basis (see Table 8.2). The works conducted consisted of trash collection, reforestation, painting walls and fences, building sanitation facilities, building access roads, and cleaning beaches (this last was the only project outside the actual pueblos jóvenes). It was expected that those who were selected for the program would be among the under- and unemployed; they were to receive minimum wage for working forty-eight-hour weeks—540 intis at the time, or approximately $36 per month.[41] This minimum was under average factory wages, but above that of domestic servants.

The PAIT came in with a bang and went out with a whimper. In January 1988 President García announced that Cooperación Popular (COOPOP)—the agency that administered the PAIT—would be dissolved and that the PAIT would be turned over to the municipalities. When García announced the proposed dissolution of the 147 COOPOP offices nationwide, he asserted that the PAIT would continue. "Who is better than a mayor to direct the PAIT, truly choosing ... the poorest and most humble in order to give them a job ... without political criteria?"[42] García's assurances were hardly credible, as in many regions municipalities were extremely weak and controlled by local party bosses or power brokers. Often local PAIT office directors had had more power than the mayors themselves. Meanwhile the PAIT had no official budget, but was merely an allocation in the central budget that had to be renewed annually.[43] In light of the ensuing economic crisis and deficit of funds, it was highly unlikely that a large budget would be approved for a project corresponding to municipalities—and from which they would reap the political benefit—that in poor areas were already short of funds for most basic services.

In the end the direction of the program never was transferred to the municipalities; it remained under the auspices of COOPOP, which also continued to function. There were two explanations for the proposal to dissolve COOPOP and transfer the PAIT. One was that García purportedly wanted to curb the power of the local COOPOP and PAIT functionaries, many of whom supported Luis Alva Castro, his main rival in APRA.[44] More important, though, the proposal was an indication that in the face of an impending budgetary crisis the government was no longer willing to invest the funds necessary to keep the PAIT running on a full scale, particularly as it had no political utility in the short term (the next elections were not until November 1989). After the January announcement the program continued to function on a much smaller scale, with the objective of maintaining existing works and using primarily the labor of the permanent program staff. Officials at all levels within the program assured people that it would continue, but none could specify how or with what funds. Those who had participated in the PAIT and hoped to continue were thus left in limbo and may have forgone other opportunities while waiting for the promised work.

Despite the fading out of the PAIT, it had lasting implications. While the program functioned in some rural areas, the focus here is Lima, where it had the most impact and highest concentration of workers, and where a money income was a prerequisite for feeding a family. The PAIT was very popular, as was demonstrated by the long lines of people waiting to sign up for the lotteries that chose eligible workers. PAIT workers were primarily women (76 percent), young (33 percent were between sixteen and twenty-five years old), uneducated (12 percent were illiterate), and poor (living standards for PAIT workers, in terms of access to basic services, were slightly below the average for inhabitants of the pueblos jóvenes)[45] (see Table 8.3).

The high percentage of female workers was a striking characteristic of the PAIT, one of the few employment options that did not discriminate between men and women. Women constituted 57 percent of the heads of household working in the PAIT.[46] The program provided women with new opportunities for both desperately needed income and relatively stable employment. Some of these women were previously domestic servants who had had to commute long hours to a job where schedules were rarely fixed, or were housewives who had had no income at all. The PAIT provided an opportunity to earn while working closer to home—often with the possibilities of going home at lunchtime and bringing young children to work—or to earn money for the first time. For those who were already working, the program served to ease their work/travel burden and at the same time yielded more income. In many cases it provided the women, for the first time, with the independence that comes from being a wage earner. The high percentage of women participating in the PAIT reflects the complex and vital positions they held in low-income Peruvian families, often acting as both principal wage earner and keeper of the home. There was a notable presence of abandoned mothers; when there are separations in low-income families, the mothers, who rarely have access to legal protection, are left with total responsibility for supporting the family.

The PAIT workers were clearly the poorest among the poor, and the program was able to provide necessary, although temporary, financial relief for its workers. Yet there were various negative effects as well. First

Table 8.3 PAIT Workers in Lima (Percentages)

Male	24.0	Single	21.0
Female	76.0	Married	64.0
		Widowed/Divorced	14.0
16–25 years old	23.0	Head of household	33.0
26–35 years old	34.0	Spouse	47.0
> 35	30.5	Son/daughter	13.0

Source: Jorge Billone, *El PAIT: funcionalidad y metodologías* (Lima: INP/OIT/PNUD, 1986).

and foremost, there were problems at the microlevel. The PAIT proved
to be a benefit for many families but also acted as a disruptive force in
some communities. Workers were selected by lottery, as there were
usually more applicants than posts. The uncertainty proved disruptive
both to families with hopes of joining the PAIT and to those with hopes
of continuing to work there; a dependence on PAIT income emerged in
many cases,[47] as some workers had given up previous employment to join
the PAIT. The PAIT also disrupted many existing community organizations, such as the mothers' clubs and communal kitchens, as responsibilities in these organizations were often dropped (no surprise) when the
opportunity to earn PAIT income arose, even though it was only temporary. In addition, rather than complement the work of such organizations
by having PAIT workers use the local kitchens at lunchtime, the program
created its own kitchen facilities. The often manipulative attitude of PAIT
functionaries was criticized by many women in mothers' clubs; others, not
surprisingly among those who were able to participate, expressed the
overriding importance of the increase to family income. Others pointed
to youth who refused to return to school when given the opportunity to
earn PAIT money.[48] The PAIT affected male-female relations, as many
women discovered the independence that accompanies a stable salary for
the first time. Finally, there were cases where the care of children at home
was severely neglected because of the time demands on the mothers
working in the PAIT;[49] and the quality of the child care at PAIT centers
was criticized as very poor. There were many cases where women worked
in very unsanitary conditions (burning trash, for example) or carried both
heavy loads and their children on their backs (as when they helped build
access roads).[50] These problems varied among districts and type of work,
and depended on the attitude of the regional functionaries.

The nature of the work itself also made it difficult for the program to
provide skills training. Low-productivity work such as painting fences and
burning trash may indeed better the conditions of the pueblos jóvenes but
it hardly provides workers with skills to enter the formal sector. The
program served as a source of temporary income but little else. The way
it was phased out in 1988 seems to have killed any long-term potential it
may have had. At the same time the desperate level of income of the
population targeted made it highly popular, despite the disruptive long-
term effects it might have had at the community level.

Garcia's—and APRA's—willingness to use the program for political
ends was demonstrated by the increase in enrollments shortly before the
November 1986 elections, and his announcement in September 1988,
while his cabinet was implementing a harsh austerity plan, that 200,000
new PAIT posts were going to be created in the near future.[51] To my
knowledge, the posts never materialized, and the program was, at the time
of this writing, functioning on a part-time basis.[52] The desperation of the

workers also increased the potential for the PAIT to be used as a political tool, a potential realized on a surprising scale among the middle-level aprista functionaries involved in local program administration. Misuse of PAIT funds was widespread; one case was so blatant that it created a rebellion of the APRA youth against the COOPOP director in Lamvayeque.[53]

The program direction was highly centralized. There was little coordination with local government, particularly in Izquierda Unida regions. Instead the posts of zone directors were used as vehicles for young apristas; fortunately, most technical posts were excluded from this process. Víctor López, the first director, built a wide reputation for utilizing the program to build up his own, and APRA's, political base.[54] There was a substantial bureaucracy in the directorate, which lent itself to politicization. For every thirty workers, or *cuadrilla,* there was a chief, and for each four cuadrillas there was a *brigada* chief. There was also a technical directorate and a district coordinator. In total there were four thousand bureaucratic functionaries, and of these most were either apristas or APRA sympathizers.[55] These bureaucrats, who wielded a great deal of power in remote rural regions, became pawns in the intraparty power struggle between Alan García and Luis Alva.

Besides the politicization of the PAIT bureaucracy, there were far more blatant cases of manipulation of PAIT workers. PAIT workers were used to disrupt strikes, as when they broke picket lines in the 1986 doctors' and SUTEP teachers' strikes, arousing a great deal of animosity against the PAIT from organized labor. In Villa El Salvador the PAIT organizers convinced their workers to march against the IU mayor, Miguel Azcueta, by claiming that he opposed the program.[56] Aprista functionaries paid by the PAIT were used in the November 1986 election campaign, and PAIT workers were often transported to APRA political rallies. There is clearly a correlation between the number of workers hired in certain regions and the November 1986 election campaign. The number hired prior to the election escalated well beyond that proposed by the Organizocion Internacional de Trabajo (OIT) consultants' team, which resulted in draining the budget, and thus in a severely curtailed PAIT in early 1987, and the transfer of the program to the municipalities in 1988. There was also a correlation between the allocation of PAIT workers going to regions where IU was strong in 1985.[57] Finally, it was rumored that in many cases an APRA *carnet* (identification card) was required to register for the PAIT lottery. More believable were the rumors of cuadrilla chiefs having to be APRA members.

It is illustrative to turn here to brief mention of the relations between apristas at the central and municipal levels in the administration of the PAIT program, as well as to the results of a survey of PAIT workers I conducted in San Juan de Lurigancho. The results of the municipal-level study demonstrate how the traits that inhibited APRA's relations with society at the central level were even more pervasive at the municipal level. The study of the PAIT was conducted in one of Lima's poorest and most populous districts, and in one town within it—Huascar. Huascar, which was settled fourteen years ago, is typical of Lima shantytowns in that it is neither tied to one political party nor exceptionally organized or disorganized. A high percentage of residents are poor; at least half of them still live in houses made of straw. All but 1 percent do not have running water and buy their water from trucks. Although none have sewage services, 95 percent do have electricity, which was extended to the town in 1986 (see Table 8.4). Yet, as in most of Lima's shantytowns, there are a host of communal kitchens and other autonomous and vibrant organizations that work in the district.[58]

The PAIT Program at the Municipal Level

Brief mention of the political record of San Juan de Lurigancho and Huascar is essential to the analysis of APRA's performance there. A surprisingly high 25 percent of those surveyed had participated in mothers' clubs; 68 percent had participated in the Vaso de Leche program. Only 10 percent had participated in a Comedor Popular.[59]

Since the late 1970s voting trends in the district have reflected those for Lima's urban poor in general; a tendency, but by no means a definitive one, to vote for the left. The urban poor, the district of San Juan included, demonstrate a great deal of pragmatism and opportunism in voting rather than any strong political allegiance. In 1985 APRA had a visible presence for the first time in the history of the district, and then took the municipality in 1986 (see Table 8.1). The 1986 outcome was swayed by García's popularity, but was also a factor of perceived opportunities. APRA offered voters a candidate backed by the government in power and produced a high level of propaganda and enrollments in the PAIT program in the district prior to the election. Alfonso Barrantes himself admitted that the IU mayor of San Juan during those same years had an extremely poor record.[60] With the demise of the García government, and the general discrediting of APRA, after a tight race between the Izquierda Unida and the conservative FREDEMO coalition, the IU took the district in the November 1989 municipal elections. In the 1990 presidential elections political dark horse Alberto Fujimori triumphed in both rounds, again demonstrating the lack of strong political allegiances.

The record of APRA municipal government is worthy of brief mention, as it reveals a great deal about the manner in which the party functioned in government. The approach at the municipal level, and of the mayor, Víctor Raúl Ortiz Pilco, was positive and pragmatic. The mayor recognized the need to organize at the most basic level, such as taking a

Table 8.4 Demographics of Huascar and Bayovar

	Number	Percentage		Number	Percentage
Huascar	195	59.8			
Bayovar	131	40.2			
Total valid cases	326				

Housing and Services

	Number	Percentage		Number	Percentage
Owns home	300	92.0	Number of floors		
Does not own	26	7.9	1	312	95.7
			2 or more	14	4.3
Wall construction			Roof construction:		
Cement/brick	155	47.2	Cement/brick	35	10.7
Straw matting	152	46.6	Straw matting	228	69.9
Cardboard or tin	4	1.2	Cardboard or tin	57	17.4
Other	15	4.6	Other	6	1.8
Buys water			Light		
From truck	322	98.8	Electric	312	95.7
Other	3	0.9	Candle/kerosene	14	4.3

Community Involvement

	Number	Percentage		Number	Percentage
Belongs to mothers' club			Belongs to communal kitchen		
No	231	70.9	No	290	89.0
Yes	94	28.8	Yes	35	10.7
Does not know	1	0.3	Does not know	1	0.3
Belongs to Vaso de Lecho			Serves on Communal Directorate		
No	101	31.1	No	229	70.2
Yes	224	68.7	Yes	81	24.8
Does not know	1	0.3	Does not know	16	4.9
Does communal work					
No	100	30.7			
Yes	224	68.7			
Does not know	2	0.6			

Source: Instituto de Investigación Nutricional, survey conducted by Dr. Francisco Lazo, March 1988.

census (the last one had been taken before the major influx of migration in 1983 from the Andes). He believed the district's lack of organization and unity resulted in a duplication of authority, with many towns having two or three competing directorates.[61] The district's high level of politicization—it had had alternately, AP, IU, and APRA leaders—had led to a duplication of effort and aid programs. For example, CARITAS, a Catholic Relief Services food program, and Organisacion Nacional de Alimenation y Abastamento, a government-run food program, both operated in the same neighborhood; other neighborhoods saw neither group. The same occurred with mothers' clubs and communal kitchens, with most being sponsored by IU, some by the central government's PAD, and some independent ones, all competing in the same area. In a district with such a lack of services, this was a pointless waste of effort and funds.

The municipality attempted to mediate and depoliticize the competing directories in several neighborhoods. In Huascar and Bayovar, for example, land titles had been held as a political ploy since 1976. One of the mayor's first acts was to press the Provincial Council to invoke an expropriations law and immediately grant titles to the residents. The land titles issue had become extremely politicized. There was a feud between the owner of the land and the dirigentes—neighborhood directors—over the value of the land, a dispute that was used by both the owner and various dirigentes as a political issue. Some dirigentes had been forcing the settlers to go to political marches, charging a fine of 500 intis (1985 value) to those who did not attend, quite a fine since the real value of a lot in Huascar and Bayovar was 350 intis. A major effort was made, admittedly with less than complete success, to support existing neighborhood organization and authority, and all existing directorates, mothers' clubs, and Vaso de Leche Program *comités* were recognized by the municipality.[62] The efforts of at least ten neighborhood organizations or associations to get water, sewage, and electric services were supported by the municipality.[63]

One of the municipality's more innovative plans was the building of low-cost occupational training workshops, with simple and inexpensive construction materials, designed to train participants in basic skills such as carpentry, electronics, welding, knitting, and leather work: all fields for which there was demand in and outside the district. Ortiz Pilco suggested this idea to President García at a meeting of district mayors. Instead of following the mayor's suggestion, the central government, with its penchant for grandiose gestures—such as the PAD's Olympic pools, one of which is in San Juan—built a huge, expensive, "high-technology institute" in the district, which has yet to open.[64] Not only is this an absurd waste of desperately needed funds, but there is no demand for high-technology experts in the district, nor would youths with the education necessary to enter high-technology institutes be the target of government aid.

At least in this case APRA at the central level proved to be much more out of touch with the poor than were its functionaries at the municipal level. This may be typical of municipalities in much of Latin America: they function with scarce resources in a system where power and money are centrally concentrated.[65]

While APRA's record in the municipality of San Juan de Lurigancho could be given a positive rating, there was also one major flaw. The fact that all the top officials were apristas clearly closed off access to other available talent and approaches, and created resentment among other political groups. Such resentment was demonstrated in APRA's administration of the Vaso de Leche program. The municipality's insistence on having an aprista in charge of the distribution of Vaso de Leche milk, and therefore with authority over the local program dirigentes, aroused a great deal of animosity from those who had been previously administering the program at the neighborhood level. This was a problem throughout Lima with the APRA takeover of the municipalities.[66] In general, the approach under the IU municipality was different; offices were open to members of other parties, and there was more collaboration with other groups.[67] The negative effects of APRA's sectarian approach are demonstrated by the implementation of the PAIT program in the district.

The PAIT in San Juan de Lurigancho and Huascar

The PAIT was set up in San Juan de Lurigancho in November 1985 but was at that point run from the central office of Cooperación Popular. The PAIT established a central office in the district in October 1986, coinciding with the expansion that occurred prior to that year's November election. When APRA won the municipal elections, it seemed that the most talented people went to work in the municipality, including the young aprista sociologist who launched the program in the district—and in Puno—who went to head the municipality's Office of Communal Services. The PAIT program was then handed over to inexperienced party rank and file[68] from the more affluent sections of the district or from outside—which may in part explain the many flaws in its implementation. After the January 1988 changes in the program's central direction, it continued to function only at a reduced level: maintaining existing works using primarily the labor of PAIT program functionaries. In its short time in full-scale operation, however, the PAIT had a substantial impact on the communities of San Juan de Lurigancho, and in particular on Huascar, which was one of the target areas.

From its inception to the 1988 reduction of the program, the PAIT employed approximately twenty-one hundred people in Huascar[69] and thus affected 17.5 percent of all households. Although there was some repetition, as many worked more than one *temporada,* or round, there were also many workers who wanted to enter the PAIT but could not, as there were not enough spaces. To inform people about the PAIT, cars were driven through the communities announcing that there would be inscriptions for the program in a rented office in Zarate; there were also advertisements on the radio and in the newspapers. Huascar was one of the first places where the administrators of the program focused, as it was an area where a great deal needed to be done and that had a very concentrated population.[70] There were four major PAIT campaigns in the district, with a relatively high proportion of spaces allotted to Huascar. Whenever an excess of applicants occurred, which was the case in almost all instances, a lottery was held to determine who could get in. After the final 1988 campaign the program operated at a substantially reduced level, primarily as maintenance or completion of existing projects, or occasional emergency ones, such as the damming of the overflowing Río Rímac near Zarate, a project that employed forty-two people.[71] In theory and practice, the program employed people regardless of their political affiliation. All positions above that of temporary squadron leader, however, were reserved for apristas.

After January 1988 the program operated primarily with permanent program workers and hired outside labor only on a part-time basis.[72] While the program was never actually transferred to the municipalities, the proposal to do so may have resulted in increased cooperation between the COOPOP offices and the municipality; this seems to have occurred in San Juan de Lurigancho.[73] This was probably less the result of a conscious effort than of a perceived need—in the face of limited funds—of PAIT administrators to rely on existing efforts and infrastructure rather than embarking on new public works.

The program had a definite effect on the district in terms of infrastructural improvement, as in almost every pueblo jóven in the district there is some evidence of PAIT labor, whether it be ditches and pipes, painted walls, a medical post, or a rudimentary road. In Montenegro, the newest pueblo joven in the district, which is located at its extreme border, the PAIT built most of the infrastructure—classrooms, sanitary facilities, floors—for a local school. This is clearly a vital need for a pueblo joven that is a substantial distance from paved roads and is serviced by only one occasional bus line, making it difficult for its children to attend school elsewhere. Works were not always finished, however. Many of the ditches and pipelines in parts of Huascar, for example, were left incomplete, and were soon rendered useless by the garbage and other waste that quickly began to fill them. In other parts of the town the piping was actually laid and the ditches filled, albeit an entire year later. Project completion was somewhat ad hoc. Regardless, and very much to its credit, the program did provide community improvements as well as employment.

The effects of the program were far more substantial than the actual works executed, particularly as the program employed a high number of women who had not previously held jobs. Thus they experienced the independence that comes with earning a salary for the first time. While in most cases the money was used to buy bread to feed the family, this new independence clearly had a more profound impact; one indication was an increase noted by community church leaders in separations and even divorces. In these cases often the husband was unhappy with his wife's newfound freedom, a freedom she was not willing to give up after the program was discontinued. There were comments such as "after that my wife was different,"[74] from a husband who wanted a divorce, claiming that his wife had got used to being away from home and, even after ending her term in the PAIT, continued to seek work and contact outside.

Another sort of instability caused by the program was a form of unemployment that resulted for those who left previous jobs in Lima for the convenience and stability of a job near home in the PAIT, only to be unable to get into another round of the program in the lottery, or to have the program discontinued. As the communities were not informed of the status of the program after the transfer to the municipalities was announced, many continued to wait for a new round of work. PAIT officials promised that there would be more work even after the transfer to the municipalities, although they would not specify when, maintaining the state of uncertainty.

General reactions to the PAIT among members of the community ranged from "for the first time they give a hand to the poor, on the part of Señor García"[75] to "there isn't a single work in the PAIT that is worth anything."[76] In almost all cases the income supplement provided by the PAIT was cited as its primary asset, and the fact that it improved the community proper as another. Among those who had worked in the program, there was definite desire for the program to be continued. Opinions among those who did not work in the program were more diverse. Some saw it as humiliating make-work and complained that it duplicated community efforts already under way. One observer cited cases of the PAIT painting school walls in the community of El Porvenir, where the fathers of the schoolchildren of the community had already pooled their resources and bought paint. The same thing had occurred with the painting of the local market walls.[77] In another case, a woman who worked in the PAIT who had children of working age said that her children refused to work in the PAIT, even though they were unemployed.[78] Another woman said that she questioned her mother's working in the program because the work was so hard and dirty, and the workers so poorly treated.[79]

The PAIT also clearly had an influence on existing organizations. As all of those were based on voluntary labor for community benefit, such as the Vaso de Leche program or the Comedores Populares—many of which were sponsored by the church groups—the prospect of a desperately needed income drew people away. A church leader who helped run one communal kitchen noted that those who had not entered the PAIT and remained working in the Comedores Populares were resentful when fellow workers came to the kitchens too tired after PAIT work to contribute to the kitchen tasks. She felt that the drop in participation reduced the effectiveness of the kitchens and disrupted community unity.[80]

This is by no means an isolated observation, and the results of my survey confirm this. Without a doubt the program, in addition to whatever positive effects it had, caused substantial disruption of San Juan de Lurigancho communities. Whether through raised expectations, competition with existing organizations, or newly discovered independence on the part of women, the program, for good or for bad, changed the communities where it was implemented.

I surveyed twenty-three inhabitants of Huascar who worked in the PAIT—a sample that represents slightly over 5 percent of the average of four hundred Huascar workers per round of PAIT work. The results give an insight into the way the PAIT functioned. A small number of interviews in Pamplona Alta, a pueblo joven in a Lima district with a two-term IU mayor, serve as a point of contrast.

The Huascar women were randomly selected but were primarily from the A section of the town (see Map 8.2 and Table 8.5). First and foremost, the survey revealed the low level of education and income of the majority of the PAIT workers: all but one worked out of desperate need for income. At least one of the women surveyed was illiterate, and another had recently arrived from Ayacucho and could not speak Spanish. Almost all had worked in more than one round of the PAIT; they had gotten in by lottery and also by signing up, depending on the situation. Those who had not worked at certain times usually had wanted to and had not gotten in. Only two of the twenty-three had left the program voluntarily because they no longer desperately needed money. The majority used the income to buy more food; and a few to save up to purchase other goods. About 50 percent had their first paid work experience in the PAIT; of those who had worked, most had had small *negocios*—usually selling food or wares on the street—or had worked as domestic servants or washerwomen in Lima. Proximity to home was an advantage often cited by the women as an advantage of working in the PAIT, as was its improvement of the community and paying a fixed salary. For a little less than half of the women the PAIT salary was the only income for the household; thus when there was no PAIT work, income was most likely less than the already low minimum wage level. Three of the twenty-three were abandoned mothers.[81]

When asked if they had felt party pressure or favoritism when joining the program, almost all said that it was easier to get in if one was an aprista or was a friend of the aprista functionaries. To become a *capataz*—a

Map 8.2 San Juan de Lurigancho

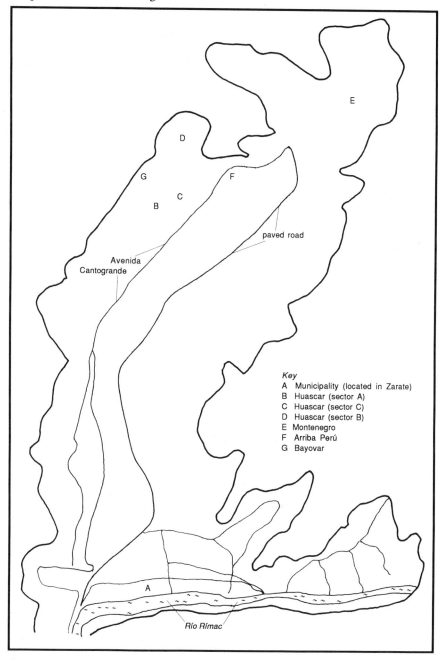

Key
A   Municipality (located in Zarate)
B   Huascar (sector A)
C   Huascar (sector C)
D   Huascar (sector B)
E   Montenegro
F   Arriba Perú
G   Bayovar

Table 8.5 PAIT Workers in Huascar

	Number	Percentage		Number	Percentage
Number of times in PAIT			**How entered the program**		
None, but tried	1	4.34	By lottery	12	52.17
1	2	8.69	Signed up	3	13.04
2 or more	7	30.43	Both	7	30.43
			Invalid	2	8.69
Why entered the program			**Abandoned mother**		
Need for income	20	86.9	Yes	3	13.04
Other	1	4.34	No	20	86.9
Invalid	2	8.68			
Was in PAD or mothers' club			**Communal kitchen/ Vaso de Leche work**		
No	10	43.4	No	10	43.4
Yes, still	4	17.39	Yes, still	0	0.0
Yes, dropped	7	30.43	Yes, dropped	3	30.43
Invalid	2	8.69	Invalid	10	43.4
First work with income			**Previous work**		
Yes	10	43.3	Selling food	1	9.09
No	11	47.8	Washing	2	18.18
Invalid	2	8.69	Street sales	4	36.36
			Lima job	1	9.09
			Domestic servant	1	9.09
			Invalid	3	27.27
Quality of PAIT work			**Wants to work again**		
Easy/OK	4	17.39	Yes	17	73.91
Hard, but OK	7	30.43	No	3	13.04
Too hard	7	30.43	Invalid	3	13.04
Invalid	5	21.73			
Went to political rallies			**Went to rally, did not mind**		
Yes, obligated	11	47.8	Yes	8	61.53
Yes, voluntary	2	8.69	No	5	38.46
No	2	8.69			
Invalid	8	34.78			
Advantages of PAIT work			**Disadvantages of PAIT work**		
Near home	10	43.3	Too hard	2	8.69
Income	3	13.04	Instability/lottery system	5	21.73
Gives women work	1	4.34	Only party members get in	1	4.34
Fixed salary	1	4.34	Only rich get to work	2	8.69
Improves community	1	4.34	Invalid	13	56.52
Illiterate/no job	1	4.34			
Invalid	5	21.73			

(continues)

Table 8.5 continued

	Number	Percentage		Number	Percentage
Felt party favoritism			PAIT income was sole salary		
Yes	12	52.17	Yes	7	30.43
No	1	4.34	No	9	39.13
Invalid	10	43.47	Invalid	6	26.08

Source: Author's survey, Huascar, January–March 1988.
Note: The total number of valid observations is twenty-three.

permanent squadron leader—one had to be of the party. The one aprista interviewed who had worked in the PAIT was no longer in the program, as she had been promoted to a job in the municipality. There were also complaints from many of the women that while they, who were the poorest, did not get into the program every time, there were some who were wealthier and owned two-story homes or stores and got work every round: "they have stores, they have big houses with two stories."[82] They also complained that often more than one person from certain households got to work, which is prohibited by the program rules. This demonstrates the difficulty of targeting social compensation programs, and also may indicate party favoritism of some form. While the lottery system seems to have been fair for inscription, any sort of promotion in the program was clearly based on party affiliation. The highest that a nonaprista worker could get was to be a temporary squadron leader when the capataz was absent.[83]

The party also clearly used the PAIT workers for political benefit by obligating them to go to the government palace to cheer for Alan García or to political marches. Only one of the women surveyed had not been obligated as part of her PAIT work to go to a march or rally.[84] Apparently, some program directors only suggested that the workers might lose a day's salary plus their *dominical,* the traditional part of the salary allocated to pay for Sunday. Marches took place both during the week and on the weekends, at times creating problems for women who had to take their children with them when they had no one else to take care of them.[85] There was not a great deal of resentment among most of the women who went to the marches; they saw them as an opportunity to see either the president or the Plaza de Armas. Resentment was evident among the two women who clearly were the more educated of those interviewed, one in Huascar and one in Pamplona. Señora Mercedes in Huascar complained of the inconvenience of having to drag her three-year-old son along with her; the other, Señora Filomina in Pamplona, resented being "put on a bus like cattle."[86] This behavior hardly gives credibility to a party that purports to represent the most disadvantaged of society.

Of the women surveyed, about 50 percent had participated in a mothers' club, Vaso de Leche program, or a Comedor Popular. Of those, about half had remained in their program, going to the kitchens after the PAIT work, or to the Vaso de Leche before work. The other half had left their respective program and had not returned, even after the PAIT had ended. Thus at least half had ended their participation with communal programs. Others continued to participate, but were exhausted after eight hours of heavy physical labor in the PAIT.[87] This disruption might have been more acceptable if the PAIT program had not been temporary.

Of the women's criticisms, the most common was the uncertainty of the program and the lottery system. The work was criticized by some as being too difficult. The majority had dug ditches; others had painted walls or burned trash. Several perceived that only party people or the wealthier members of the community got into the program.[88] Opinions were in general split about whether or not the people's situation was better, but almost all wanted the PAIT to be reinstated. A few complimented the work of the mayor.

APRA, THE PAIT, AND THE MARGINALIZED: CONCLUSIONS

The results of the survey in Huascar and of the analysis of the PAIT's operation in San Juan de Lurigancho in general seem to complement the overall conclusions that can be drawn about the PAIT; and to demonstrate the complex issues raised by government-sponsored aid for the poor. Yet the program's temporary nature was a drawback, and the system of inscription by lottery precipitated a sense of instability and made the acquisition of a job a function of luck and government patronage. The program raised expectations and caused disruption in some communities and then was ended without warning. People did not know what to expect, as the government announced the drastic reduction of its funding for the program in a roundabout manner: the dissolution of COOPOP and the transfer of its programs to the municipalities. It is highly unlikely that most poor people would associate the PAIT with COOPOP. The government's announcement was made in January; as late as March many Huascar residents were still waiting for another round of PAIT work. Officials in San Juan de Lurigancho and the central PAIT office in La Molina both insisted that the PAIT would continue, but no one could specify how or with what funds.[89] This kept many poor in a position of uncertainty: not looking for other work or participating in programs that they had dropped for the PAIT, in hopes that there would soon be another round, thus creating a sense of dependency on the government.

On the other hand, the program did provide many women with a first employment experience and a newfound independence. It also contributed, with the labor of members of the very communities, to the development of several of the district communities' sorely inadequate infrastructure. These positive aspects, however, are undermined by the sudden termination of the program, which left the heightened expectations unfulfilled and public works unfinished in many parts of the district.

While the PAIT may have been designed with the best of intentions, the rather ad hoc manner in which it was implemented, without research into the side effects it might have on the target communities, as well as the abrupt way in which it was ended, reveal the pervasive lack of training and capable people in APRA ranks. The behavior of Acción Democratica in the *barrios* of Venezuela during its first tenure in power in the 1950s was characterized by lack of planning, inadequate training of local officials, and a high degree of sectarianism that limited the performance of local aid projects. These traits are analogous to APRA's performance in implementing the PAIT. With experience, however, AD changed its approach and now functions less exclusively and defensively.[90] In APRA's case it is unlikely that such an evolution occurred, given the polarized atmosphere and highly confrontational tone of the political debate of the latter part of its tenure in power.

The PAIT's potential as a long-term solution to the problems of chronic unemployment and inadequate income levels was clearly diminished by the lack of planning and foresight in terms of funding and side effects on community life, and by the usurping of the program for political purposes by both the García administration and party functionaries. The García government blatantly manipulated the program to fit its political timetable. Party functionaries, meanwhile, in implementing the PAIT, demonstrated the sectarianism and reliance on clientelism that APRA was traditionally known for. The use of patronage occurred from the highest level—most clearly demonstrated by the many cases of friends of apristas getting a chance to work when spots were short, and by the reserving of leadership positions for party members.

Yet the program clearly raised expectations and awareness. These hopes were hardly fulfilled by the termination of the program and the economic crisis that set in, leading to the frustration that has so often been a part of the history of pueblos jóvenes such as Huascar. The economic crisis, by mid-1988, was such that it eroded any short-term benefits the PAIT may have bestowed; in the meantime the PAIT disrupted autonomous community organizations, which were all the more crucial to survival in the face of the unprecedented deterioration of living standards that marked the latter part of the APRA regime. The result was political polarization and the ultimate rejection of traditional parties altogether by the poor. The extent to which APRA was willing to manipulate the poor, and the blatant manner in which it did so, seems more characteristic of authoritarian governments such as the Odría and Velasco regimes than of reformist parties.[91]

The urban poor, meanwhile, supported APRA when that support yielded tangible benefits, yet became aware of the clientelistic and manipulative nature of the government, particularly as programs were discontinued precisely before economic crisis set in. Support for the government plummeted: García's approval rating, which was over 90 percent early on, fell to 16 percent by September 1988. APRA attained only 13.5 percent of the vote of Lima's poor in the first round of elections in 1990[92] (see Table 8.1).

Traditionally the urban poor have turned to communal efforts to survive in times of crisis, and it is likely that the importance of communal kitchens and other such organizations—precisely those that were disrupted by some of APRA's programs—will grow in importance. However, the role of radical alternatives, given the focus of Sendero on disrupting existing communal organization, and given the severity of the crisis and the extent to which the government was discredited, cannot be discounted. Anecdotal evidence indicates that the presence of Sendero was much more pronounced in the pueblos by the latter half of the APRA regime;[93] actual support for the group is a different matter.

The PAIT in theory and the PAIT in practice proved to be largely different, and exposed certain undemocratic traits of the APRA government and party. This should not totally dispel our impression of the program's initial potential, despite its flaws, as an attempt to better the conditions of the workers of Lima's pueblos jóvenes. For the first time in Peru's history a program directed at the pueblos was, in theory at least, part of a coherent plan to make the poorest sectors active and central participants in the economic strategy. Even the "revolutionary" military regime failed to recognize the economic potential of the urban poor—focusing instead on building political support through SINAMOS and basing its strategy largely on state investment in large-scale infrastructure projects. However, while the APRA approach was conceptually different from those of its predecessors, there were serious flaws in implementation.

The apparent coherence in theory between the government's programs for the poor and its overall economic strategy was lost in practice. The tendency to operate from the central level with no regard for coordination with existing organizations—or even with its own municipalities— caused misallocation of funds and duplication of effort, as well as alienation of non-APRA-directed organizations. Party favoritism was pervasive. The PAIT's potential was undermined by the manner in which its fate was determined by political criteria. Indeed the way in which the program was used as a tool for clientelism and co-optation was sadly more reminiscent of how the military regime implemented SINAMOS, rather than of the behavior one might expect from a reformist democratic party. "Operating on the basis of the tremendous necessity for employment and income among the popular sectors, the administration attempted . . . the creation of direct control of the population by the government. In all cases, an explicit characteristic of the program was the marginalization of the neighborhood organizations . . . including its own local governments."[94]

There is nothing new in political parties' relying on patronage; it is pervasive in parties such as the AD in Venezuela. And aid programs are often used for political patronage ends, even in advanced industrial democracies. The balance between goals and overall policy objectives is important, however. Patronage in Venezuela is more prevalent among party leaders vying for posts in the government[95] than in the overt manipulation of programs for the extremely poor, who have little interest or stake in party affairs. As is described in the opening chapter, patronage is a common practice among political parties in developing countries, and the poor often manage to use clientelistic politics to their own advantage. There is, however, a tension between the use of patronage to build a political support base on the one hand, and the party's role in implementing comprehensive reform and consolidating democracy on the other. The party leaders' ability to maintain a commitment to longer-term goals of reform seems important in determining the extent to which patronage goals are allowed to supersede policy objectives. It seems that the AD's evolution in approach coincided with progress on the reform front and the consolidation of democracy in Venezuela. In APRA's case such a commitment was clearly lacking.

In political development terms, autonomous community organization is clearly one of the most basic foundations of democratic government and thus of democratic consolidation. Rather than serving as a bridge between state and society, the APRA party—because of its authoritarian and sectarian structure and behavior—served primarily to alienate much of nonparty society and thus to widen the gap. Clearly the task of consolidating democracy in societies where large sectors are marginalized is no easy task. Yet it is the premise of this study that the *nature* of the party in power can be a determining factor in this process, and that certain types of reformist parties are able to establish the conditions necessary for successful democratic reform and ultimately consolidation. Nowhere is it more clearly demonstrated than in APRA's relations with the marginalized— relations that the party itself stressed as vital—why the nature of the party made it incapable of establishing such conditions. Instead, by widening the gap between state and society, the party instigated the polarization that set in.

3
Conclusion

9

APRA 1968–1990: Impossible Revolution, Relinquished Reform

APRA's first experience in power as a single governing party began as a potential success story in democratic reformist government—unprecedented in Peru—yet then deteriorated into political polarization and severe economic collapse. In this analysis of the recent evolution of APRA I have sought, first and foremost, to lend insight to the difficult and fragile process of democratic consolidation in developing countries. The barriers to democratic reform and consolidation are particularly acute in countries such as Peru, where social mobilization and politicization have far outpaced the ability of the formal economy and polity to respond.

Huntington sees stable political institutions as integral to progress in development, and the sorry outcome of APRA's "experiment" in Peru lends credibility to his thesis. The case of APRA points to the critical role of the party as an institution. Parties have a fundamental representative role. Reformist parties in particular must also build and maintain a consensus for a viable macroeconomic strategy on the one hand, and incorporate the participation of the marginalized of society in that process on the other. This highlights the importance, particularly in the context of reformist parties in polarized societies, of ideological or doctrinal coherence. In APRA's case the party's ambiguity vis-à-vis reform versus revolution, coupled with its age-old authoritarian tendencies—and thus ultimately its commitment to electoral government—acted as a catalyst to polarization. The governing party's revolutionary rhetoric destroyed the consensus and confidence it initially built in the private sector and middle class, and at the same time was neither credible nor radical enough for the opposition on the left. The lack of agreement on doctrine within the party made it incapable of setting and abiding by "rules of the game," which are critical to the consensus necessary for democratic reform.

The lack of internal cohesiveness and agreement on the pace of change, the domination of the party by the erratic and autocratic García, and sectarian traits that precluded cooperation with nonparty members of society, all served to alienate opposition on both sides of the political spectrum—as well as society from polity more generally—and resulted in polarization and chaos similar in some respects to the Allende regime at the time of its breakdown. Peru had all of the characteristics that Sartori points to as typical of polarized polities: relevant antisystem parties; opposition from both sides of the political spectrum; a party or group of parties in the center; a wide spectrum of political opinion with deep cleavages and low consensus, questioning the legitimacy of the system; irresponsible oppositions; and a prevalent politics of outbidding or over-promising.[1] In Peru underlying economic conditions were far worse and the challenge from the armed left more formidable than in the case of Chile. Peruvian society in 1990 could be described as praetorian: social forces conflicting directly with each other, with a lack of agreement on a legitimate means for conflict resolution.[2] As Haggard and Kaufman conclude in a multicase comparison,[3] such a context is the least conducive to macroeconomic stability, and is one in which necessary stabilization measures are likely to be delayed. The dramatic deterioration that occurred in Peru—policymaking paralysis in the face of hyperinflation and hyperrecession—demonstrates their point well.

The APRA party's disastrous performance in power resulted in a rejection of parties in general by society, boding considerable uncertainty for the future of democratic consolidation in Peru. This rejection originated at the grassroots level and reflected the increased importance of autonomous local groups and the informal economy. That electoral results reflect this ongoing phenomenon should be no surprise, and indeed support from this sector of society was key to the 1990 victory of Alberto Fujimori.

Yet the rejection of parties also indicates a crisis of representation in Peru. The overwhelming support for a candidate who had no ties with the state or with the traditional polity reflected the existing breach between state and society. The basic representative function of parties has a role in virtually all consolidated democracies: channeling demands from society to state and from state to society. In developing countries such as Peru, where demands exceed state capacity to respond, the role of parties in channeling these demands *and* indicating their relative importance is critical.

Parties also play a role in guaranteeing institutional stability for nondemocratic actors such as the military. APRA filled this role during the transition to civilian rule and at the height of the García government's crisis. With the current scenario—an unstable coalition without a party basis—there is no institutional fallback in the event of a loss of leadership coherence. Ultimately the rejection of parties may result in a process of internal reform and adaptation to new societal realities within the parties themselves, which would clearly strengthen the democratic process in Peru. However, such a future will occur only with the solution of the current crisis of political polarization, economic collapse, and unrestrained social violence—a daunting task for any government, particularly one with a weak institutional base.

Tragically, APRA's tenure in power resulted in the increased im-
poverishment and the total alienation of the marginalized of society, the
very group that the party purported to represent. Its performance was in
keeping with Peru's age-old paradox: an extremely poor record of social
reform in spite of the long-term presence of a strong reformist party. This
raises the questions of why the implementation of reform is so difficult in
Peru, and why APRA in particular was so inept once in power. The failure
of APRA in government can be attributed to a variety of factors: the
nature of the party; the backwardness of Peru's political institutions in
general and politicians' inexperience or unwillingness to learn from past
errors; the behavior of individual leaders—primarily Alan García; and
finally, and perhaps most important, the severity of the challenges Peru
faced in the mid-1980s. The outcome was by no means preordained, and
the analysis of the disintegration that occurred highlights the prerequisite
conditions for successful reform: the emergence of a party system that can
guarantee economic elites a semblance of economic stability, and the
growth in strength of civil society. The performance of APRA in power,
and its failure to maintain the consensus that was so necessary to reform,
adds to the understanding of parties and more generally of the barriers to
democratic consolidation in countries such as Peru, where large sectors of
society are marginalized from the formal economy and polity.

THE APRA PARTY IN RETROSPECT

Since its inception, the APRA party has aroused more intense emotions
than any other force in Peruvian politics. This occurred for two reasons.
The first was that the party began with a revolutionary doctrine that sought
to challenge if not transform the existing order. The young Haya's penchant for action placed APRA much more in the forefront of the nation's
attention than its counterpart on the left, the Communist party. Because
the APRA machinery developed faster and much more extensively than
that of the Communists, and early on launched insurrectionary activity, it
was feared and opposed by the traditional elites more than any other
political force. The second reason was the nature of the party itself. The
sectarianism and sense of mission of party members, which in part grew
out of the persecution they suffered, made APRA exclusionary by nature
and prohibited effective political cooperation with other progressive
forces. Ironically, by the mid-1960s, tired of persistent persecution, the
party entered into an alliance with the conservative forces in Congress in
exchange for legality, and acted as a counterforce to reform. Its blocking
of reform was not only a function of its convivencia with the conservatives,
but also of a deeply imbedded party sentiment that it alone could implement reform—"solo el APRA salvara el Peru." This sectarianism exacer-

bated existing cleavages in polity and society, and created its own as well. Cleavages were made more extreme by political violence both outside and within APRA's ranks, a situation analogous to that of the Peronist party in Argentina in 1973–1976.

The belief that only APRA could implement reform was strongly shaken when the Velasco regime enacted a virtual carbon copy of the party's original program. APRA's was forced to revamp its strategy and renovate its doctrine and leadership ranks, which culminated in the election of Alan García. This involved an opening up of the party's image, including the temporary shelving of traditional APRA symbols that were seen as exclusive by outsiders. This opening up was neither complete nor permanent. The party's performance in government demonstrated that the sectarian tendencies, the sense of mission that prevailed over realism, and the hierarchical party structure that had led many external observers to attribute to it quasi-fascist rather than democratic characteristics, were all still evident. As the political situation increasingly became a crisis, these traits grew more pervasive and served to aggravate existing tendencies toward polarization in the system. The eventual result was the rejection of parties altogether, although not by the military as in the case of Argentina, but by the marginalized of society. The rejection of parties could be largely attributed to the manner in which the APRA operated among the poor.

The party's traits were evident not only at the central government level, but were even more prevalent at the municipal and middle-rank party levels, where sectarianism and the hierarchical approach resulted in the implementation of policies designed to help the poor in a way that often did more harm than good. This was most evident in APRA's implementation of the PAIT program. The party operated without any concern for existing organizations and community structure, and merely superimposed its own order. The commitment of community self-help groups such as communal kitchens is an autonomous and democratic means that the poor themselves have developed to cope with economic crisis and chaos. APRA's approach in implementing programs such as the PAIT, without any concern for the effects that it would have on such efforts, coupled with its insistence on party members' dominating existing leadership structures in the highly successful Comités de Vaso de Leche, was disruptive and authoritarian.

These traits were mirrored in the manner that APRA implemented the Rimanacuy—avoiding existing campesino organizations—and in its total disregard for labor unions and small-business organizations in its concertación strategy. This centralist, authoritarian approach fostered clientelism and dependence. It was an approach that was largely out of touch with the increase in activity and importance of autonomous local organizations, and ultimately was rejected by them, as the 1990 elections demonstrate. It served to undermine efforts at independent municipal government, even those of its own party, as the experience of San Juan de Lurigancho showed. This behavior was in part a function of the concentration of power in the central government coupled with a scarcity of resources, which is not unique to Peru. Yet the extent to which APRA manipulated programs for the poor, for political reasons, and the bluntness with which it did so, indicates that it was not only a function of municipalities in developing countries, but of traits inherent to the APRA party. A comparison with Chile during the Frei and Allende years is relevant. "[The] ubiquity (of particularistic transactions) was reinforced by two important and continuing characteristics of Chilean society: centralization and scarcity. The centralization of the political system not only cut back on the autonomy of municipalities . . . it transformed local officials into brokers between the distant offices of an omnipotent government and community people who became dependent on its regulations and services."[4]

In Peru the traditional government approach to the issue of urban poverty has been either co-optation or neglect. APRA's behavior at the municipal level and its implementation of policies to help the urban poor are particularly important in light of this tradition and APRA's rhetorical commitment to the poor, as well as of the expansive nature of urban poverty, which has also become inextricably linked with the growth of Sendero Luminoso and the additional migration that it has caused. As the APRA government's policies raised expectations and disrupted the poor's existing organizations, and then severely exacerbated their plight, their frustration with an economic and political system that ignored their concerns increased. The analysis of APRA's behavior toward the urban poor was a means to determine its nature as a reformist party; the results vividly demonstrate the traits that were the party's downfall at the central level as well. The approach in implementing the PAIT, in retrospect, was not very different from Odría's co-optative granting of land titles or from Velasco's attempts to control the autonomous organizations of the poor through SINAMOS, in that it was an approach from above that attempted to supersede vibrant and autonomous forms of popular organization with one designed to force political support. The most frustrating aspect of the APRA government's failure is the initial success of the regime and the potential success of its programs for the informal sector. Initially the García regime clearly had the support and potential to alleviate the problems of urban poverty and unemployment. Instead the party's own traits as well as García's erratic behavior resulted in the implementation of those programs in a manner that undermined their potential and alienated the very sector of society they were intended to benefit. This alienation coincided with Sendero's onslaught and the extension of terrorist violence on a widespread scale to the slums, a factor that would challenge autonomous popular organizations and fundamentally threaten democratic consolidation at the grassroots level.

APRA AND THE ARMED LEFT

I cannot conclude without mention of armed insurrectionary groups and the ideological and practical challenges that they posed for the APRA party and for democracy in Peru more generally. APRA began as the first political party in the nation's history to launch insurrection, and was subsequently a monopoly holder of the political space on the left until the 1950s convivencia. APRA as a movement and as an ideology influenced other revolutionary groups in Latin America, such as the sandinistas in Nicaragua, a heritage the party took pride in. Thus ideologically the party was in a difficult position when faced with insurrection from the left. The APRA links of many leftist leaders—from Polay Campos to Alfonso Barrantes to Luis de la Puente Uceda and the 1960s guerrillas—coupled with the strong appeal and support for insurrectionary activity among the APRA youth, made the party's position in formulating a coherent approach to the armed left a difficult one. The contradictory position of APRA, a supposedly revolutionary party, in the face of armed insurrection from groups either frustrated with the pace of reform or seeking to destroy existing social structures and government, points to the difficulty of implementing substantial social reform in a democratic context.

APRA's position was made more complex by the ambiguities in its doctrine and in the attitudes of its leaders about insurrection and commitment to democratic government. García's contradictory stances toward guerrilla movements and his blatant disdain for democratic leadership substantially undermined the legitimacy of the legislative system. APRA's predicament points to the importance of a commitment, both doctrinal and practical, to the democratic system on the part of reformist parties. Ambiguity and attempts to circumvent or dominate the system will ultimately serve to undermine it, particularly in the face of armed insurrection. Alan García could not act as both the leader of a democracy and a revolutionary at the same time. In this sense, his "different future," his "revolution in absolute liberty," given the polarized nature of Peruvian society and the severity of the challenges that it faced, was indeed an impossible one. García made the oft-repeated mistakes of radical reformers. By acting in a manner that was characterized by "provocativeness, abruptness, and lack of planning," he created for himself the dilemma of the battling reformer, victimized by entrenched opposition from both sides. Given that the early years of his regime had shown that consensus for reform was possible, that the elites were not inextricably entrenched, this was a sorry outcome, and the worst victims were the marginalized population whose cause APRA had espoused as a priority.

Under the APRA government, democracy was functioning only as a formality, and while a substantial sector of society was actively engaged in armed insurrection, the debates in the halls of Congress grew increasingly irrelevant and polemical. This was indeed a product of the lack of political institutionalization that Huntington describes, but more fundamentally it was a result of the lack of agreement both within APRA and in Peruvian society in general about basic societal and political values. "Value sharing endows a social system with a homeostatic capacity. . . . Dahrendorf has observed, 'For effective conflict regulation to be possible, both parties to a conflict have to recognize the necessity and reality of the conflict situation, and in this sense, the fundamental justice of the cause of the opponent.' The antagonists must, in short, share some of the same values."[5]

This lack of agreement was also reflected in an institutional crisis: the inability of political institutions to represent the interests of society, and of the state to address its basic needs. In electoral terms this was demonstrated by the rejection of traditional parties by the majority in 1990, creating considerable uncertainty for Peru's political future. More damaging, though, and far more threatening to democratic consolidation, this phenomenon manifested itself most vividly by an increase of political violence from all sides of the political spectrum.

APRA'S POLITICAL CULTURE: MÍSTICA

Amid all of this, APRA continued to function, at a very different level, as a spontaneous force that provided many Peruvians with a sense of integration, a sense that so much of the nation was lacking. One observer noted that Haya de la Torre's foremost achievement in founding APRA was his attempt to provide a means to integrate Peru culturally and politically. Haya provided Peruvians with a political movement that was uniquely their own, with an ideology that was based on Peru's realities, and with a Latin American interpretation of history and a view of the world. APRA's influence outside Peru provided apristas with a sense of pride; the party's activities inside the country and the persecution that it faced because of them, with a sense of mission and an identity. The ideology that Haya introduced was clearly Marxist and antiimperialist in its origins. However, his coining of the term *Indo-America*, his focus on issues of Latin concern such as the Panama canal, and his inclusionary nature rather than a focus on class struggle—the alliance of manual and intellectual workers—combined to give the party an original and eclectic vision, one Peruvians of diverse origins could identify with. This effect was augmented by the mercurial nature of Haya's philosophy, such as the

theory of *espacio-tiempo histórico,* which could justify APRA's ideological compromises and shifts, facilitating its appeal to a broader base. Haya's
concern for the oppressed, and his position as the first actor in modern
Peruvian politics to challenge the nature of Peruvian society, gave him a
stature that remains unequaled.

The APRA mística—its appeal to followers on a cultural and almost
religious level rather than on a political one—was still evident in the 1980s
within the party, and was what set it apart from all other political parties
in the country. Aprismo at this level involved unquestioning loyalty—not
so much to Alan García as to Haya de la Torre and his ideals—and a sense
of shared experiences, including that of persecution. These loyalties were
analogous to familial rather than political ties, and included groups who
had very little interest in politics.

The one crucial group that did not share in these experiences, and thus
had very different loyalties, was the APRA youth, who had never known
Haya and for whom the party leader was Alan García. This youth may
clearly have admired García, but his youth and the realities of being
president provided a very different image from that of the mythical Haya.
Young apristas sought their own myths, and in their impatience were
drawn by the allure of the MRTA and even of Sendero. The desperate
socioeconomic situation in the country added to their need for a myth or
a cause to inspire faith.

APRA under Haya had been able to provide, at least for its adherents,
a cause, a sense of belonging, a sense of integration. The post-Haya APRA
was less able to do so. The partial loss of mística was in part a product of
the different behavior that holding power dictated for the party leaders,
and the necessary relegation of party affairs to secondary importance. It
was also, however, due to the sort of leader and personality that Haya de
la Torre was, and the stature that he held in Peruvian politics and history.
Alan García, despite his oratorical skills and his complex emotional
baggage, could not replace the figure of Haya, and thus the party lost an
important part of the glue that had held it together—through persecution
and imprisonment, convivencia with Prado, alliances with Odría, and
finally the military's "usurping" of APRA's revolution.

This cultural aprismo will continue to exist and to give Peruvian
politics a unique quality. However, because of the difficulties the party
faced in power, the growth of the left—both armed and unarmed, the
radicalization of the party's own youth; and ultimately the absence of
Haya and his contemporaries, aprismo popular will become less and less
influential. The APRA mística remains a hope increasingly separate from
political realities. This is in part due to the lack of real intellectual debate
and even of intellectuals in the party, and thus the inability to respond with
a coherent party platform designed to deal with the nation's problems.
The lack of intellectuals was in part the result of the prevalence of mística

over realistic debates on policy. Neither García's update of Haya's ideas in *El futuro diferente* nor endless debates over Haya's works could fill this gap. Ideological shifts were far less important to the party faithful than was their *mística*; yet this had little appeal to intellectuals who were not born into the party. The sectarianism that was part and parcel of this political culture also had limited appeal and created a cleavage between APRA and the rest of society that was to act as a substantial obstacle to its ability to govern.

When Haya first introduced the APRA program he provided Peru, and in some ways Latin America, with a new way—one not imported from abroad—of looking at and overcoming existing realities and injustices. Haya's success also lay in his political genius, which managed to transform APRA from a front of students with a support base among a few labor groups into a party of national and international renown. While APRA under García was able to provide the crisis-stricken Peruvian nation with a temporary sense of hope, its efforts were short-lived and its plans empty. The APRA of the 1980s, lacking the brilliance that had characterized the generation of the 1920s, had to rely on an underskilled party apparatus and on a party doctrine that was revolutionary and innovative in 1920, but hopelessly outdated in 1985. Thus APRA *mística* continued, but continued to relive Haya's past "glories," not to provide a solution for Peru's realities. "Without the ghost of Haya and the contradictory dreams of Aprismo, García would be but another helpless reformer in the morass of Peru's present social tragedy. Haya and Aprismo provide a ray of hope and faith and a banner of struggle in a nearly impossible situation; perhaps ultimately this is the most important of Haya's contributions to Peru."[6]

APRA AND DEMOCRATIC CONSOLIDATION IN PERU

Peru by the end of the 1980s faced what José Matos Mar has called a *desborde popular*, or a popular overflow. The nation's institutions, economic as well as political, were totally incapable of dealing with the demands placed upon them by society, and thus society functioned primarily outside them. Peruvian society has yet to be integrated politically, economically, and culturally, and this lack of integration is expressed in the economic sphere by the dominance of the informal economy, and in the political and cultural spheres in its most extreme form by Sendero Luminoso and other groups involved in armed insurrection.

> One of the fundamental processes that make up the situation today in Peru is the accelerated growth of an unusual dynamic that affects its entire social, political, economic, and cultural structure. It is an overflow, in all dimensions, of the institutional guidelines that direct national society . . . the popular sectors that, questioning the authority of the state

and falling back on multiple strategies and parallel mechanisms, are altering the established rules and changing the face of Peru.[7]

APRA's ideology, its message, its disciplined party machine, and finally the personality of Haya de la Torre made the party a point of departure for cultural and political integration. Yet the polarized nature of Peruvian society made the unifying element of APRA—from the time it originated—a threat to the nation's elites. APRA's confrontational behavior coupled with the repression of its opponents early on served to polarize the debate: one was either for or against APRA. While the nature of the debate changed with the military revolution and the emergence of the left, APRA remained a unique and prevalent force in Peruvian politics. Despite a history of ideological compromise, the party retained its sense of mission, as well as the sectarianism that grew out of that sense of mission and of the party's struggle to survive. However, once APRA finally attained power, the very traits that had enabled it to survive were in large part responsible for its inability to provide the national integration that its mission called for.

APRA's historical role as the most prevalent organized political force in Peru has linked it, either directly or indirectly, with most attempts to reform or transform the nation, whether through the Velasco regime's use of prista doctrine or Haya de la Torre's role in the transition to civilian rule; whether directly through Alan García's government or indirectly through its links with the left: Barrantes, Polay Campos of the MRTA, and many in the guerrilla movement of the 1960s all began their political careers as apristas. Perhaps most ironically, the traditional rivalry between Haya and Mariátegui—and between apristas and Communists—became prevalent in a most extreme form, between the struggling APRA government and those who claim to be following Mariátegui's "Shining Path."

Despite APRA's own efforts and its direct links to other attempts to transform Peru, none have succeeded. APRA's inability was the result of characteristics of the party and parties like it, which tended to exacerbate existing cleavages and polarizing tendencies in the system; of the extent of polarization that existed in Peruvian society; and of the extent to which that polarization was aggravated by the past decade of economic crisis. In Peru, "more than any other South American country, the economic depression of the early 1980's and the associated debt crisis exposed fundamental internal weakness."[8] In the face of increased social mobilization and economic pressures, there was a total lack of agreement among the nation's leaders about basic political tenets, with particularistic ideologies and interests taking precedence over issues of national concern. "A society with weak political institutions lacks the ability to curb the excesses of personal and parochial desires . . . for the sake of general social objectives."[9]

In the case of Peru such personal and parochial impulses included fundamental disagreements among politicians over whether democracy was a permanent system or a stage before a violent transition to socialism. The fact that the total commitment to democratic government did not exist among all the ranks of the governing party or of the democratic left—many advocated armed struggle—put pressure on the capacity of already weak institutions. In society in general, as was demonstrated by the rise of Sendero Luminoso, there was an absence of agreement on the basic values, the homeostatic equilibrium that Dahrendorf describes as essential to stable societies. In the face of overwhelming pressures on insufficient institutions and of a lack of agreement on basic values, the political system grew increasingly polarized, dominated by what Sartori labels centrifugal tendencies.[10] He notes that the position of the center party in polarized systems is often untenable, as APRA's became, largely because of its own behavior. "A center party that attempts to outdo the parties located on its left or right will contribute, more than anything else, to a crescendo of escalation and extremism."[11]

As is noted in the opening chapter, rigid, hierarchically organized parties that manage affairs in a highly centralized manner have utopian philosophies, and a sectarian approach to society, are most likely to clash with local organizations and aggravate polarizing trends. This was the case of, for example, the Christian Democrats during the Frei years in Chile. The loss of a coherent center coalition led to the polarized situation of the Allende period. Sectarianism and sense of mission are distinct from ideological coherence, however. APRA shared the former traits with the Christian Democrats, but not the latter, and disagreements on fundamental issues such as armed insurrection added to the chaos in APRA's case.

In light of APRA's shortcomings, the contrasts made in the first chapter with a successful reformist party, AD, and the similarities noted with the Peronists are relevant. AD's commitment to reform within the democratic system, its ability to temper its sectarian approach with experience, and its ability to maintain the support of its own left wing, enhanced both its position in the political spectrum—as it was not the untenable center—and the possibilities for pursuing pragmatic reform. The Peronists, on the other hand, shared APRA's lack of doctrinal clarity—its inability to satisfy more-radical elements within its own ranks; and maintained the strong sense of party affiliation as a social identity that alienated much of the rest of society. In both cases economic mismanagement and radical rhetoric alienated the private sector, yet did not satisfy the radical left. Highly ideologized discourse and authoritarian behavior created cleavages in society and polity, precluding the building of consensus and exacerbating polarization.

A key factor in this polarization process—which was determined by the nature of the party—was the manner in which the reformist debate was presented. Initially the APRA government distinguished itself from other efforts at radical reform, which had all resulted in polarization. The way in which reform is presented—the instruments used, the rhetoric chosen and the extent of provocation, "the willingness of policymakers to improvise and calibrate their measures despite ideological qualms, [as] opposition coalitions form as much from feelings of threat as from actual deprivations,"[12]—are all more important than the stated ideology or political category of the reformers. The success of Communist reformers in a private enterprise setting that Kohli points to is a case in point. The creation of a predictable environment, in which the rules of the game, the extent of reformist intents, are clear, is critical to successful reform. Governments of different ideological bent, military or civilian, have all fallen into the same quagmire. Ascher compares Allende in Chile, Campora in Argentina, and Velasco in Peru. "The commonality of these efforts lay not in ideological uniformity, for neither Campora nor Velasco were Marxists, but rather in the provocativeness, abruptness, and lack of planning of each attempt."[13] The result of the reliance of these reformers on an increase in the public sector, leftist rhetoric, and confrontations to mobilize workers, was "the adamant opposition of a private business sector that feared massive expropriation."[14] In some cases, such as Velasco's, this was the very sector that he had hoped to rely on for investment, and he was then forced to turn to an inadequate state. Surprisingly, after a very different start, the APRA government repeated the same mistakes.

In the first years of García's government the debate was presented in such a way as to avoid antagonism and thus polarization. The term *marginal* was used instead of *class*, a tactic also utilized in the past by Chile's Christian Democrats. This contrasts sharply with García's later phrases about exterminating the middle class—as well as all owners of electric blenders—and calling for a "war economy." García's avoidance of unnecessary confrontation was key to consensus early on in his regime, and his surprise shift at the time of the bank nationalizations was a major factor in its breakdown.

The shift from an inclusive and cooperative approach to a winner-take-all, "us versus them" approach proved fatal to democratic consensus. Economic elites in Peru, although their power was substantially reduced by the military and while clearly accepting of the need for some social reform, still maintained enough strength so that their cooperation was necessary for an effective economic growth strategy, particularly in the absence of any foreign capital and the weak capacity of the state. Lower-income groups, on the other hand, may have at first relished García's rhetoric—although the ownership of the banks was hardly an issue of import in most poor households—but were quickly disillusioned as economic collapse yielded hyperinflation and acute shortages of both jobs and basic goods. Imposed in an autocratic and poorly planned manner, the banks nationalization was the classic case of alienating the private sector while failing to build support for reformist initiative among other crucial groups. Most ironic is that the measure was imposed primarily for political reasons, and had no positive effect on distribution. "The ideological rigidity of [the] governments, and their preoccupation with macropolitics rather than economic detail, inhibited the concrete planning and policy flexibility required."[15]

Ideological rigidity is not the same as ideological coherence. Ideological coherence entails a key distinction between democratic reformist and revolutionary approaches. Democratic reform involves inclusion of as many social sectors as possible and requires eliciting their cooperation; key to its success is a delicate process of consensus building in which the nature of the political party in power plays a major role. Revolutionary change most often involves coercion. Elites, as during Velasco's time, would not cooperate when threatened with coercion. García—unclear himself about whether he was a democratic reformer or a revolutionary— tried to play both games, which was impossible. APRA had the same lack of clarity in its doctrine, which was not resolved in the 1980s renovation of the party. The lack of ideological coherence and García's penchant for radical rhetoric and grandiose gestures made the maintenance of consensus and therefore democratic reform impossible. "Attention to detail, when the world seems to require radical transformation, is often regarded with disdain by radicals, giving rise to economic 'romanticism' or 'naivete'."[16]

Reform in Peru required substantive policies to alleviate poverty and create employment, something the APRA government at first recognized. Ironically, with the banks nationalization, García focused the debate in the same way that it had been during Velasco's time: on the structure of property relations. As with the transfer of resources from private property to large state enterprises, the poor fared no better with the nationalization of the banks. Instead their position was made worse by the ensuing economic collapse.

PERUVIAN DEMOCRACY AND REFORM IN THE FUTURE

In many ways the barriers to effective democratic reform in Peru have existed throughout its history. Certainly APRA, whose history is a struggle against a conservative and antireformist military-elite alliance, was frustrated by such barriers. During the first Belaúnde regime APRA itself acted as such a barrier, unwilling to accept the political costs of reforms being implemented by an opposition party. The stalemate of all reformist attempts in Congress was one of the main factors in the military's frustration with and overthrow of the civilian political system. What is striking—and extremely disappointing—is that after the military docenio, the transition to civilian rule, and the supposed renovation of the APRA party and its initial success, the barriers to reform are as evident as before. The nation's leaders seem to have learned few lessons, which is both a result of the "freezing" of political activity by the military, closing opportunity for political experience, and of the absence of political institutionalization.

The social pressures in Peru are indeed the most extreme on the continent. Society is in a process of violent disintegration. The irony is that as the problems facing society grow larger, so does the temptation to revert to dogmatic debate, precisely at the time that pragmatic and careful solutions are most vital. The result has been polarization, both within the political system and between the system and the society that it supposedly represents. APRA as a party and government was a major catalyst in this process. While weak institutions, heightened political mobilization, and the need for coherent economic policy and social reform pointed to a critical role for a reformist party like APRA in the transition to and the consolidation of democracy, the party's machinery and complex ideological baggage made it incapable of fulfilling that role.

The question remains whether another political force could have performed better, given the constraints facing Peru in 1985. Success was not preordained, but neither was disaster; the nature of the party was the determining factor. It suffered a lack of skilled personnel within its ranks, and at the same time sectarian and authoritarian traits acted as obstacles to the consensus building that is necessary for democratic government. Alan García was a unique orator and energetic leader, yet his autocratic style and volatile personality, coupled with the unresolved dilemma in his own mind and in his party between democratic reform or radical confrontation, led to incoherence in policymaking. While at first the APRA government was able to elicit the unprecedented cooperation of the nation's elites behind a reformist government, the haphazard shift of the president to a confrontational and exclusionary approach quickly upset the delicate balance that was required for this consensus. This, coupled with APRA's lack of experience with expressing dissent with its leaders, and the tendency of both the left and right to attempt to benefit from APRA's errors rather than seek consensus, resulted in the virtual breakdown of policymaking and regime coherence. The reformist debate again became—as it has been historically in Peru—one of confrontation, of winner-take-all, of the opposition's behaving as if it had a greater stake in the failure of the government than in the success of the civilian political system.

In Peru there are several obstacles to successful democratic reform. First and foremost is the lack of agreement on basic societal values and tenets—homeostatic equilibrium—as is evidenced by the relatively widespread support for groups involved in armed struggle. This presents a challenge for any government, but particularly for a reformist democracy that, without the backing of strong institutions, must rely totally on consensus building for effective government. The transition to democracy in the context of a severely underdeveloped economy with a massive employment shortage, with capital highly concentrated in either a few private firms or large state enterprises, a burgeoning informal sector, and a continuing economic crisis led to an increasingly doctrinaire approach to the nation's problems precisely at the time that they dictated pragmatism and consensus. The result was the termination of reformist initiatives, deepening economic crisis and social upheaval, and a plethora of endless and pointless ideological debates in the halls of Congress. The system was clearly disconnected from the society that it supposedly represented. There was indeed the desborde popular that Matos Mar describes.

Democracy exists in Peru only in the sense that political freedom is not restricted. Democratic consolidation remains an elusive goal. The *vieja democracia verbal* that Haya originally challenged still prevails, although it now includes even the Marxist left. Until the nation's divergent political forces can forge some sort of consensus to work toward progress and social reform, there will not be the "fated progress towards equality"[17] that Toqueville says must accompany democracy.

Two conditions were identified as critical to the consolidation of democracy in the beginning of this study: the emergence of a party system that can provide a minimum degree of economic stability; and the growth in the strength of civil society. Peru in 1990 was further from meeting those conditions than it was in 1985: political parties in general were rejected by the electorate, and the system was both fragmented and polarized. Civil society, meanwhile, was being undermined by political violence and economic turmoil. APRA, the nation's only truly institutionalized party as well as the governing party during this period, bears a primary responsibility. The party was the first force in Peru to recognize the dire necessity of its task of reform; its performance in power was in keeping with a history of frustrated attempts to achieve its elusive goal.

On the other hand, there is perhaps room for cautious optimism. Despite the challenge from armed insurrectionary groups and from extreme economic crisis, elections were successfully held, and the results reflected a movement—from civil society itself—to go beyond a polity that was out of touch with Peru's realities. While the rejection of traditional parties and ideologies does not signify the rejection of democracy per se, it does signify a crisis of representation. Democratic consolidation will depend on the ability of political institutions, parties in particular, to adapt to new realities, especially the increased importance of autonomous local organizations. Another prerequisite is the attainment of economic stability in the short term and renewed growth in the longer run. A prolongation of the current economic crisis and associated social turmoil is a cost that the already impoverished Peruvian society cannot afford.

This study demonstrates that the *nature* of political institutions, parties in particular, can be critical. In other cases, such as that of the Acción Democrática in Venezuela and the Christian Democrats in Chile,[18] parties were able to adapt to new social and political realities, and by doing so greatly enhanced the process of democratic consolidation in their respective nations. If institutions in Peru—APRA and other political parties in particular—do not adapt, then the prospects for even minimal economic and political stability are bleak. The current situation is a political experiment of sorts: democratic politics operating outside the realm of traditional democratic institutions. Like all experiments, it may have a favorable outcome. The hope is that democratic consolidation moves beyond the experimentation stage.

POSTSCRIPT

On April 5, 1992, President Fujimori suspended Peru's constitution, dissolved the Congress and the judiciary, and placed several Congressional leaders and members of the opposition under house arrest. The measures, which were fully supported by all three branches of the armed forces, were announced in the name of guaranteeing order and stability, eliminating corruption, and fighting drug traffic. They amounted to an "autogolpe" or self-coup: a military coup against the government led by the president himself. In the days following, the government announced a referendum on the measures for July of 1992, and new elections for Congress for February 1993.

There are many plausible explanations for the "autogolpe." The most significant, which is noted in Chapter 7, was Fujimori's lack of organized or party-based support, resulting in his increasing reliance on the armed forces and on rule by decree. By early 1992, the APRA, which had originally supported Fujimori, had coalesced the opposition in Congress—rather ironically—under the leadership of Alan García. After the coup, APRA leaders, García included, were specifically targeted by government repression, indicating that the government felt threatened by APRA opposition. In March there had been a politically damaging scandal among Fujimori's close circle of advisors: his wife publicly accused his brother—his closest advisor—of misuse of foreign aid donations. Another of Fujimori's close advisors, Vladimiro Montesinos, a retired army intelligence officer with questionable links to the drug traffic, had been pressuring the president for some time to free the counter-insurgency struggle from judicial "interference." This coincided with a major Sendero assault on Lima. At the same time, relations with the United States were at an all time low due to disagreements over counter-narcotics strategy, possibly leading Fujimori to conclude that there was not much to lose from jeopardizing relations with the United States.

The international community's reaction to the coup was negative. Most international financial organizations delayed loans, and the United States government suspended all aid other than humanitarian assistance. This threatened the entire economic recovery strategy, which was based on "reinsertion" into the international economic community. Despite international condemnation, Fujimori refused to rescind the suspension of constitutional government, and the armed forces reasserted their support for the measures. The situation posed a serious threat to democratic government and to respect for human rights. It also played into Sendero Luminoso's strategy of provoking a coup in order to polarize society into military and non-military camps. As of late April, the prospects for democratic government—much less democratic consolidation—were minimal at best.

Notes

Throughout the manuscript, quotations that originally were in Spanish are my own translation.—C.G.

CHAPTER 1

1. Huber-Stephens, p. 171.
2. Angell, *Politics and the Labour Movement in Chile,* p. 177.
3. Thoumi, p. 44.
4. Huntington.
5. Sartori.
6. Angell, "Trade Unions in Chile in the 1980's," p. 32.
7. Oxhorn.
8. Guillermo Campero, cited in Angell, "Trade Unions."
9. Nelson covers the voting behavior of the urban poor in a wide array of countries throughout the Third World and concludes that they are markedly pragmatic in their political behavior, rather than potential revolutionaries, as is often assumed. In Peru the urban poor have at times provided a significant base of support for dictators who provided, or promised to provide, them with tangible benefits, as did Manuel Odría and Juan Velasco, for example.
10. Gay, p. 107.
11. Ibid.
12. Huber-Stephens, pp. 158-159.
13. The well-known work of Guillermo O'Donnell, Phillippe Schmitter, and Laurence Whitehead, *Transitions to Democracy,* focuses on transitions to democracy in Latin America rather than on democratic consolidation, as does the edited volume of James M. Malloy and Mitchell A. Seligson, *Authoritarians and Democrats: Regime Transition in Latin America.* Works on consolidating democracy, such as Alfred Stepan's *Democratizing Brazil* and Cynthia McClintock's "The Prospects for Democratic Consolidation in a Least Likely Case: Peru," have focused more on single cases.
14. McClintock, ibid.
15. J. Samuel Valenzuela.
16. Huber-Stephens.
17. Samuel Huntington, speaking to the annual meeting of the American Political Science Association, Washington, DC, September 2, 1988.

18. Toqueville.

19. Petras, p. 12.

20. Huber-Stephens, p. 166. Seymour Martin Lipset, "Social Requisites of Democracy: Economic Development and Political Legitimacy. *American Political Science Review* 53, March 1959; and James M. Mallory and Mitchell A. Seligson, *Authoritarians and Democrats: Regime Transition in Latin America* (Pittsburgh: University of Pittsburgh Press, 1987), among others, note the correlation between economic development and democracy.

21. Haggard and Kaufman, p. 1.

22. Ibid.

23. Kohli. I thank Atul Kohli also for discussing these ideas with me in detail on several occasions.

24. Ibid.

25. Randall.

26. Samuel Huntington, cited in Randall, ibid.

27. Duverger.

28. Randall, p. 42.

29. Huber-Stephens, p. 164.

30. Randall.

31. Ibid.

32. Migdal.

33. Duverger, p. 2.

34. Ibid.

35. Sartori, p. 134. This tendency among opposition parties is also noted by Duverger.

36. Duverger, p. 390.

37. Randall.

38. Paul Drake, cited in Dornbusch and Edwards.

39. Dix.

40. Dornbusch and Edwards add that they "emphasize that the redistributive objectives are a central part of the paradigm. Whether they are moderated by a strategy of massive social reform is consequential but is not central to our discussion" (p. 4).

41. Paul Drake, cited in Stein.

42. Ascher, p. 303. "Opposition coalitions form as much from feelings of threat as from actual deprivation" (p. 304).

43. Ibid., p. 292.

44. Oxhorn, p. 43.

45. Angell, "Some Problems in the Interpretation of Recent Chilean History," p. 537.

46. Sartori.

47. Coppedge, p. 75.

48. Ibid.

49. Ibid., p. 88.

50. Gillespie, p. 223.

51. Rock, p. 185.

52. Gillespie, p. 46.

53. Rock.

CHAPTER 2

1. Klaren, p. xviii.
2. Thorp and Bertram, p. 3.
3. See, e.g., Klaren; Pike, *A Modern History of Peru;* and Stein.
4. Pike, *Modern History,* p. 238. Like the democratic populists that Dix describes, APRA was international in its orientation.
5. Ibid., p. 240.
6. Klaren, p. xvii. Klaren's view of the extent to which the north coast was dominated by the Graces and Gildemeisters may be exaggerated. However, his interpretation is useful in understanding the resentment of foreign influence that was a key factor in the support for APRA.
7. North, p. 41.
8. Ibid.
9. Stein, p. 145.
10. Ravines. Ravines, who was initially friendly with Haya, then became a leader of the Peruvian Communist party, and subsequently defected and became an informer for the US Central Intelligence Agency, must be read with caution. However, his proximity to both Haya and Mariategui in the crucial 1920s make his insights worthy of note.
11. Alexander, p. 21.
12. Cotler, "Democracy and National Integration in Peru." A neutral view of the party seemed virtually impossible, even among foreign scholars.
13. Vega Centeno, *Aprismo popular,* p. 131.
14. Angell, *Peruvian Labour and the Military Government Since 1968,* p. 1.
15. Stein, p. 188. Sánchez Cerro received slightly over 49 percent of the vote versus Haya's slightly over 34 percent. Stein makes a convincing case that APRA's claims of widespread fraud were untenable. Sánchez Cerro maintained a substantial popular following because he overthrew Leguía.
16. Bourricaud, *Pouvoir et Société dans la Pérou contemporaine,* p. 156. ("Nous sommes les citoyens exemplaires d'un parti exemplaire. Et si nous sommes exemplaire c'est parce que nous avons souffert et que nous avons su suffrir").
17. Bourricaud, "Ideología y desarrollo," p. 24.
18. Angell, "The Difficulties of Policymaking and Implementation in Peru," p. 1.
19. Ibid.
20. Ibid.
21. Jaquette, pp. 57–58.
22. Long and Roberts, p. 13.
23. Ibid., pp. 13–15.
24. Ibid.
25. Nancy R. Johnson.
26. Angell, "Classroom Maoists."
27. Long and Roberts.

28. Angell, *Peruvian Labour and the Military Government Since 1968.*

29. For an account of APRA in control of the legislature during the Bustamante years, see Bustamante y Rivero; Thorp and Bertram, pp. 187–188. For the Odría and Prado years, see Sánchez, vol. 3; Hilliker; Jaquette; and Long and Roberts. For the 1963–1968 Belaúnde years, see Kuczynski; Webb, *Government Policy and the Distribution of Income in Peru, 1963–1973.*

30. Sánchez, vol. 6, p. 243. The unofficial name of Venezuela's Acción Democrática—like APRA's—is Partido del Pueblo, the party of the people.

31. Bourricaud, *Pouvoir et société dans la Pérou contemporaine,* p. 160. ("Comment expliquer cette réussite. Le courage, la détermination des clandestines apristes y ont leur part. Mais pour apprécier plus exactment ces vertus, il fait ajouter la hypothèse: si l'Apra a si bien tenu le coup entre 1933 et 1945, et encore entre 1948 et 1956, c'est qu'a cette époque, pour un apriste, j'entends pour un militant engagé, aucune autre voie n'e concevable que l'Apra").

CHAPTER 3

1. Interviews with Sánchez, Lima, February 5 and March 16, 1988.

2. Jaquette, pp. 82–84.

3. Collier, p. 155.

4. Thorndike, *La revolución imposible,* p. 88. Thorndike's book is a semiofficial biography of Alan García. He has published a historical novel about APRA, *El año de la barbarie,* and also served as an advisor to the Velasco regime. The accuracy of his facts in *La revolución imposible* was confirmed by my interview with César Atala (a member of APRA and Peruvian ambassador to the United States) in Washington, July 11, 1988.

5. Interview with Javier Valle Riestra, Lima, March 3, 1988. Valle Riestra is a high-ranking member of APRA, and at one point was slated as a possible candidate for the 1985 elections.

6. For a comprehensive evaluation of the successes and failures of the military revolution, see Lowenthal and McClintock.

7. Franco.

8. Interview with General Anibal Meza Cuadra, in del Pilar Tello (1983).

9. Pike, "Visions of Rebirth." The military's turning to precisely the same parties it previously overthrew is the scenario described by Vicky Randall, noted in Chapter 1.

10. Interview with Jorge Fernández Maldonado, in del Pilar Tello (1983).

11. Sánchez, vol. 5. Sánchez asserts, both in his book and in my interviews with him, that 90 percent of the text of the law adopted by the military was the same as that proposed by APRA. While this may be an exaggeration, most observers agree that the land reform that the military implemented was not vastly different from the various proposals circulating in Congress prior to the coup.

12. Kus. I verified Kus's conclusions with data from the Peruvian Ministry of Agriculture, which confirm the drop in productivity of Peruvian sugar farms as well as the drop in wages. The sugar haciendas are now heavily in debt to the government, and Peru is a net sugar importer.

13. Sánchez, vol. 5, p. 209.

14. Angell, *Peruvian Labour and the Military Government Since 1968.*

15. Kus, p. 23.

16. Cotler, "The New Mode of Political Domination in Peru." For detail on the General Industries Law, see also Angell, *Peruvian Labour and the Military Government Since 1968.* Also see Angell for detail on the Labor Stability Law.

17. For detail see Webb, *Government Policy and the Distribution of Income in Peru.*

18. Townsend Escurra.

19. Angell, *Peruvian Labour and the Military Government Since 1968.*

20. Ibid.

21. Ibid., p. 15.

22. Angell and Thorp, p. 876.

23. Collier, pp. 145–153. The Pamplona invasion coincided with the meeting in Lima of the Board of Governors of the Inter-American Development Bank. The term *pueblo jóven* was first used by Bishop Bombaren, but then was picked up by the military.

24. Ibid., pp. 145–153.

25. Ibid., p. 157.

26. Dietz.

27. Ibid. The poor display similar hostility to parties that threaten their independent organizations, as is noted in Chapter 1 and detailed in Part 3.

28. Ibid., p. 131.

29. Delgado, *Revolución peruana.*

30. Ibid, p. 21.

31. Collier, p. 145.

32. Interview with Carlos Franco, Lima, March 8, 1988. Franco worked closely with Delgado during the Velasco years.

33. Delgado, *Revolución peruana,* p. 60.

34. Franco, quoted in Vásquez Bazan, p. 184. It is unlikely that Franco is exaggerating here. Delgado's influence has been noted by both critics and supporters of the regime.

35. Interview with Carlos Franco, Lima, March 8, 1988.

36. Thorp, "Evolution of Peru's Economy." Debt service was 37 percent of exports, and inflation was over 20 percent for 1975.

37. Angell and Thorp. Even the officially sponsored CTRP did not remain loyal to the government.

38. *Perú: cronología política,* vol. 4 (Lima: Centro de Estudios y Promoción del Desarrollo, 1975).

39. Crabtree, "Peru," p. 231.

40. Townsend Escurra, p. 2.

41. Thorndike, *La revolución imposible,* pp. 28–32.

42. *Perú: cronología política,* vol. 1 (1968).

43. Interview with Andrés Townsend Escurra, Lima, March 3, 1988. Townsend received the message through his own military attaché, which, at that time, Chamber presidents had.

44. Sánchez, vol. 5, p. 116.

45. Thorndike, *La revolución imposible,* p. 248.

46. Interview with César Atala, Washington, July 11, 1988.

47. Ibid. At the time, A. Villaneuva contacted Atala, a loyal aprista and the Inter-American Development Bank representative in the Caribbean, to explore the possibility of a meeting of Haya and APRA leaders in Trinidad.

48. Sánchez, vol. 5, p. 291. See also Kus's conclusions, discussed above.

49. Ibid., p. 295. This is confirmed by *Perú: cronología política* (1972).

50. Sánchez, vol. 5, p. 289. Mulder also recounts these incidents in his article, but with less detail. The person who was rumored to be after Haya, "Compadre Silvio," turned out to be a hairdresser rather than a villain, and the plot was afterward called the *complot de peluqueros.*

51. Mulder.

52. Sánchez, vol. 5, p. 290. Again this can be confirmed by the relevant dates in *Perú: cronología política* (1972).

53. Sánchez, vol. 5, p. 188; confirmed in *Perú: cronología política.* Sánchez's interpretation of the deportation of Idiaquez as a direct stab at Haya is probably correct, given Haya's dependence on Idiaquez, particularly as he grew older. The Velasco regime, meanwhile, must have been aware of the public uproar and opposition that deporting Haya would have caused.

54. Interview with Luis Alberto Sánchez, Lima, February 5 and March 16, 1988.

55. Interview with Pedro Richter Prada, former prime minister, Republic of Peru, Lima, February 11, 1988.

56. Interview with General Javier Tantalean, in Pilar Tello.

57. Interview with Antonio Flores Roncero, secretary of organization of APRA until 1972, Lima, March 14, 1988.

58. Interview with Andrés Townsend Escurra, Lima, March 3, 1988.

59. Interview with General Meza Cuadra, quoted in Pilar Tello, p. 362.

60. Interview with Pedro Richter Prada, Lima, February 11, 1988.

61. Interview with Andrés Townsend Escurra, Lima, March 3, 1988. This has been confirmed by my conversations with both apristas and nonapristas.

62. Interviews with Luis Alberto Sánchez, Lima, February 5 and March 16, 1988.

63. Delgado, *El proceso revolucionario,* p. 87.

64. Rodríguez Elizondo.

65. Even diplomatic channels were affected. Allende apparently had been very friendly with APRA and visited the party every time he came to Peru. "Nos tratabamos como verdaderos correligionarios" (We treat each other as true coreligionists). Once the Velasco government was in power, Allende apparently ignored APRA overtures and maintained relations with antiapristas. He invited a group of "antiapristas and antiadecos" (those against the AD in Venezuela) to his swearing in. Sánchez, vol. 5, p. 337.

66. Ibid., vol. 6, p. 60.

67. Thorndike, *La revolución imposible,* p. 89.

68. Interview with Wilbert Bendezu Carpio, congressional deputy, APRA, and director, Casa Central de Pueblos Jóvenes, Lima, March 5, 1988.

69. Thorndike, *La revolución imposible,* p. 255.

70. Ibid.

71. Ibid.

72. Interview with François Bourricaud, Washington, October 5, 1988.

73. Vega Centeno, *Aprismo popular,* p. 3.

74. Ibid.

75. Ajuero.

76. Interview with the directors of Generación en Marcha (young Lima wing of APRA), Lima, January 27, 1988. See also Vega Centeno, "Aprismo popular," or her published works, in which she describes in detail the remoteness of much of the APRA party from the central leadership.

77. Interviews with Tito Ajuero, José Barreto, and Coco Mora, directors of Juventud Aprista Peruana, March 8, 1988.

78. Ajuero. The crucial role of the student movement in pressing the leaders of APRA into a more radical stance was also discussed in detail in my interview with Pedro Richter Prada, former prime minister and interior minister during the military years.

79. Ibid.

80. Thorndike, *La revolución imposible,* p. 88.

81. *Cronologia Politica* 5 (February 1975). Haya's tacit approval of APRA insurrection as a way to destabilize the military regime is analogous to Juan Perón's relationship with the Montoneros from his exile in Spain.

82. "Entrevista: Manuel García," *Claridad* 10 (February–March 1980).

83. "Impresiones del 5 de Febrero 1975," *Claridad,* 10, February–March 1980).

84. "Entrevista: Manuel García." The events are confirmed by *Perú: cronología política* (February 1975). There are few, if any, other accounts by the actors, such as García's.

85. Ibid.

86. *Perú: cronología política,* vol. 5 (February 1975).

87. Interview with Richter Prada, Lima, February 11, 1988.

88. *Perú: cronología política,* vol. 5 (February 1975).

89. Interviews with Luis Alberto Sánchez, Lima, February 5 and March 16, 1988.

90. Pilar Tello, preface.

91. *Perú: cronología política,* vol. 5 (August 29, 1975).

92. General Morales Bermúdez, in Pilar Tello.

93. Sánchez, vol. 6, p. 29. This is confirmed by *Perú: cronología política (1975).*

94. Crabtree, "Peru."

95. Interview with César Atala, Washington, July 11, 1988. An earlier meeting was proposed between Atala and Morales Bermúdez in 1973.

96. *Perú: cronología política,* vol. 6 (August 30, 1976).

97. Sánchez, vol. 6, p. 31. While there may have been other contacts between APRA and the military, I was unable to find any other documented accounts, and Sánchez's indeed may be the first ones.

98. Ibid., p. 32.

99. *Perú: cronología política* (May 7, 1976).

100. Interview with César Garrido Lecca, Lima, February 1, 1988.

101. Sánchez, vol. 6, p. 34. The AP boycotted the entire Constituent Assembly

process.

102. Ibid., p. 35.

103. Interview with Javier Valle Riestra, Lima, March 2, 1988.

104. Thorndike, *La revolución imposible.*

105. Bendezu Carpio.

106. Woy-Hazelton, p. 34.

107. Ibid., p. 35.

108. Interview with Tito Ajuero, Lima, March 7, 1988.

109. Woy-Hazelton, p. 37.

110. Ibid., p. 39.

111. Ibid., p. 40.

112. Thorndike, *La revolución imposible,* p. 322. See also Bendezu Carpio.

113. Sánchez, vol. 6.

114. *Perú: cronología política,* vol. 7 (July 1978).

115. Woy-Hazelton, p. 40.

116. Ibid., pp. 40–42.

117. Bendezu Carpio.

118. Woy-Hazelton, p. 49.

119. Crabtree, "Peru." A strong executive is not necessarily good for Peru. Recent comparative studies by Arturo Valenzuela suggest that parliamentary systems are better for dealing with polarized political systems, as the emphasis is on coalition building rather than on intransigent opposition in an all-or-nothing game. See his "Party Politics and the Failure of Presidentialism in Chile: A Proposal for a Parliamentary Form of Government," paper for presentation at the Eighty-third Annual Meeting of the American Political Science Association, Chicago, September 3–6, 1987.

Haya had voiced concerns in late 1977 that there could be a repetition of 1962 in Peru and 1970 in Chile, where, because of the failure of the majority vote, the president was elected by the Congress. François Bourricaud suggested to him the French system, where a second runoff is held in the absence of a majority; this system was adopted, to begin with the 1985 elections (interview with Bourricaud, Washington, November 1, 1988).

120. Woy-Hazelton, p. 48.

CHAPTER 4

1. Miller.

2. Rodríguez Elizondo.

3. Miller.

4. Matos Mar.

5. Ibid.

6. Sánchez, vol. 6, p. 65.

7. Interview with a Peruvian government official who preferred to remain anonymous. This interpretation is strengthened by the account of the transition to democracy in Woy-Hazelton.

8. Villanueva, p. 188.

9. Ibid.

10. Crabtree, "Peru."

11. "Left Sweeps Board in Major Test for Belaúnde," *Latin America Weekly Report,* November 18, 1983.

12. Inter-American Development Bank, *Economic and Social Progress in Latin America.*

13. "Mensaje Anual al Congreso del Presidente de la República, Arq. Fernando Belaúnde Terry," *El Peruano,* July 28, 1983.

14. McClintock, "Peru's Sendero Luminoso Rebellion."

15. Gonzales Elizondo, "Los olvidados."

16. Mulder.

17. Sánchez, vol. 6, p. 164. This is confirmed by the survey of major press reports for the relevant years in *Perú: cronología política,* vols. 7–9.

18. Interviews with César Garrido Lecca, Lima, February 1 and March 8, 1988. Garrido Lecca, a former military officer, joined APRA in the 1950s and was a very close friend of both Andrés Townsend and Armando Villanueva. This was confirmed by my interview with Townsend and telephone conversation with Villanueva.

19. Interview with Andrés Townsend Escurra, Lima, March 3, 1988.

20. Woy-Hazelton.

21. Gonzales Elizondo, "Los olvidados." This is confirmed by Vega Centeno's various works on aprismo as political culture, in particular by her "Aprismo Popular."

22. Interviews with Luis Alberto Sánchez, Lima, February 5 and March 16, 1988. Ramiro Priale was another aprista who dropped his support for Townsend when he formed his own party.

23. North and Doyer.

24. Interview with Andrés Townsend Escurra, Lima, March 3, 1988. This is confirmed by accounts in Thorndike, *La revolución imposible,* and Bendezu Carpio.

25. Bendezu Carpio.

26. Vásquez Bazan, p. 154. This was confirmed by my interviews with César Garrido Lecca, Lima, February 1 and March 8, 1988.

27. Interviews with César Garrido Lecca, Lima, February 1 and March 8, 1988.

28. Letters from Armando Villanueva in Paris, January 2, 1983, and Madrid, March 27, 1983, to César Garrido Lecca in Lima.

29. Mulder.

30. Gonzales Elizondo, "Los secretos del Señor García."

31. Ibid.

32. Interviews with François Bourricaud, Washington, October 5, 14, and 21, and November 7, 1988. I thank Bourricaud also for reading the entire manuscript and for his helpful comments.

33. Interview with Javier Valle Riestra, Lima, March 3, 1988.

34. Interview with Tito Ajuero, Lima, March 8, 1988. Ajuero, along with other APRA youth members I interviewed, such as Coco Mora, Pepe Barreto, and Ivan García, knew Alan García as a fellow member of the APRA youth—of the next generation in age—prior to his quest for general secretariat and the presidency.

35. Interviews with César Garrido Lecca, Lima, February 1 and March 8, 1988; a Peruvian government official; and François Bourricaud, Washington, October

5, 14, and November 7, 1988.

36. Gonzales Elizondo, "Los secretos del Señor García."

37. Ibid.

38. Ibid.

39. "Consagre al mozallon," *Caretas* (Lima), February 27, 1988.

40. DESCO, compilation of press coverage of Alan García, 1980–1987, Lima, 1988.

41. Riding, "Peru's Alan García Puts Democracy to the Test."

42. Cotler, "The Political Radicalization of Working Class Youth in Peru."

43. Gonzales Elizondo, "Los olvidados."

44. Mulder.

45. Interviews with Luis Alberto Sánchez, Lima, February 5 and March 16, 1988; and directors of Generación en Marcha, Lima, January 27, 1988.

46. "Left Sweeps Board in Major Test for Belaúnde," *Latin American Weekly Report,* November 18, 1983.

47. "Es un angelito," *Caretas* (Lima) January 9, 1984.

48. Sánchez, vol. 6, pp. 245–255.

49. Roett.

50. Interviews with a Peruvian government official; Luis Alberto Sánchez, Lima, February 5 and March 16, 1988.

51. "Retorno a la quinta," *Caretas* (Lima) May 28, 1984.

52. "APRA Looks to 1985," *Andean Report* 10, no. 9 (September 1984).

53. Ibid.

54. "El APRA pacta con el ejército," *Oiga* (Lima), March 12, 1982; "El APRA pacta con el ejército," *El Correo* (Lima), March 21, 1982; "El APRA y los militares rebeldes," *Kausa Chum* (Lima), July 15, 1982.

55. "APRA Looks to 1985," *Andean Report* 10, no. 9 (September 1984).

56. Quoted in Vergara.

57. Interview with François Bourricaud, Washington, October 5, 14, and 21, and November 7, 1988. Bourricaud was one of García's main advisors when he was at the Sorbonne in the 1970s. García continued to consult Bourricaud after he returned to Lima. In particular, García visited Bourricaud in Paris after his election, prior to his inauguration; and Bourricaud spent ten days in Lima, at the presidential palace, in December 1987.

58. "Retorno a la quinta," *Caretas* (Lima), May 28, 1984.

59. Miller.

60. Riding, "Peru's Alan García Puts Democracy to the Test."

61. Vergara.

62. "APRA Looks to 1985," *Andean Report* 10, no. 9 (September 1984).

63. Sethi, "Alan García: An Interview." *Naila Report on the Americas,* October 1985.

64. Gonzales Elizondo, "Los secretos del Señor García." The original quotation is "primero ganemos, después discutimos."

65. Roett, p. 279.

66. Cotler, "The Political Radicalization of Working Class Youth in Peru."

67. Ibid.

68. "IU Platform," *Andean Report* 11, no. 1 (February 1985).

69. Ibid.

70. "Results: April 14 Election," *Andean Report* 11, no. 4 (May 1985).

71. "Peru: Second Round Election Doubts," *Latin American Regional Reports,* May 17, 1985.

72. Ibid., p. 9.

73. McClintock, "Peru's Sendero Luminoso Rebellion."

74. Ibid. Null and blank votes nationwide fell from 21.7 percent in 1980 to 8.2 percent in 1986, in conjunction with an increase in the total number of voters; Tuesta Soldevilla.

75. "Si la jungla estuvo aqui," *Oiga* (Lima), September 9, 1986.

76. "El modelo de Alan García y los éxitos iniciales," *Qué Hacer* 36 (August–September 1985).

77. Miller.

78. Riding, "Peru's Alan García Puts Democracy to the Test," p. 42.

79. Gonzales Elizondo, "Los olvidados," p. 20.

80. Ibid. Delgado Parker remained a close advisor and friend of the president even when he did not have an official government role. He was kidnapped by the MRTA in late 1989, and released after several months in captivity.

81. Ortiz de Zevallos, "Falta de una frente democrática."

82. Riding, "Peru's Alan García Puts Democracy to the Test."

CHAPTER 5

1. Iguiniz, *Política económica 1985–1986.*

2. "President García's Inaugural Address," *Andean Report* (August 1985).

3. Ibid.

4. Ibid., pp. 7–8. For details of measures, see the entire article.

5. McClintock, "APRA and the Peruvian Army Since the Constituent Assembly."

6. Roett.

7. Thorp, "The APRA Alternative in Peru." (A version of this paper appeared as "The APRA Alernative in Peru: Preliminary Evaluation of García's Economic Policies," in the *Bulletin of Latin American Research* 6, no. 2 [1987].)

8. Webb, Richard. "Special Report on the Debt." *Andean Report* (June 1986).

9. *Andean Report* (September–October 1985).

10. *Andean Report* (February 1986). The February measures included increases in the minimum wage and in pay for state workers and teachers; a reduction of 5 percent in the general sales tax; and another cut in interest rates. Electricity rates were cut for industry and for farmers. A multiple exchange-rate system was set up, with a frozen base rate for imports of basic-need items, and a free-market rate—approximately 25 percent higher—for luxury items or items competing with local production. Exporters were allowed to exchange 30 percent of their foreign currency earnings on the parallel market.

11. "Los empresarios y la primavera democrática," *Qué Hacer* 44 (December 1985–January 1986). Joel Migdal notes that the primary difference between

corporatism and concertation is that in concertation organized labor is not included in the bargaining process in any significant manner. Thus the course that concertación took under the APRA government should perhaps not have been such a surprise, with the difference possibly being that APRA opted to negotiate with the "twelve apostles" and exclude other entrepreneurial groups such as the National Industrial Society.

12. Stallings, p. 145.

13. Thorp, "The APRA Alternative in Peru."

14. Webb, "Special Report on the Debt." Richard Webb served as an unofficial representative for debt negotiations for the government for its first two years in power (interview with Webb, Lima, March 11, 1988). The extent to which García's stance affected international creditors is not clear. While it did not change their public stance toward Peru, it may have been the impetus for the October 1985 Baker Plan, as is suggested by Baker's former advisor Robin Broad (see Broad's article in *The New York Times*).

15. Thorp, "The APRA Alternative in Peru." Thorp points to the rapidly rising number of bank deposits in agencies located in *sectores populares* as indicative of this concentration, and to the evidence of dynamic growth on the production side. There was a flurry of auto construction activity, as judged by the increase of demand in materials; an increase in such construction reflects increases in income.

16. Schuldt.

17. Thorp, "The APRA Alternative in Peru." The so-called April package also included subsidies—through a Fondo de Inversión e Empleo—for some industrial projects, particularly those outside of Lima. However, the positive benefits of the package were undermined by poor policy coordination and the announcement of the compulsory bond repatriation at the same time.

18. Ibid.

19. Stallings.

20. *Peru Report* (May 1987).

21. *The Financial Times*, July 31, 1987. A key member of the concertación process, Ricardo Vega Llona—president of the Exporters Association and of the National Federation of Private Business Institutions (CONFIEP)—resigned in protest from two top committees that coordinated state and private sector activity.

22. *Oiga* (Lima), March 23, 1987, p. 13.

23. Thorp, "The APRA Alternative in Peru."

24. *Peru Report* (May 1987). The government's attempts to incorporate union concerns were indeed minimal: even spokesmen from large companies openly stated that they preferred the government to decree wage increases so they could avoid negotiating with the unions; *Qué Hacer* 47 (June–July 1987).

25. Iguiniz, "Economía."

26. "Sindicalismo: nueva etapa?" *Qué Hacer* 47 (June–July 1987.

27. Interview with Tito Ajuero, Lima, March 8, 1988. Ajuero's observations are confirmed by the minimal role played by the CTP in all the general strikes of the García regime. For trends in the late 1970s, see Angell, *Peruvian Labour and the Military Government Since 1968,* and "Classroom Maoists"; and Taylor, "Maoism in the Andes," p. 5.

28. *Caretas* (Lima), March 23, 1984, pp. 12–13.

29. *Caretas* (Lima), July 11, 1988. APRA was aware of its weak position among organized labor, as was evidenced by the CEN's call for a renovation effort on the part of all directors with responsibilities for union affairs.

30. Sánchez, p. 237.

31. Riding, "Peru, in Disarray, Directs Its Fury at the President." The size of the fiscal deficit is less relevant than how the money is spent. The US deficit at its peak was 4.8 percent of GDP, and Mexico's is 8.7 percent. However, in both cases a much greater percentage was spent on investment, guaranteeing future growth, as opposed to Peru's, which was primarily spent on subsidizing imports of consumer goods and food (interview with Edward M. Bernstein, Washington, August 17, 1988).

32. *El Comercio* (Lima), March 15, 1988. García consulted such outside advisors as Javier Silva Ruete, who was economics minister under Morales Bermúdez, and Felipe Ortiz de Zevallos, who was a high-level functionary during the Belaúnde years. PetroPerú's deficit was $900 million for 1986/87, and $90 million was spent on the import of crude, a product Peru used to export.

33. *El Comercio* (Lima) March 9, 1988.

34. Durr, "Peru Economic Policy Submerged By Politics." Seventy percent of those polled said that the measures would not help, and 58 percent said that they disapproved of the García administration.

35. Lago Gallego, "Pursuing Redistribution Through Macropolicy," and "Del crecimiento record a la hiperinflación."

36. Interview with Richard Webb, Lima, March 11, 1988.

37. Stallings, p. 38.

38. Interview with Richard Webb, Lima, March 11, 1988. It was rumored that Jeffrey Sachs, the Harvard professor who designed Bolivia's plan, was in Peru prior to the announcement of the shock plan, a rumor that was later confirmed by my informal conversations with Sachs.

39. Dornbusch and Edwards, p. 15.

40. Ibid.

41. Riding, "Peru, in Disarray, Directs Its Fury at the President"; and *The Wall Street Journal,* September 6, 1988.

42. Interview with Carlos Paredes, research associate with the Grupo de Análisis pare el Desarrollo, Brookings Institute, Washington, October 14, 1988.

43. Interviews with François Bourricaud, Washington, October 5, 14, and 21, and November 7, 1988; and Richard Webb, Lima, March 11, 1988.

44. Interviews with François Bourricaud, Washington, October 5, 14, 21, and November 7, 1988. Bourricaud's assessments are based on both his experience with García as a student in the 1970s and on his conversations with García in Lima—after the banks nationalization—during Bourricaud's stay at the government palace in December 1987.

45. Lago Gallego, "Illusion of Pursing Redistribution"; and interview with Richard Webb, Lima, March 11, 1988. See also "Remigio destapa la olla," *Oiga* (Lima), December 19, 1988; "Cusco: APRA o muerte?" *Qué Hacer* 47 (June–July 1987); "La Juventud se rebela," *Oiga,* October 26, 1987; and "Revienta la IPSS," *Caretas* (Lima), January 11, 1988.

46. Iguiniz, "Las chances y las restricciones de la política del APRA," p. 42. For a demonstration of such practices, see the case study in Part 3.

47. Angell and Thorp. The inadequacy of the state mechanism, coupled with García's autocratic tendencies, resulted in the executive's, more often than not, bypassing the state, which only served to further undermine it. Demonstrative was García's purported refusal to deal with the Central Bank team, and his reliance on his personal team of advisors who had a basis in the Instituto Nacional de Planificación. The economists from the Central Bank, however, are some of the most talented in the state apparatus (my off-the-record conversations with a Central Bank official and with an independent Peruvian economic analyst in Washington, DC). For more on the Peruvian state and economic policymaking, see relevant sections of Thorp and Whitehead; and Thorp and Bertram.

48. Velarde.

49. Interview with Hernán Garrido Lecca, chairman, Committee on External Debt, Lima, August 26, 1987. See also Velarde; and Institute for Liberty and Democracy. "State banks" here refers to noncommercial state banks, rather than the associated banks—Popular, Continental, and Interbanc—that function like private banks and lend a similar percentage of their funds to large-scale enterprises.

50. Webb, "Falta de confianza," p. 14.

51. *Caretas* (Lima), August 10, 1987. The largest group, the Romero group, controlled 128 enterprises through the Banco de Crédito. While associated banks controlled 44.4 percent of commercial credit, the private banks controlled 55.6 percent. In terms of credit concentration, the five hundred largest entrepreneurial groups controlled 33.8 percent of total commercial credit; the ten largest, 9.9 percent; and the largest, the Romero group, 2.2 percent. (*Si* [Lima], August 10, 1987).

52. Moreyra. Ironically, García had christened 1987 the "Year of Investment," and later claimed that the primary motive behind the measure was to force businesses to invest, as they had not invested as much as he needed (Durr, "To Govern Must Be to Change").

53. The five foreign bank branches that operate in Peru—although they had been scaling down their operations and held only 2 percent of credit—were exempted, most likely for practical reasons. The government was in the process of opening the door to foreign credit, and it stood to lose over $80 million per year in trade credit lines, which foreign bank branches were required to extend by law in proportion to their deposits. See Durr, "To Govern Must Be to Change."

54. "Disciplina sin salida," *Caretas* (Lima), August 31, 1987.

55. "Adios al Chi-Cheno," *Oiga* (Lima), July 20, 1987.

56. Interview with Carlos Franco in *Debate* (September 1985).

57. *Peru Report* (October 1987).

58. Durr, "To Govern Must Be to Change." Supply bottlenecks may have played a role in determining the continued willingness of entrepreneurs to invest; see Thorp, "The APRA Alternative in Peru," p. 176.

59. Lago Gallego, "Illusion of Pursuing Redistribution"; and Dornbusch and Edwards.

60. *Andean Report* (September 1987).

61. Moreyra; it is relevant to note that state banks loaned 50–60 percent of their credit to businesses with which they had links.

62. Ortiz de Zevallos, "En defensa del sistema democrático."

63. *Caretas* (Lima), August 10, 1987; interview with Carlos Franco, Lima,

March 8, 1988.

64. "Alfonso Barrantes y la estatización de la banca," interview in *La República* (Lima), August 22, 1987.

65. Interviews with Alfredo Barnechea, Lima, September 1, 1987; an anonymous Peruvian government official.

66. Interview with Alfredo Barnechea, Lima, September 1, 1987.

67. Coppedge.

68. Ortiz de Zevallos, "Bank Nationalization Signals End of Peru's Spending Spree." The first week that the expropriation proposal was announced, public opinion on the issue was split fifty-fifty; as the controversy deepened and dragged on into October and November, García's approval rating fell as low as 39 percent. Regional opposition in Arequipa and Piura was so strong that García withdrew the *bancos regionales* from the expropriation list. See ibid.; and "Paso Ligero," *Caretas* (Lima), January 11, 1988.

69. Quoted in Stallings. At the time the government was also revamping its strategy on external debt, moving toward a cautious opening to foreign credit and negotiations with the World Bank (Javier Iguiniz, "Economic Debt and Politics in Peru," a lecture given at St. Antony's College, Oxford, October 20, 1987).

70. Mexico's López Portillo nationalized that nation's banks also for primarily political reasons. See Diane Stewart, "Nationalization of the Banking Sector and its Consequences," in *Politics in Mexico,* ed. George Philip (London: Croom Helm, 1985).

71. Interview with Alejandro Toledo, Escuela de Altos Estudios de Negocios, August 24, 1987.

72. The law was finally approved by the Senate on September 28 and was promulgated as law on October 9. The debate in the Senate led to many modifications, such as Armando Villanueva's article 16, which exempted over 250 enterprises linked to the banks from takeover. The voting in favor of the modifications pitted APRA, in conjunction with the AP and the PPC, against the IU. Alva Castro was able to gain points with the left at the expense of García by leading a movement in protest of the modifications in the Chamber of Deputies. See "Qué tal sancochado," *Oiga* (Lima), September 21, 1987.

Bank owners attempted a plethora of tactics, including physically moving—beds included—into their banks, and several copied the Banco de Crédito's devolution of its shares to its employees. High-level officials approved the sale as a means to solve the controversy. It was rumored that García changed his mind when the Banco de Crédito leaked to the press copies of two checks that proved him guilty of tax fraud in the payment for a house. The Crédito sale was then declared illegal by the government, and on October 15 several banks were forcibly taken over by riot policemen and armored cars (see *Caretas* [Lima], October 19, 1987). Subsequently, the government removed a judge who ruled that the government's taking control of the banks prior to a legal ruling was unconstitutional, and replaced him with an APRA judge who reversed the ruling. This semiridiculous situation could hardly be to the government's credit, nor did it contribute to a supposedly democratic climate. García called an extraordinary legislature in January and finally approved the Crédito solution in March 1988. Several other banks followed suit, but the Banco Wiese remained under government control until October 1989. In another highly publicized controversy in July 1988, police—supposedly on orders from the interior minister—stormed the bank in order to eject Guillermo Wiese (see "A la bruta," *Caretas,* July 4, 1988).

73. Sánchez, vol. 6, p. 292.

74. Interview with an anonymous Peruvian government official.

75. Apoyo, S.A., opinion polls, September and November 1987. Opinion polling in a country such as Peru, with volatile public opinion, is clearly fraught with difficulties. As a result, even polling agencies with acceptable survey methods are held to be unreliable. Apoyo is a generally well-respected firm, although it may at times underestimate support for the left.

76. Cotler, "Entrevista," p. 14.

77. Angell, "Some Problems in the Interpretation of Recent Chilean History," p. 94.

78. Lago Gallego, "Illusion of Pursuing Redistribution."

79. Ibid., p. 58.

80. Ibid.

81. Ibid.

82. Paredes and Sachs.

83. Prisma survey of a periurban community in Lima, reprinted in *The Peru Report* (March 1990); interviews with health workers from the Nutrition Research Institute, Cantogrande, Lima, June 1990.

84. "Brutal maquinazo," *La República* (Lima), July 20, 1989; and Lago Gallego, "Illusion of Pursuing Redistribution."

85. Interview with Hernán Garrido Lecca, Lima, July 18, 1990.

86. "Presente griego," *Caretas* (Lima), June 5, 1990; and Francisco Sagasti, in a lecture on the results of the 1990 elections given at the Washington Office on Latin America (WOLA), Washington, June 28, 1990.

CHAPTER 6

1. Randall.

2. Planes.

3. Ibid. This is confirmed by several conversations I had with both high-level APRA party members and with government officials.

4. Torres Guzmán.

5. Interviews with François Bourricaud, Washington, October 5, 14, 21, and November 7, 1988. Bourricaud claims that García said this when he was visiting Bourricaud in Paris in mid-1985, after his election and prior to his inauguration. García's lack of trust in either friends or advisors has also been noted by government and party functionaries, and by other acquaintances.

6. Sánchez, vol. 6, p. 288.

7. Vásquez Bazan, p. 26.

8. John Crabtree, "The Consolidation of the APRA Government in Peru," lecture at St. Antony's College, Oxford, May 26, 1987. See also Stein; and Paul Drake, cited in Dornbusch and Edwards.

9. Vásquez Bazan, p. 172.

10. Miller.

11. Crabtree, "Consolidation of the APRA Government." See also Tuesta Soldevilla.

12. García.

13. "El cassette de Ayacucho," *Caretas* (Lima), July 4, 1988.

14. Interview with Alexander Watson, US ambassador to Peru, Lima, February 1, 1988.

15. "La carta," *Caretas* (Lima), July 25, 1988.

16. Baruffati, "Peruvian General Retires Amid Coup Rumours."

17. Interviews with François Bourricaud, Washington, October 5, 14, 21, and November 7, 1988.

18. "Se fue el tango y se quedo el tongo," *Oiga* (Lima), September 19, 1988.

19. "Alan García: Open Letter to the APRA Party," *Caretas,* July 17, 1988.

20. "El APRA no es socialismo," *Oiga* (Lima), August 8, 1988.

21. Group interview with Generación en Marcha leaders, Lima, January 27, 1988.

22. Ibid.

23. "Perestroika en el PAP," *Oiga* (Lima), August 29, 1988.

24. Chalmers Johnson, pp. 55–58.

25. "Cusco: APRA o muerte?" *Qué Hacer* 47 (June–July 1987).

26. Gonzales Elizondo, "Los olvidados," p. 18.

27. Vego Centeno, "Aprismo Popular." The isolation of regional apristas was also noted in my interviews with members of Generación en Marcha.

28. Ramos Tremolada.

29. Interviews with Miguel Hurtado, Generación en Marcha leader and advisor to the Chamber of Deputies' Development Commission, Lima, February 2, 1988; Tito Ajuero, Lima, March 8, 1988.

30. APRA Party Official Document, February 1988.

31. Hilliker.

32. "La juventud se rebela," *Oiga* (Lima), October 26, 1987.

33. Gonzales Elizondo, "Los olvidados."

34. Interview with Tito Ajuero, Lima, March 8, 1988.

35. Gonzales Elizondo, "Los olvidados."

36. "Tenemos mística," *Caretas* (Lima) July 11, 1988.

37. Interview with Tito Ajuero, Lima, March 8, 1988.

38. In early 1986 García himself instructed the national secretary of organization, Walter Cuestas, to organize a series of coloquia for party youth, which was based on the ideas behind Haya's coloquia. Seminars were given by prominent party leaders, and several of the youth were sent to observe the Rimanacuy. This effort seems to have been short-lived and concentrated primarily in Lima, however. See *Coloquios: Revista de la Juventud* 1, no. 1 (August–September 1986).

39. Interview with Ivan García, former APRA militant, Lima, March 8, 1988.

40. Interview with Tito Ajuero, Lima, March 8, 1988.

41. "En busca del cambio prohibido," *Cambio* (Lima), March 3, 1988.

42. Ramos Tremolada, p. 12.

43. Interview with Tito Ajuero, Lima, March 8, 1988. See also *Caretas* (Lima), July 11, 1988.

44. Interview with Tito Ajuero, Lima, March 8, 1988. This was confirmed by my tracing of the press coverage of the APRA student movement in *Perú: cronología política* (1977–1980).

45. "Arena de contienda o 'zona liberada'?" *Oiga* (Lima), April 25, 1988.

46. "Caso Bedón: buscado vivo o muerto," *Oiga* (Lima), October 26, 1987.

47. "Cusco: APRA o muerte?" *Qué Hacer* 47 (June–July 1987).

48. Vega Centeno, "Aprismo Popular," p. 7.

49. Interview with the Barreto family, formerly persecuted apristas, March 15, 1988. There are hundreds of APRA families that have a history of some sort of persecution, Alan García's included. A good example of aprismo popular are the icons that loyal Apristas invariably have. Almost all APRA government officials interviewed had at least a picture, if not a bust, of Haya de la Torre in their office. The APRA families I met with had pictures of Haya de la Torre in the bedrooms, placed on the wall either next to a religious cross or in the place where it might normally have hung.

50. Vega Centeno, "Aprismo popular."

51. Ibid.

52. Ibid.

53. Interview with Ivan García, Lima, March 8, 1988; and members of Generación en Marcha; and with Tito Ajuero and Coca Mora, members of the APRA youth, Lima, March 8, 1988.

CHAPTER 7

1. Angell and Thorp, p. 878.

2. Felipe Ortiz de Zevallos, in a lecture read at St. Antony's College, Oxford, May 23, 1988. This assertion is confirmed by several of Barrantes's own statements in the press, and in my interview with him, Lima, March 9, 1988.

3. Interview with Julio Calderón. DESCO, Lima, March 4, 1988.

4. Javier Iguiniz, "Economic Debt and Politics in Peru," lecture read at St. Antony's College, Oxford, October 20, 1987. See also "Tiempo de pactar," *Caretas* (Lima) April 10, 1990.

5. Urrutia.

6. Interview with Alfonso Barrantes, Lima, March 9, 1988.

7. Wise, p. 7.

8. Interview with Alfonso Barrantes, Lima, March 9, 1988.

9. Official elections results for the first round of elections, 1990, Peruvian Embassy document, Washington, DC.

10. Interview with Alfonso Barrantes, Lima, March 9, 1988.

11. "APRA versus PUM," *Andean Report* 14, no. 3 (March 1987). Also see Taylor, "Agrarian Unrest and Political Conflict in Puno."

12. *Latin American Regional Report,* May 14, 1988.

13. Interview with Javier Iguiniz, Oxford, October 29, 1988.

14. Iguiniz, *Política Económica,* p. 116. This is not a surprise, given the lack of skilled technicians in APRA, the absence of APRA-related think tanks, and the poor quality of the education offered at the APRA-affiliated university,

Villareal. In contrast is the plethora of left-affiliated world think tanks—many of them set up during the Velasco years—such as DESCO and CEDEP, and the better quality of education offered at the Universidad Católica, one of the main training institutions of the IU.

15. "Agustín Haya—entrevista," *Oiga* (Lima) February 29, 1988.

16. Interview with Miguel Cruchaga, Lima, February 29, 1988.

17. Interview with Mario Vargas Llosa, Lima, March 1, 1988. This assertion is made more credible by statements from dissenting apristas, such as Barnechea and Torres Vallejo, as well as in my conversations with several APRA youth leaders.

18. Interview with Miguel Cruchaga, Lima, February 29, 1988.

19. Palma. This was also hinted at in my conversations with Vargas Llosa's campaign manager.

20. "Libertad: vuelo propio," *Caretas* (Lima), March 21, 1988.

21. Interview with Felipe Ortiz de Zevallos, Lima, January 27, 1988.

22. Incidents such as Vargas Llosa's opening a press conference by responding to a French journalist's questions in French and spending a purported $1 million to hire the US advertising consultant firm Sawyer-Miller are examples; see Brooke. While APRA spent $2 million total on the campaign, Izquierda Socialista $1 million, IU $150,000 and Cambio 90 $200,000, FREDEMO spent a total of $12 million; see "Balance final," *Caretas* (Lima), April 10, 1990.

23. *Qué Hacer* 64 (May–June 1990) contains several pieces on the elections. See also "Catedráticos y evangelistas," *Caretas* (Lima), April 16, 1990.

24. Election results are from a Peruvian Embassy document, Washington, DC, and press coverage of the June 10 elections. Official results were not yet available at the time of this writing.

25. *Caretas* (Lima) May 21, 1990, p. 14.

26. The analysis was gleaned from my conversations with members of several political parties as well as independents, Lima, June 16–22, 1990.

27. Letters from Sofía Madrid, a field worker at the Instituto de Investigación Nutricional, Huaraz, to Dr. George Graham, president of IIN, Lima, dated April 6 and 10, 1990.

28. This was expressed in my off-the-record conversations with several of Fujimori's top advisors, Lima, June 18–20, 1990; and during my attendance/participation in the GRADE/Brookings Conference on a Plan for Stabilization and Growth for Peru, Lima, June 19, 1990. Conversations were held there with leaders from FREDEMO, the IU and ASI, Cambio, and APRA, as well as independents. Perhaps not surprising, given Fujimori's support base among small businessmen and the informal sector, was Hernando de Soto's position as unofficial advisor to the president elect.

29. This opinion is based on my observations of Fujimori's appearances on television, Lima, June 16–22, 1990; and on press coverage in both the United States and Peru of Fujimori's statements, April 9–June 30, 1990.

After a visit to the IMF/World Bank as well as to several potential donors, including Japan in July, Fujimori returned to Lima convinced of the need for an orthodox stabilization plan, and on August 8, 1990, Prime Minister Juan Carlos Hurtado Miller announced what most observers had deemed inevitable. Yet the severe nature of the shock surprised even the harshest Fund/Bank critics: gas prices rose by 3,000 percent and most other basic goods by 500 percent. Subsequently a series of sorely needed structural reforms, including tariff and trade reforms, reform of the labor code, and privatization of some state industries, have also been implemented. The severity of the shock is largely due to the desperate financial straits that the APRA government passed on to its successors.

30. Haggard and Kaufman. I gathered further support for this view at the conference where Haggard and Kaufman presented and discussed their work, at The World Bank, Washington, DC, June 26, 1990.

31. Sachs used this phrase during a presentation to the GRADE/Brookings Conference on a Plan for Stabilization and Growth for Peru, Lima, June 19, 1990; he reiterated this idea during my conversations with him at the same conference.

32. Francisco Sagasti, lecture on the results of the Peruvian elections, Washington Office on Latin America, Washington, June 28, 1990.

33. Vásquez Bazan.

34. McClintock, "Peru's Sendero Luminoso Rebellion." See also "Cifras macabras," *Caretas* (Lima), June 12, 1990; and Rosenberg. From 1982 to 1988 more than six thousand people were killed in Ayacucho alone; this is twice the number killed or "disappeared" in Chile during the entire Pinochet regime.

35. McClintock, "Peru's Sendero Luminoso Rebellion."

36. "Labrando la reactivación del agro," *Oiga* (Lima), September 8, 1986.

37. "El mensaje," *Caretas* (Lima), August 1, 1988.

38. "El cassette de Ayacucho," *Caretas* (Lima), July 4, 1988.

39. Granados, p. 3.

40. Quoted in "The Shining Path Mystery," *The Washington Post,* March 24, 1985. While there is not a great deal of published work on the ideology of Sendero Luminoso, there are some reliable sources. For Peruvian sources, among others, see the various works of Raúl Gonzales Elizondo in *Qué Hacer* (1985–1988), in particular "La cuarta plenaria del Comité Central de Sendero Luminoso"; and Degregori. For foreign sources see Harding; McClintock, "Peru's Sendero Luminoso Rebellion"; and Taylor, "Maoism in the Andes." For the most detailed publicized statement made by Sendero Luminoso, see Abimael Guzmán. A good anthology is forthcoming from St. Martin's Press, edited by D. S. Palmer.

41. See note 40. Sendero's tactics have been compared to those of the Khmer Rouge, and indeed the similarities in terms of ideology seeking a revolution more radical than that of China or the Soviet Union, and also romanticizing ancient civilizations—the Incas in Peru and the Angkor in Cambodia) and tactics (Maoist encircling of cities; willingness to use revolutionary violence in an extremely brutal manner, including assassinations of entire families in front of villages as "warnings") are both striking and frightening. For detail see William Shawcross, *Sideshow* (New York: Simon and Schuster, 1979); and François Ponchaud, *Cambodia: Year Zero* (New York: Holt, Rinehart, and Winston, 1977).

42. I spoke with private transportation workers on July 20, 1989, and visited Lima's center on July 29. See also the press coverage of the strike, July 20, 1989; and Baruffati, "Strong Support for Peruvian Stoppage."

43. "Alcaldes muertos," *Caretas* (Lima), June 19, 1989; Treaster.

44. See the coverage of the April 8, 1990, elections in *Caretas* (Lima), April 10 and 16, 1990. I spoke with voters in the Lima shantytown Huascar, where

Sendero has a visible presence, on June 20, 1990. One voter recounted how she went to vote as early as possible, and then ran home hiding her inked index finger, so that she would not be seen by senderistas.

45. Gonzales "Sendero: duro desgaste y crisis estratégica."

46. United States Department of State. Atrocities committed in the name of counterterrorism resulted in a depopulation of much of Ayacucho, with entire villages migrating to Lima's pueblos jóvenes, such as Huanta in Cantogrande. See also McClintock, "Prospects for Democratic Consolidation in a Least Likely Case."

47. Partido Comunista del Perú–Sendero Luminoso, Comité Central,"Desarrollar la guerra popular sirviendo a la Revolución Mundial" (August 1986).

48. "La iglesia católica en mira," *Caretas* (Lima), December 7, 1987.

49. Interview with social workers and parish nuns, Pamplona Alta, Lima, February 11, 1988. In 1991 Sendero Luminoso killed two Polish priests and an Australian nun, as well as several Japanese engineers working on a development project near Lima, specifically targeting foreign clergymen for the first time.

50. "Arena de contienda o 'zona liberada'?" *Oiga* (Lima), April 25, 1988.

51. "Lima University Raids Signal Launch of New Get Tough Drive," *Latin American Weekly Report,* February 26, 1987.

52. "SL's Urban Political War Indicating Increased Military Presence in Government Anti-terrorist Decisions," *Andean Report* (June 1988).

53. *El Comercio* (Lima), January 29, 1988. I discuss this event in detail in my "New Guerrilla Group Adds to Peruvian Pressure Cooker."

54. "SL's Urban Political War."

55. "El costo del terror," *Oiga* (Lima), December 21, 1987. An example of such sabotage was the assassination in late 1987 of the director and other high-level functionaries of a long-awaited multimillion dollar irrigation and hydroelectric development plan for the Andean Trapezoid, the Río Cachi plan. Sendero was also able to sponsor highly successful general strikes in Ayacucho and Huancayo in late 1988; "Recuperamos Junín y Ayacucho," *Oiga,* December 26, 1988.

56. "Asesinato intencionado," *Caretas* (Lima), August 1, 1988.

57. Javier Iguiniz, "Economic Debt and Politics in Peru," lecture read at St. Antony's College, Oxford, October 20, 1987.

58. Interview with Hernán Garrido Lecca, Lima, January 21, 1988; and conversations with several members of the APRA youth.

59. "El cassette de Ayacucho," *Caretas* (Lima), July 4, 1988.

60. "El foco," *Caretas* (Lima), November 16, 1987. For detail, see my "New Guerrilla Group Adds to Peruvian Pressure Cooker."

61. Graham, "New Guerrilla Group."

62. "Extraña propuesta de paz," *Caretas* (Lima), November 16, 1987.

63. "El foco," *Caretas* (Lima), November 16, 1987.

64. Ibid. In late November the government had attempted to negotiate by sending INP chief Tantalean to Tarapoto. His efforts were thwarted by the presence in the village of a reunion of the military command for the region; see "Tantalean en Tarapoto: en busca de diálogo," *Caretas* (Lima), November 16, 1987.

65. "El foco," *Caretas* (Lima), November 16, 1987.

66. "Extraña propuesta de paz," *Caretas* (Lima), November 16, 1987.

67. Javier Iguiniz, "Economic Debt and Politics in Peru," lecture read at St. Antony's College, Oxford, October 20, 1987.

68. Internal document of the Partido Aprista Peruano, 1988.

69. "Bejar," *Caretas* (Lima), April 4, 1988.

70. "Revienta la IPSS," *Caretas* (Lima), January 11, 1988.

71. "Mas armas para mantilla," *Oiga* (Lima), March 7, 1988; interviews with Congressman Manuel Piqueras, head of Congressional Commission to Investigate Paramilitary Violence, Lima, July 18–19, 1989.

72. Interview with Javier Valle Riestra, Lima, March 3, 1988.

73. "Vuelvan las manoplas," *Caretas* (Lima), June 13, 1988.

74. Graham, "Peruvian Death Squad's Links to the Government"; interviews with Manuel Piqueras, Lima, July 18–19, 1989, and with Carlos Enrique Escobar, Washington, December 6, 1988. The command followed through on its threats and killed Ayacucho journalist Júvenal Farfán, as well as his wife and two children.

75. McClintock, "Prospects for Democratic Consolidation in a Least Likely Case." The number of "disappearances" decreased from 1,750 in 1984 to 368 in 1986, and 350 in 1987. The halving of the Mirage order saved the government $300 million.

76. "García Pushes for Defence Ministry," *Latin America Weekly Report,* March 19, 1989; and "El General Flores defiende la Defensa," *Qué Hacer* 47 (June–July 1987).

77. Thorndike, *La revolución imposible,* pp. 1–10. See also, John Crabtree, "The Consolidation of the APRA Government in Peru," lecture read at St. Antony's College, Oxford, May 26, 1987; and McClintock, "Prospects for Democratic Consolidation in a Least Likely Case."

78. "El General Flores defiende la Defensa," *Que Hacer* 47 (June–July 1987).

79. "Andean Mayors Resign," *The Guardian* (Manchester), December 21, 1989. See also "Sierra de fuego," *Caretas* (Lima) December 19, 1988; and "Recuperamos Junín y Ayacucho," *Oiga* (Lima) December 26, 1988.

80. Carlos Enrique Escobar, lecture read at WOLA, Washington, DC, December 11, 1988. Also see documentation of the Cayara massacre in *Caretas* and *Sí,* May 1988.

81. "Ampay Polay," *Caretas* (Lima), February 13, 1989. Polay, along with forty other MRTA members, escaped from Lima's Cantogrande prison in the final months of the APRA government by building a three hundred-meter tunnel. Public outcry at police negligence was understandable!

82. For more detail, see my "The Latin American Quagmire" and "Terrorism, Economic Woes Ravaging Peru." Also see *Caretas,* February 6, 13, and 20, 1989.

83. McClintock, "APRA and the Peruvian Army Since the Constituent Assembly," p. 5.

84. Ibid. Most of the polls were taken by a respected firm, DATUM. The 1987 poll was taken by APOYO, which at times may underestimate support for the Marxist left.

85. Ibid. This is also confirmed by my interviews with Hernán Garrido Lecca, leader of the APRA group Generación en Marcha, Lima, August 24, 1987, and January 21, 1988; with Javier Valle Riestra, an APRA senator who is active in

human rights issues, Lima, March 3, 1988; and with members of the APRA youth.

CHAPTER 8

1. Thorp, "The APRA Alternative in Peru."
2. This section is drawn from a detailed account of these programs and their implementation in my "The APRA Government and the Urban Poor."
3. Thumm, p. 2.
4. Altimir, pp. 83–84. For a detailed account of poverty trends in Lima from 1985 to 1991, see Webb, *Ajuste y economía familiar.*
5. Inter-American Development Bank, *Annual Report—1987.* See also Peredes and Vigier, p. 1. Lima's population during this period grew from 1 to 6 million.
6. Perú, Ministerio de Vivienda, Oficina de Estadística.
7. Peredes and Vigier. For a detailed account of the decline in living standards of the poor from 1985 to 1990, see Webb, *Ajuste y economía familiar.*
8. Robert Graham. See also Soto, *El otro sendero;* Alarco; and interview with Carlos Wendorff, Lima, August 19, 1987. (Wendorff called the informal sector Peru's social security system.)
9. Carbonetto, "El sector informal urbano." The labor surplus in Peru became most evident after industrialization, as the number of migrants coming to the capital in response to perceived opportunities was greater than the number of jobs available in the modern sector. At the turn of the century there was actually a labor shortage in the agriculture sector; see Thorp and Bertram.
10. Soto, "The Informal Sector as a Tool for Development"; and interview with Anna Lucía Camaiora, Instituto Libertad y Democracia, Lima, August 17, 1989. See also Durr, "Peru Banks to Make Credit More Available"; and "Siguen las invasiones: alternativas de solución de la union formal-informal," *El Comercio* (Lima), March 7, 1988. In a recent and highly publicized study of the informal sector, *El otro sendero,* Peruvian economist Hernando de Soto describes the excess of government regulations for entrance to the formal economy as a legal and economic apartheid. Soto makes a strong case; the amount of time and funds that he cites as necessary if one does not wield some sort of influence or is unable to expedite the process with a hefty bribe, to obtain essential permits such as land titles, operating licenses, or legal credit is daunting for any entrepreneur, and prohibitive for those of small scale. Soto has been active in lobbying the state to remove or simplify impediments for the informal sector's access to legality and credit. He was a key sponsor of a law that was decreed in April 1988, requiring all banks to lend 10 percent of their credit to small-scale entrepreneurs. While he clearly opened new roads in his analysis of crippling and discriminatory state regulations, his thesis overlooks the drastic shortage of social infrastructure other than jobs and homes, such as health and education services. Because of this, his argument is often used as a political tool by the right.
11. Campero, p. 39.
12. Ibid., p. 252.
13. Ibid.

14. Ray, p. 177.

15. Nelson.

16. Tuesta Soldevilla.

17. Talton, p. 59.

18. Tuesta Soldevilla.

19. Ibid.; and "El voto de los pobres," *Caretas* (Lima), May 14, 1990.

20. For a detailed account of APRA's predecessors' approaches to urban poverty, see my "The APRA Government and the Urban Poor."

21. Carbonetto, "Políticas de mejoramiento," pp. 115–118.

22. "Desciende el empleo bajo el regimen PROEM," *El Comercio* (Lima), March 4, 1988.

23. *Caretas* (Lima), April 4, 1988. D'Ascueta's assertions are confirmed by Julio Velarde's work on credit to the informal sector; I heard the same estimates voiced at a Friedrich Ehbert Foundation conference on the role of the informal credit market, Lima, August 20, 1987.

24. Interview with Ramón Barua, Acción Comunitaria, September 1, 1987, and Jorge Carbonel, IDESI, Lima, August 26, 1987; see also Pinilla.

25. "IDESI dio mas del millón a trabajadores informales," *El Pueblo* (Lima), February 25, 1988. See also Pinilla; "Bancos del estado prestaran 300 millónes de intis a informales," *El Comercio* (Lima), March 5, 1988; Durr, "Peru Banks to Make Credit More Available." See also Institute for Liberty and Democracy; "Gran apoyo para los informales," *La Crónica* (Lima), February 26, 1988; interviews with Jorge Fernández Baca, Instituto Libertad y Democracia, Lima, August 20, 1987, Alejandro Toledo, Escuela de Altos Estudios de Negocios, August 24, 1987, and Susanna Pinilla, director, IDESI, Lima, August 31, 1990. The April 1988 decree was sponsored by Hernando de Soto.

26. Perú, Instituto Nacional de Planificación.

27. "Historia de un tren y algunas piscinas sin agua," *Oiga* (Lima), February 9, 1987. I conducted site visits to the Olympic pool in San Juan de Lurigancho, as well as to a government-built high-technology institute, which towers above most of the buildings in the modest district but remains empty and nonfunctional.

28. Franke Ballre.

29. Centro de Investigación Social y Educación Popular. This was confirmed by my interview with Mary Fukumoto, Instituto de Investigación Nutricional/Universidad Católica, and conversations with a health survey team in Cantogrande. I also attended a meeting of a Vaso de Leche Committee that had previously been run by the IU and was then being run by APRA.

30. Franke Ballre.

31. Burgess.

32. Ibid., p. 64. The Spanish is "Comedores APRA–AP: fácil aparecen, fácil desaparecen."

33. Ibid. See also Centro de Investigación Social y Educación Popular; and my conversations with PAIT/PAD officials, both in San Juan de Lurigancho and in the central offices.

34. Burgess, p. 72.

35. Ibid.

36. Ibid., p. 72.

37. Centro Estudios Alternativos.

38. Interviews with Javier Camara, director of community services, San Juan de Lurigancho, Zarate, Lima, January 26 and 29, February 15, and March 14, 1988. Sectarianism and a penchant for grandiose schemes also characterized APRA's governance of this municipality, which lacked any coherent approach toward the pueblos jóvenes. A central office attempted to coordinate the extension of services to the pueblos jóvenes, but, in contrast to the highly publicized SINAMOS, APRA's Casa Central de los Pueblos Jóvenes (CCPJ) was neither funded nor run by the García government; instead it was run as an APRA program by party volunteers (interview with Wilbert, Bendezu Carpio, director, CCPJ, Lima, March 5, 1988). While the organizers may have been well-intentioned, the left claimed that the Casa was a mixture of state and party apparatus that turned citizens' rights into a gift from the party. The government, meanwhile, made no attempt to address in any coherent manner the issues of pressing concern to the pobladores: land titles and basic services such as water and electricity. Instead the government focused on grandiose schemes such as García's famous electric train, which was designed to solve the city's transport problems. Construction of the train, whose projected cost was $1 billion, was begun with a donation from the Italian government, but not a single route was ever completed, because of shortage of funds. Basic services, such as garbage collection, meanwhile, deteriorated dramatically, in large part because APRA filled the directorates of agencies responsible for basic service provision with party loyalists who had no technical skills (see "Lima sin tren, sin rumbo," *Debate* 9, no. 48 [December 1987]). Government policy on land invasions, meanwhile, was often vague and contradictory. While Alan García would rush to the scene of dislocated invasions, such as that of Paraguay in September 1985, and pontificate on the fate of the urban poor, the central government continued to violently repress many invasions. Party members at the local level, on the other hand, continued their past policy of sponsoring invasions, as did, for example, Chorrillos mayor Jorge Meneses (see Zolezzi; and "Concertación a Palos," *Oiga* [Lima], March 7, 1988). I went to an APRA rally in Surquillo the day of an APRA-led invasion march—March 3, 1988.

39. The information in this section was previously published, in a slightly different version, as my "The APRA Government and the Urban Poor."

40. Peredes and Vigier; Pinilla.

41. Ibid.

42. "El jefe de estado fundamento el proyecto de disolución de Coopop," *El Comercio* (Lima), January 19, 1988.

43. Interviews with Nicholas Houghton, Organisación Internacional de Trabajo, Lima, August 19, 1987, and February 12, 1988.

44. Ibid.

45. Peredes and Vigier. Many of Peredes and Vigier's conclusions are supported by the results of my own study of the PAIT in practice. In addition, the rural PAIT, which is beyond the scope of this study, functioned differently. As "machismo" is much more persistent, there was a much lower percentage of female workers: in Piura, for example, only 40 percent of the workers were women. The rural program was also more a response to seasonal unemployment. Its impact on Andean farming communities was limited, as many campesinos could provide food for self-consumption (interviews with directors of PAIT programs for Suyana, Piura, and Cora Cora, Ayacucho, Cooperación Popular Offices, Lima, Feb-

ruary 10, 1988).

46. Peredes and Vigier.

47. Interview with Mary Fukumoto, Lima, August 28, 1987.

48. Centro de Estudios Alternativos.

49. Interview with Hilary Creed Kanashiro. Instituto de Investigación Nutricional, Lima, August 28, 1987.

50. Group interview with health survey team for Cantogrande, Instituto de Investigación Nutricional, Cantogrande, Lima, August 29, 1987.

51. See *Oiga* (Lima), September 19, 1988. The timely announcement of the PAIT posts was in keeping with past policy, such as the raising of enrollments prior to the November 1986 elections.

52. Conversations with PAIT and municipal officials, Lima, January–March 1988, and return visit to the San Juan de Lurigancho municipality, July 1989.

53. "La juventud se rebela," *Oiga* (Lima), October 26, 1987. See also Gonzales Elizordo, "Los olivados."

54. Interviews with Nicolas Houghton, Lima, August 19, 1987, and February 12, 1988; and with Generación en Marcha.

55. Interview with Peri Peredes, ADEC/ATC, Lima, August 25, 1987. Peredes's description of the practices within the PAIT bureaucracy were confirmed by my conversations with PAIT officials, both at the central level and in San Juan de Lurigancho, and also by observations in the field.

56. Ibid.

57. Interviews with Nicolas Houghton, Lima, August 19, 1987 and February 12, 1988. The study of the PAIT in practice (Part II) confirms Houghton's conclusion about the willingness of APRA party officials to use the program for political ends.

58. Group interview with health survey team, Lima, August 29, 1987. Details of this survey can be found in my "The PAIT" (1991). The study of the PAIT involved interviews with the apristas who set up and administered the program in the district; with municipal administrators of other community service programs; with the mayor of San Juan de Lurigancho; with church leaders in Huascar; and with twenty-three women who worked in the PAIT in Huascar. As a comparison, a small group of women who worked in the PAIT in another peublo joven, Pamplona Alta, in a different district, were also interviewed.

59. See note 58.

60. Interview with Alfonso Barrantes, Lima, March 9, 1988.

61. Interview with Víctor Raúl Ortiz Pilco, Lima, February 3, 1988.

62. Ibid. The mayor's assertions were confirmed by interviews with four social workers who operate in the area; none of the four were apristas. In addition, my interviews in the municipality with the women who worked in the PAIT resulted in high ratings for the mayor, lending support to his claims of attempting to operate in a nonpartisan manner. Interviews with Huascar residents confirmed that Ortiz Pilco was a substantial improvement over his predecessors.

63. Ortiz Pilco. The tax system was revamped so that at least 40 percent of the population was reached, an effort at least partly successful, as—at least according to municipal accounts—the income from property tax doubled in 1987. If the extension of electric service to Huascar is a viable indicator, then these efforts were somewhat successful.

64. Ortiz Pilco; and interview with Ortiz Pilco, Lima, February 3, 1988. This was also confirmed by my visit to the district's nonfunctioning "high-technology institute."

65. See Arturo Valenzuela, who points out that municipal officials in Chile, even during democratic governments, functioned much more as brokers between their electorate and the central government, than as the executers of significant projects within their districts.

66. Interview with Mercedes Cabanilla, Municial Offices, Municipality of San Juan de Lurigancho, Lima, February 20, 1988. The highly popular milk distribution program relied on community-organized autonomous committees to distribute donated milk to over 1 million children per day. With the APRA takeover of the Lima municipality, there was an increase in tension in several areas, as district committees clashed with newly appointed APRA coordinators. I observed distribution of Vaso de Leche milk at the San Juan municipality and attended meetings of the neighborhood dirigentes with the APRA municipality officials.

67. Interview with Alfonso Barrantes, Lima, March 9, 1988. Barrantes's assertions are confirmed by my interviews with social workers who have worked in such communities both under the Barrantes (IU) and del Castillo (APRA) administrations; and by my field observations, particularly at Vaso de Leche committee meetings.

68. Interviews with Nicolas Houghton, Lima, August 19, 1987, and February 12, 1988. This was confirmed by my extensive interviews with various APRA officials in charge of the PAIT in San Juan de Lurigancho; and my interviews with Javier Camara, director of community services, San Juan de Lurigancho, January 26 and 29, February 15, and March 14, 1988.

69. PAIT Program Directorate figures.

70. Interviews with Javier Camara, San Juan de Lurigancho, January 26 and 29, February 15, and March 14, 1988.

71. PAIT Program Directorate figures.

72. Interview with Víctor García, PAIT program functionary, Zarate, February 3, 1988; also my observation of voluntary PAIT workshops in San Juan de Lurigancho in early 1988.

73. Interview with Víctor Raúl Ortiz Pilco, Lima, February 3, 1988. The mayor felt that there had been much more coordination of effort between the PAIT office and his own since the proposed transfer. He attributed this to the increased interest in the PAIT on the part of the mayors who had expected to receive control of the program. While the transfer did not occur, he believed that mayors had asserted themselves more in the direction of the program. Javier Camara, one of the original organizers of the PAIT, also expressed this impression in our interview.

74. Interview with Sister Wilma Carrasco, Damas Apostólicas, Catholic parish, Huascar, March 10, 1988.

75. Interview with Señora Judith, Huascar PAIT worker, January 1988.

76. Interview with Señora Jubilia, Huascar PAIT worker, January 1988.

77. Ibid.

78. Ibid.

79. Interview with Gladys de la Cruz, Huascar resident, January 20, 1988.

80. Interview with Sister Wilma Carrasco, Huascar, March 10, 1988.

81. Survey of Huascar PAIT workers, 1988.

82. Ibid.

83. Señora Mercedes, speaking during my survey of Huascar PAIT workers, 1988.

84. Survey of Huascar PAIT workers, 1988.

85. Ibid.

86. Survey of Pamplona Alta PAIT workers, 1988.

87. Survey of Huascar PAIT workers, 1988.

88. Ibid.

89. Survey of Huascar PAIT workers; and my conversations with San Juan de Lurigancho PAIT officials.

90. Ray.

91. For a detailed account of the deterioration of living standards of the poor of Lima in the late 1980s, see Webb, *Ajuste y economía familiar.* From 1985 to 1990 the purchasing power of the poorest sectors fell by approximately 60 percent. It fell an additional 20 percent with the August 1990 "shock" stabilization package.

92. "El voto de los pobres," *Caretas* (Lima), May 14, 1990.

93. See Chapter 7 for Sendero's strategy in the slums and its results. My own observations of Sendero's increased influence in San Juan de Lurigancho occurred one year after the original fieldwork was conducted, in a follow-up visit to the district in July 1989. Social and municipal workers complained of Sendero attacks on colleagues, including assassinations, and also of Sendero's increased influence in local schools. Those interviewed remain anonymous for obvious reasons of safety.

94. Monge, p. 22. For details on a similar program—the PEM—in Chile, see my "From Emergency Employment to Social Investment."

95. Coppedge; Ward and Chant.

CHAPTER 9

1. Sartori, pp. 134–138.

2. Huntington, p. 196.

3. Haggard and Kaufman.

4. Arthur Valenzuela, p. 79.

5. Charles Johnson, p. 55.

6. Davies, p. 18.

7. Matos Mar, p. 17.

8. Riding, "Peru's Alan García Puts Democracy to the Test," p. 42.

9. Huntington, pp. 22–23.

10. Sartori, pp. 132–138.

11. Ibid, p. 134.

12. Ascher, pp. 16–17, 19.

13. Ibid.

14. Ibid., p. 18.

15. Ibid., p. 291.

16. Riordan Roett, lecture read at the Johns Hopkins School of Advanced International Studies, Washington, DC, September 20, 1988.

17. Toqueville, p. 21.

18. For a good description of the role of parties in the Venezuelan transition, see the work of Daniel Levine and Terry Lynn Karl, some of which can be found in O'Donnell, Scmitter, and Whitehead. For an account of the role of parties in the Chilean transition, see the work of Manuel Antonio Garretón. For a brief account, see my "Chile's Return to Democracy."

Selected Bibliography

Ajuero, Tito. "Una generación desconocida." *Piru* (January, 1988).

Alarco, Germán, ed. *Desafíos para la economía peruana, 1985–1990.* Lima: Centro de Investigación, Universidad del Pacífico, 1985.

Alexander, Robert J. *Aprismo: The Ideas and Doctrines of Victor Raul Haya de la Torre.* Kent State, OH: Kent State University Press, 1973.

Altimir, Óscar. *The Extent of Poverty in Latin America.* Washington, DC: The World Bank, 1982.

Amat y León, Carlos. *Niveles de vida y grupos sociales en el Perú.* Lima: Universidad del Pacífico, 1983.

Angell, Alan. "Classroom Maoists: The Politics of Schoolteachers Under Military Government." *Bulletin of Latin American Research* 1, no. 2 (1982).

———. "The Difficulties of Policymaking and Implementation in Peru." *Bulletin of Latin American Research* 3, no. 1 (1984).

———. "Peruvian Labour and the Military Government Since 1968." Institute of Latin American Studies Working Papers. London: University of London, 1979.

———. *Politics and the Labour Movement in Chile.* London: Oxford University Press, 1972.

———. "Some Problems in the Interpretation of Recent Chilean History." *Bulletin of Latin American Research* 7, no. 1 (1988).

———. "Trade Unions in Chile in the 1980's," in Paul Drake, ed. *The Struggle for Democracy in Chile.* Lincoln: University of Nebraska Press, 1991.

Angell, Alan, and Thorp, Rosemary. "Inflation, Stabilization and Attempted Redemocratization in Peru, 1975–1979." *World Development* 8 (November 1980).

Ascher, William. *Scheming For the Poor.* Cambridge, MA: Harvard University Press, 1984.

Ballon, Eduardo. "Alan, La Piramide y El Movimiento Social," *Que Hacer* 41, Junio-Julio, 1986.

Baruffati, Veronica. "Peruvian General Retires Amid Coup Rumors." *Financial Times* 13 (October 1988).

———. "Strong Support for Peruvian Stoppage." *Financial Times* 21 (July 1989).

Bendezu Carpio, Wilbert. *Los últimos días de Víctor Raúl.* Lima: Editora Tempus, 1986.

Billone, Jorge. *El PAIT: funcionalidad y metodologías.* Lima: INP/OIT/PNUD, 1986.

Bourricaud, François. "Ideología y desarrollo: el caso del Partido Aprista peruano." *Jornadas* 58 (El Colegio de México, 1966).

———. *Pouvoir et société dans la Pérou contemporaine.* Paris: Armand Colin, 1967.

Broad, Robin. "How About a Real Solution to Third World Debt?" *The New York Times,* September 29, 1987.

Brooke, James. "Obscure Engineer Now the Favorite to Lead Peruvians." *The New York Times,* April 10, 1990.

Burgess, Stephen. "The Communal Kitchens of Lima: An Analysis of Women's Organization in the Barriadas." M.Phil. thesis, Oxford University, October 1986.

Bustamante y Rivero, José Luis. *Tres años de lucha por la democracia en el Perú.* Buenos Aires: published by the author, 1949.

Campero, Guillermo. *Entre la sobrevivencia y la acción política: las organizaciones de pobladores en Santiago.* Santiago: Ediciones ILET, 1987.

Carbonetto, Daniel. "Políticas de mejoramiento en el sector informal urbano." *Socialismo y Participación* 25 (1984).

———. "El sector informal urbano: estructura y evidencias." In *Desafíos para la economía peruana, 1985–1990,* ed. Germán Alarco. Lima: Centro de Investigación, Universidad del Pacífico, 1985.

Centro de Estudios Alternativos. Centro de Investigación Social y Educación Popular."Primer conversatorio sobre PAIT-PAD." Lima, March 1987.

Centro de Investigación Social y Educación Popular. "Reflexiones de mujeres organizadas y la ley del PAD." Lima, December 1986.

Collier, David. "Squatter Settlements and Policy Innovation in Peru." In *The Peruvian Experiment,* ed. Abraham Lowenthal. Princeton, NJ: Princeton University Press, 1975.

Coppedge, Michael John. "Strong Parties and Lame Ducks: A Study of the Quality and Stability of Venezuelan Democracy." Ph.D. diss., Yale University, New Hartford, CT, December 1988.

Cotler, Julio. "Democracy and National Integration in Peru." In *The Peruvian Experiment Reconsidered,* ed. Abraham F. Lowenthal and Cynthia McClintock. Princeton, NJ: Princeton University Press, 1983.

———. "Entrevista." *La República* (Lima), September 2, 1987.

———. "The New Mode of Political Domination in Peru." In *The Peruvian Experiment,* ed. Abraham Lowenthal. Princeton, NJ: Princeton University Press, 1975.

———. "The Political Radicalization of Working Class Youth in Peru." *CEPAL Review* 29 (August 1986).

Crabtree, John. "Peru: From Belaúnde to Alan García." *Bulletin of Latin American Research* 4, no. 2 (1985).

Davies, Thomas M. "Víctor Raúl Haya de la Torre and the APRA: The Politics of Ideology." Paper presented at the University of California at San Diego Conference on APRA, March 21, 1988.

Degregori, Carlos Ivan. "Sendero Luminoso: los hondos y mortales desencuentros." In *Movimientos sociales y crisis: el caso peruano,* ed. Eduardo Bannón. Lima: DESCO, 1990.

Delgado, Carlos. *El proceso revolucionario: testimonio de lucha.* México: Siglo Veintiuno Editores, 1972.

———. *Revolución peruana: autónoma y deslindes.* Lima: Libros de Contratiempo, 1974.

Dietz, Henry. *Poverty and Problem Solving Under Military Rule.* Austin: University of Texas Press, 1980.

Dix, Robert H. "Populism: Authoritarian and Democratic." *Latin American Research Review* 20, no. 2 (1985).

Dornbusch, Rudiger, and Edwards, Sebastian. "The Macroeconomics of Populism in Latin America." Policy Planning and Research Working Papers, WPS 316. Washington, DC: World Bank, December 1989.

Durr, Barbara. "Peru Banks to Make Credit More Available." *The Financial*

Times (London), April 12, 1988.

———. "Peru Economic Policy Submerged by Politics." *The Financial Times,* March 22, 1988.

———. "To Govern Must Be to Change." *The Financial Times,* September 9, 1987.

Duverger, Maurice. *Political Parties: Their Organization and Activity in the Modern State.* London: Methuen, 1967.

Franco, Carlos. *Del marxismo eurocéntrico al marxismo latino americano.* Lima: Centro de Estudios para el Desarrollo y la Participación, 1981.

Franke Ballre, Marfil. "Weathering Economic Crisis: Urban Women's Response to Recession in Lima, Peru." Paper presented at International Center for Research on Women, Conference on the Nature and Evolution of Economic Crisis in Peru: 1975–1987, Spring 1988.

García, Henry Pease. "El populismo aprista." *Que Hacer* 47 (June–July 1987).

Gay, Robert. "Neighborhood Associations and Political Change in Rio de Janeiro." *Latin American Research Review* 25, no. 1 (1990).

Gillespie, Richard. *Soldiers of Peron.* Oxford: Oxford University Press, 1983.

Gonzales, Raúl. "La cuarta plenaria del Comité Central de Sendero Luminoso." *Qué Hacer* 44 (December 1986–January 1987).

———. "Los olvidados." *Qué Hacer* 47 (June–July 1987).

———. "Qué Paso en Puno." *Qué Hacer* 43 (October–November 1986).

———. "Los secretos del Señor García." *Qué Hacer* 21 (February 1983).

———. "Sendero: duro desgaste y crisis estratégica." *Qué Hacer* 64, May–June 1990.

———. "Sendero vs. MRTA." *Qué Hacer* 46 (April–May 1987).

Graham, Carol L. "The APRA Government and the Urban Poor: The PAIT Programme in Lima's Pueblos Jóvenes." *Journal of Latin American Studies* 23, pt. 1 (February 1991).

———. "Chile's Return to Democracy." *The Brookings Review* (Spring 1990).

———. "From Emergency Employment to Social Investment: Alleviating Poverty in Chile." *Brookings Occasional Papers* (November 1991)

———. "The Latin American Quagmire: Beyond Debt and Democracy." *The Brookings Review* (Spring 1989).

———. "New Guerrilla Group Adds to Peruvian Pressure Cooker." *The Wall Street Journal,* February 26, 1988.

———. "Peruvian Death Squad's Links to the Government." *The Wall Street Journal,* August 11, 1989.

———. "Terrorism, Economic Woes Ravaging Peru." *The San Diego Union,* April 2, 1989.

Graham, Robert. "Debt Crisis Swells Informal Economy." *The Financial Times* (London), September 16, 1987.

Granados, Manuel Jesús. "El PCP Sendero Luminoso: approximaciones a su ideologia." *Hueso Humero* 21 (1987).

Guzmán, Abimael. "La entrevista del siglo." *El Diario* (Lima), July 24, 1988.

Haggard, Stephan, and Kaufman, Robert. "The Political Economy of Inflation and Stabilization in Middle-Income Countries." Policy, Research, and External Affairs Working Papers, WPS 444. Washington, DC: World Bank, June 1990.

Harding, Colin. "Antonio Díaz Martínez and the Ideology of Sendero Luminoso." *Bulletin of Latin American Research* 7, no. 1, (1988).

Hilliker, Grant. *The Politics of Reform in Peru.* Baltimore, MD: Johns Hopkins University Press, 1971.

Huber-Stephens, Evelyne. "Democracy in Latin America: Recent Developments in Comparative Historical Perspective." *Latin American Research Review* 25, no. 2, (1990).

Huntington, Samuel P. *Political Order in Changing Societies.* New Haven, CT: Yale University Press, 1968.

Iguiniz, Javier. "Las chances y las restricciones de la política del APRA." Paper presented at the University of California at San Diego Conference, "APRA as Party and Government: From Ideology to Praxis," March 21, 1988.

——. "Economía: vísperas del abismo?" *Qué Hacer* 47 (June–July 1987).

——. *Política económica 1985–1986: deslindes mirando al futuro.* Lima: DESCO, 1987.

Institute for Liberty and Democracy. "Democratizing Peru's Banks: Extending Credit to the Informal Sector." Unpublished manuscript, Lima, 1988.

Inter-American Development Bank. *Annual Report—1987.* Washington, DC: IADB, 1988.

——. *Economic and Social Progress in Latin America.* Washington, DC: IADB, 1989.

Jaquette, Jane S. "The Politics of Development in Peru." Cornell University Dissertation Series 33, Ithaca, NY, 1971.

Johnson, Chalmers. *Revolutionary Change.* Stanford, CA: Stanford University Press, 1982.

Johnson, Nancy R. *The Political, Economic, and Labor Climate in Peru.* Latin American Studies, Multinational Industrial Relations Series no. 4. Philadelphia: University of Pennsylvania, 1979.

Klaren, Peter F. *Modernization, Dislocation, and Aprismo: The Origins of the Aprista Party, 1870–1932.* Austin: University of Texas Press, 1973.

Kohli, Atul. *The State and Poverty in India.* Cambridge: Cambridge University Press, 1987.

Kuczynski, Pedro Pablo. *Peruvian Democracy Under Economic Stress: An Account of the Belaunde Administration, 1963–1968.* Princeton, NJ: Princeton University Press, 1977.

Kus, James S. "The Sugar Cane Industry of the Chicama Valley, Peru." Unpublished manuscript, Department of Geography, California State University, 1986.

Lago Gallego, Ricardo. "Del crecimiento record a la hiperinflación." *Caretas* (Lima), April 4, 1988.

——. "The Illusion of Pursuing Redistribution through Macropolicy: Peru's Heterodox Experiment 1985–90." In *Macropolicies and Income Distribution in Latin America: The Economics of Populism,* Chicago: University of Chicago Press, 1991.

Long, Norman, and Roberts, Bryan. *Miners, Peasants, and Entrepreneurs: Regional Development in the Coastal Highlands of Peru.* Cambridge: Cambridge University Press, 1984.

Lowenthal, Abraham, and Cynthia McClintock, eds. *The Peruvian Experiment Reconsidered.* Princeton, NJ: Princeton University Press, 1983.

Matos Mar, José. *Desborde popular y crisis del estado.* Lima: Instituto de Estudios Peruanos, 1984.

McClintock, Cynthia. "APRA and the Peruvian Army Since the Constituent Assembly." Paper presented to University of California at San Diego Conference, "APRA as Party and Government: From Ideology to Praxis," March 21, 1988.

——. "Peru's Sendero Luminoso Rebellion: Origins and Trajectory." Unpublished manuscript, George Washington University, Washington, DC, October 1986.

——. "The Prospects for Democratic Consolidation in a Least Likely Case: Peru." *Comparative Politics* 21, no. 2 (1989).

Migdal, Joel S. *Strong Societies and Weak States: State-Society Relations in the Third World.* Princeton, NJ: Princeton University Press, 1988.

Miller, Rory. "Continuity and Change in Contemporary Peruvian History." Paper (draft) presented to a seminar on contemporary Peru, University of Liverpool, March 30–31, 1987.

Moreyra, Manuel. "El proyecto de estatización es clamorosamente inconstitucional." *El Comercio* (Lima), August 17, 1987.

Mulder, Mauricio. "Buscando el camino." *Qué Hacer* 47 (June–July 1987).

Nelson, Joan M. *Access to Power.* Cambridge, MA: Harvard University Press, 1976.

North, Liisa. *Orígenes y crecimiento del Partido Aprista: el cambio socioeconómico en el Perú.* Lima: Universidad Católica, 1975.

North, Liisa, and Doyer, Jacques. "The Peruvian Aprista Party and President Alan García: Contradictions and Convergence." Unpublished manuscript, CERLAC, York University, 1987.

O'Donnell, Guillermo, Philippe C. Schmitter, and Laurence Whitehead. *Transitions from Authoritarian Rule: Latin America.* Baltimore, MD: Johns Hopkins University Press, 1986.

Ortiz de Zevallos, Felipe. "Bank Nationalization Signals End of Peru's Spending Spree. *The Wall Street Journal,* August 14, 1987.

———. "En defensa del sistema democrático." *El Comercio* (Lima), August 30, 1987.

———. "Falta de una frente democrática: joven, cholo, y optimista." *Oiga* (Lima), February 16, 1987.

Ortiz Pilco, Víctor Raúl. "Gestión municipal y participación popular: un proyecto municipal para la juventud no escolarizada." Paper presented to Fundación de Friedrich Ebert Conference for District Mayors of the South, Cusco, Peru, December 1987.

Oxhorn, Philip David. "Democratic Transitions and the Democratization of Civil Society: Chilean Shantytown Organizations Under Authoritarian Regime." Ph.D. diss., Harvard University, Cambridge, MA: September 1989.

Palma, Diego. "Un discurso eficaz para un proyecto político." *Que Hacer* 51 (March–April 1988).

Palmer, David Scott. *Peru: The Authoritarian Tradition.* New York: Praeger, 1980.

Paredes, Carlos, and Sachs, Jeffrey. "Estabilización y crecimiento en el Perú: una propuesta independiente." Plan proprosed at a public forum sponsored by GRADE and The Brookings Institute, Lima, June 18–19, 1990.

Peredes, Peri, and Vigier, María Elena. "Los trabajadores del Programa Nacional de Apoyo de Ingreso Temporal en Lima metropolitana." Lima: OIT/INP, January 1986.

Perú. Instituto Nacional de Planificación. "Distribución del ingreso 1986." Lima, 1987.

Perú. Ministerio de Vivienda. Oficina de Estadística. "Boletín No. 2." Lima, June 1982.

Petras, James. "State, Regime, and the Democratic Muddle." *LASA Forum* 18, no. 4 (Winter 1988).

Pike, Frederick B. *A Modern History of Peru.* London: Weidenfield and Nicholson, 1967.

———. "Visions of Rebirth: The Spiritual Facet of Peru's Haya de la Torre." *Hispanic American Historical Review* 63, no. 3 (August 1983).

Pilar Tello, María del. *Golpe o revolución: hablan los militares del 68.* Lima: Ediciones Sagsa, 1983.

Pinilla, Susanna. "Políticas y programas de promoción del empleo: el PAIT y el

IDESI." Paper presented at the University of California at San Diego Conference, "APRA as Party and Government: From Ideology to Praxis," March 21,
1988.

Planes, Pedro. "La alanización del estado." *Debate* 8, no. 42 (December 1986).

Ramos Tremolada, Raúl. "El APRA en vísperas de su XVI Congreso." *Que Hacer*
53 (July–August 1988).

Randall, Vicky. *Political Parties in the Third World.* London: Sage, 1988.

Ravines, Eudocio. *The Yenan Way.* New York: Charles Scribner's Sons, 1951.

Ray, F. Talton. *The Politics of the Barrios of Venezuela.* Berkley: University of
California Press, 1969.

Riding, Alan. "Peru, in Disarray, Directs Its Fury at the President." *The New York
Times,* October 19, 1988.

———. "Peru's Alan Garcia Puts Democracy to the Test." *The New York Times
Magazine,* July 14, 1985.

Rock, David. *Argentina in the Twentieth Century.* London: Duckworth, 1975.

Rodríguez Elizondo, José. "Un futuro diferente?" *Debate* 9, no. 43 (March–April
1987).

Roett, Riordan. "Peru: The Message from García." *Foreign Affairs* (Winter
1985–1986).

Rosenberg, Tina. "Guerrilla Tourism." *The New Republic,* June 18, 1990.

Sánchez, Luis Alberto. *Testimonio personal: Memorias de un peruano del siglo
XX.* 6 vols. Lima: Mosca Azul, 1988.

Sartori, Giovanni. *Parties and Party Systems.* Cambridge: Cambridge University
Press, 1976.

Schuldt, Jurgen. "Desinflación y reactivación selectiva en la economía peruana."
Unpublished manuscript, Lima, March 1986.

Soto, Hernando de. "The Informal Sector as a Tool for Development." Unpublished manuscript, Instituto Libertad y Democracia, Lima, 1986.

———. *El otro sendero.* Lima: Editorial El Barranco, 1986.

Stallings, Barbara. "The Political Context of Economic Decision-making: Chile,
Peru and Colombia in the 1980's." In *The Politics of Stabilization and Adjustment in Developing Countries,* ed. Joan Nelson et al., forthcoming.

Stein, Steve. *Populism in Peru.* Madison: University of Wisconsin Press, 1980.

Taylor, Lewis. "Agrarian Unrest and Political Conflict in Puno." *Bulletin of Latin
American Research* 6, no. 2 (1987).

———. "Maoism in the Andes: Sendero Luminoso and the Contemporary Guerrilla Movement in Peru." Working Paper 2. Centre of Latin American Studies,
University of Liverpool, 1983.

Thorndike, Guillermo. *El Año de la barbarie: Perú 1932.* Lima: Mosca Azul
Editoras, 1969.

———. *La revolución imposible.* Lima: EMISA, 1988.

Thorp, Rosemary. "The APRA Alternative in Peru." Paper presented at a University of Liverpool seminar on contemporary Peru, March 31, 1987.

———. "The Evolution of Peru's Economy." In *The Peruvian Experiment Reconsidered,* ed. Abraham Lowenthal and Cynthia McClintock. Princeton, NJ:
Princeton University Press, 1983.

Thorp, Rosemary, and Geoffrey Bertram. *Peru, 1890–1977: Growth and Policy in
an Open Economy.* London: Macmillan, 1979.

Thorp, Rosemary, and Lawrence Whitehead. *Inflation and Stabilization in Latin
America.* London: Macmillan, 1980.

Thoumi, Francisco E. "Some Implications of the Growth of the Underground
Economy." *Journal of InterAmerican Studies and World Affairs* 29, no. 2
(1987).

Thumm, Ulrich. *Peru: Major Development Policy Issues and Recommendations.* Washington, DC: The World Bank, 1981.

Toqueville, Alexander de. *Democracy in America.* New York: Anchor Press, 1969.

Torres Guzmán, Alfredo. "Los caminos de Alan García." *Debate* no. 33 (July 1985).

Townsend Escurra, Andrés. "El aprismo, las fuerzas armadas, y una 'revolución' sin pueblo." Unpublished manuscript, Fundación Friedrich Ebert, San José, Costa Rica, 1973.

Treaster, Joseph. "Despite Guerrilla Threats, Elections Go on in Peru." *The New York Times,* November 8, 1989.

Tuesta Soldevilla, Fernando. "Pobreza urbana y participación política: clases populares y cambios electorales en Lima." Unpublished manuscript, DESCO, Lima, 1988.

United States. Department of State. "Human Rights Practices Report—1987." Washington, DC: US Government Printing Office, 1988.

Urrutia, Carlos. "La larga marcha del ideologismo a la política." *Debate* 9, no. 43 (March–April 1987).

Valenzuela, Arturo. *Political Brokers in Chile: Local Government in a Centralized Polity.* Durham, NC: Duke University Press, 1977.

Valenzuela, J. Samuel. *Democratización via reforma: la expansión del sufragio en Chile.* Buenos Aires: Ediciones Ides, 1985.

Vásquez Bazan, César. *La propuesta olvidada.* Lima: Editorial La Juventad, 1988.

Vega Centeno, Imelda. "Aprismo popular: Cultura, Religión, y Política." Paper presented at University of California at San Diego conference, "APRA as Party and Government: From Ideology to Praxis," March 21, 1988.

———. *Aprismo popular: mita, cultura, e historia.* Lima: Tarea, 1986.

Velarde, Julio. "El financiamiento de la actividad informal." Paper presented at Fundación Friedrich Ebert seminar, "El Mercado Financiero no Organizado y Financiamiento de la Actividad Económica Informal," Lima, August 20, 1987.

Vergara, Ricardo. "Un futuro diferente . . . al del Haya primigenio." *Qué Hacer* 21 (February 1983).

Villanueva, Víctor. "Peru's New Military Professionalism: The Failure of the Technocratic Approach." In *Post-Revolutionary Peru: The Politics of Transformation,* ed. Stephen Gorman. Boulder, CO: Westview Press, 1982.

Ward, Peter, and Chant, Sylvia. "Community Leadership and Self-Help Housing." *Progress and Planning* 27, part 2 (1987), pp. 31–54.

Webb, Richard. *Ajuste y economía familiar.* Lima: Instituto Cuanto, 1991.

———. "Falta de confianza." *Sí* (Lima), August 10, 1987.

———. *Government Policy and the Distribution of Income in Peru, 1963–1973.* Cambridge, MA: Harvard University Press, 1977.

———. "Special Report on the Debt." *Andean Report* (June 1986).

Wise, Carol. "Alfonso Barrantes." *NACLA* (September–December 1986).

Woy-Hazelton, Sandra. "The Return to Partisan Politics in Peru." In *Post-Revolutionary Peru: The Politics of Transformation,* ed. Stephen Gorman. Boulder, CO: Westview Press, 1982.

Zolezzi, Mario. "Terrenos urbanos: Lima, Hora Cero." *Qué Hacer* 37 (October–November 1985).

Index

About the Book
and Author

When Peru's APRA—one of the oldest and most controversial political parties in Latin America—came to power in 1985, expectations were high for the new government, and in part because a decade of economic decline and social crisis had discredited both the military and the right as alternatives. APRA did manage to maintain an unprecedented consensus for two years. But a sudden shift in strategy to confrontational rhetoric and authoritarian tactics led to policy stagnation, economic collapse, and a surge of reaction and political violence from extremes of the left and right. Rather than playing the role of the strong center, APRA acted as a catalyst to the polarization process. The party's sectarian and authoritarian strains, coupled with the increasingly erratic behavior of its once-popular young leader, Alan García, created damaging and perhaps irreparable cleavages between the party and the rest of society, and between society and polity more generally.

This book examines the evolution of APRA from its origins in the 1920s through its tenure in government, ending with the 1990 elections. Graham explores the consensus that the party built and the reasons for its breakdown, looking at party-government relations, the party's role in economic policymaking, its relations with the opposition, and finally, its relations with the marginalized sectors of society, in particular the urban poor. Beyond explaining the extreme crisis in Peru, she contributes to an understanding of the role of parties in the difficult process of democratic consolidation in developing countries.

CAROL GRAHAM is guest scholar in the Brookings Institution's Foreign Policy Studies Program and adjunct professor of government at Georgetown University.